W9-BLV-713

DEATH OF THE CHURCH

DEATH OF THE CHURCH

**The Church has a choice:
to die as a result of its resistance to change
or to die in order to live.**

MIKE REGELE
with Mark Schulz

Percept™
America's Religion Data Source

ZondervanPublishingHouse
Grand Rapids, Michigan

A Division of HarperCollinsPublishers

Death of the Church
Copyright © 1995 by Percept Group, Inc.

Requests for information should be addressed to:

Zondervan Publishing House
Grand Rapids, Michigan 49530

Library of Congress Cataloging-in-Publication Data

Regele, Mike.
    Death of the church / Mike Regele.
       p.   cm.
    Includes bibliographical references and index.
    ISBN: 0-310-20006-7
    1. Christianity—United States—Forecasting. 2. Church renewal. 3. United States—
Civilization—20th century. 4. United States—Moral conditions. 5. United States—Church
history—20th century. I. Title.
BR526.R44 1995
277.3'0829—dc 20
                                       95-26175
                                         CIP

This edition printed on acid-free paper and meets the American National Standards Institute
Z39.48 standard.

Published in association with Sealy M. Yates, Literary Agent, Orange, CA.

Edited by Ed van der Maas and Robin Schmitt
Interior design by Sherri L. Hoffman

Printed in the United States of America

---

98 99 00 01 02 /❖ DH/ 10 9 8 7 6 5 4

In gratitude to

*Ray Stedman (in memory) and Ron Ritchie
who taught me the Hope of the Gospel: that God's
power is revealed in bringing life out of death.*

*The entire Percept Team for their commitment
to see the church alive and effective in the
twenty-first century.*

*My wife, Debbie, and our five children for their
demonstration of God at work in everyday lives.*

Contents

Appendixes

Acknowledgments

EVERY CREATIVE WORK borrows, expands, or enhances ideas from other creative thoughts and ideas. This is especially true of *Death of the Church*. I have drawn on many sources in an attempt to find the pattern within all of the forces that are reshaping our world in general and the mission of the church more specifically. From futurist to theologian, from philosopher to sociologist, have come the essential ideas presented here.

However, it is not just from these disparate sources that the issues within *Death of the Church* have been derived. In a very real sense, this book is a collective enterprise of the entire Percept team. Though only one of us "put pen to paper," everyone within our small firm participated to a lesser or greater degree. We exist primarily to assist the church in addressing the issues outlined here. It is the hope of true renewal of the institutional church in American culture as a structure of meaning and a means of infinite grace that compels our whole team to wrestle with the challenges facing the institutional church.

This is especially true of three individuals with whom I work in total collaboration, namely Mark Schulz, Peter Wernett, and Tom Hoyt. Their keen interest in the church and culture provided the rich environment in which many of the ideas germinated and took on early form.

Mark Schulz, cofounder of Percept, and I have worked from our company's inception as the primary conceptualizers. Indeed, it is practically impossible to discern the original contributer of our ideas and the subsequent programs and products that have evolved out of them. This book is no different. Mark's thoughts are found on every page.

Tom Hoyt and Peter Wernett each contributed their share of ideas and soul to the project as well. Tom is a master at translating complex ideas into meaningful graphic illustrations. Peter lives each day in the field with our clients and knows too well their challenges. He forces us to keep our feet tied to the real turf where the institutional church finds itself today.

It is also appropriate to recognize the rest of our team who tirelessly work to assist churches and denominations across America. In the field with Peter is Bob Clary. In the office are Georgiana Armstrong, David Bleeker, Debra Regele, Barb Schulz, and Jennifer Wernett.

Mention must also be made of Tim and Valerie Cook. These dear friends have supported our efforts on several levels. Without them, the Ethos research conducted by our firm and reflected in some sections of the book would have never been more than an idea.

I am greatly indebted to our agents, Sealy Yates and Tom Thompson. Their vision, patience, and wisdom were invaluable in the process of transforming many relatively loose and vague ideas into a singular concept.

Finally, I appreciate the commitment of Zondervan to publish a somewhat unusual work for them. This extends especially to Ed van der Maas, who as editor demonstrated great enthusiasm that in turn set me free to write the book that was in my heart.

Mike Regele
Irvine, California 1995

What This Book Is About

AUTHORS GENERALLY IDEALIZE THE response they hope their book will provoke. Some authors write to inspire and only feel successful if the reader has been lifted to new heights of spiritual reflection. Others write simply to inform, and their basic goal is met if the reader walks away with better knowledge on a particular subject. We too have given serious thought to the intended response, and we want to let you, the reader, know what that is from the beginning.

It is our hope that you have a strong reaction. Even if your anger is aroused, we will have accomplished our task. If you find yourself energized, great. *Death of the Church* is intended to provoke, although we have been careful to be accurate and responsible in our statement of the issues. We will have failed if you only yawn.

You may not like what we say, but you must at least acknowledge the issues, for they are very real. The institutional church in America will look very different twenty-five years from now. Indeed, several denominations may no longer exist. We are sure that there will be hundreds of local congregations that won't. The forces reshaping our culture are too many and too strong. We see signs of social fragmentation and collapse everywhere.

But we also believe deeply in the hope of the Gospel and the security of the church. Both will survive. But *how* the church universal is expressed in and through the churches in America will look very different. This is the issue we write about.

Death of the Church is divided into three main sections:

- Part One focuses on the kinds of change that are reshaping our world.
- Part Two examines four focal points of change: changing reality, changing structures, changing players, changing faith.
- Part Three, "The Church in a Defining Moment," is the heart of the book. It examines the life-and-death issues facing the church as we enter the twenty-first century.

The flow of these three sections is very intentional. They are designed to build on one another. Part One, which focuses on the dynamic of change, is foundational. However, it is also the most abstract. We have chosen to use two models for interpreting social change as a framework. These are laid out in Part One.

The second section addresses the forms that change is taking in our culture and is therefore more concrete. It also flows increasingly from general cultural reflection to a focus on religious faith and the church.

Part Three answers the "so what" question of all that has preceded. Some may be inclined to peruse this section before digging in to the first two. However, the reader must understand that what is found in the third section only has contextual meaning because of the first two.

Finally, several extensive appendixes provide supporting data and information. We put these data in appendixes to keep them from cluttering the text and obscuring the main argument of the book.

We would like to make one final comment about how to read this book. *Death of the Church* is intentionally impressionistic. If the reader attempts to get too close to the detail, the overall message will be lost. While we have drawn on history, we have not written as a historian would write. While we have drawn extensively on sociological analysis, we have not written as a sociologist would write. While we have engaged philosophical issues, we have not written a philosophical treatise.

We have attempted to provide a faithful impression of the context in which the church finds itself today and the forces reshaping it. Many of the subjects we have touched beg for far better treatment than we have given them. But our purpose is not academic investigation. Our purpose is assisting the church in moving through a death process.

We write as one church leader to another. Founded on our own deep faith and commitment to the Gospel, we envision a church reborn and vital, carrying forth the Good News into the twenty-first century. But the road to this life leads through the valley of the shadow. Ours is an attempt to provide insight into that shadow.

CHAPTER 1

We're Not in Kansas Anymore!

Toto, I've a feeling we're not in Kansas anymore.

Dorothy in *The Wizard of Oz*

WHILE WAITING, I WONDERED how well the kids would do. After all, *The Wizard of Oz* is filled with singing parts. The kids playing the solo parts were fifth- and sixth-graders. But like any parent filled with pride, I knew that quality wasn't the issue. It was the experience that made it special.

I was not prepared for what happened. These kids were *very* good. Here were twelve-year-old children singing solos to a large audience and doing a very professional job of it. I found myself pulled into the story, and its magic began to work on me.

We all remember the classic scene wherein Dorothy steps out of Auntie Em's house into the Land of Oz and speaks the classic line, "Toto, I've a feeling we're not in Kansas anymore." As she spoke those words, I found myself resonating with the notion on several levels—so much so that my mind took a brief excursion.

Something is happening in American culture today that makes the phrase "I've a feeling we're not in Kansas anymore" a more vivid metaphor than we'd like to admit. My firm, Percept, works with churches and denominations all over the United States. Percept came into existence to assist the many leaders who are struggling to formulate effective mission strategies in today's environment. The more traditional models are breaking down. We find ourselves struggling to find adequate ways to understand and respond to a world that is not what we have known. The institutional church is going through a radical change in this country, and the entire system is breaking under incredible stress.

I also serve as a school board member in a large California school district. Twenty-five years ago, California led the nation in education. That has changed. In terms of dollars-per-student we currently invest, we rank near the bottom today. Yet as financial support is rapidly deteriorating, the complexity of the issues and problems that face education is increasing at an equal or greater rate. The system is under incredible stress. This is not limited, I might add, to California. Education throughout the U.S. is fighting for its life. Like the church, the world of education is finding that the traditional models are breaking down, and educational leaders are struggling to know how to respond.

My world is also changing on a personal level. Nothing makes this more apparent than when I think about the future of my five children. Every day, our kids must cope with friends without both parents in the home; unprecedented levels of violence in the media; health problems, such as AIDS, that hover over their entire generation; increasing violence on school campuses; and projections that they will be the first generation in this century that will not exceed the financial and professional accomplishments of the generations that preceded them. They may not yet know it, but they too are under great stress.

"Toto, I've a feeling we're not in Kansas anymore." No kidding!

Meanwhile, the play progressed. More and more characters came across the stage. It occurred to me that this particular presentation was a metaphor on top of a metaphor. In the movie version, the Land of Oz was inhabited by White people, albeit many quite short. At Westwood, I noticed African-American, Asian, Indian (as in India), Persian, and other Near Eastern actors. Judy Garland's Land of Oz was more similar to the image most of us hold of Kansas than were Westwood's actors!

We live in Irvine, California, an upper-middle-class, highly educated, and affluent community. Yet, over sixty-eight different native languages are spoken, and 25% of the children who attend our schools do not speak English as their primary language.

A recent public-television documentary discussed the general prevailing attitudes in America during the thirties and forties as the winds of war began to blow. There was a desire to remain separate and isolated from the events emerging in Europe and Asia. It noted that *The Wizard of Oz* was a symbol of the American mind-set. We felt we had woken up in a foreign land but we wanted to get back to Kansas. The narrator pointed out that the entire story drove that theme home.

Why Kansas? For many of us, Kansas is a symbol of traditional America. A place where family is important and stability prevails, with good, hardworking people of the land—a secure place for children and adults. Kansas is an image of an era.

The Land of Oz is a place of uncertainty where evil witches are at work. It is a place where things out of the ordinary occur. Where else do scarecrows talk and walk, are men made of tin, and do lions fail to be fierce and courageous? Oz is a place where things just are not the way they are supposed to be. It is an unstable place where the predictable is stood on its head.

LIVING IN OZ

OZ THUS BECOMES SYMBOLIC of a world out of control, characterized by stress and uncertainty. How often today do we hear muttered reflections on how it used to be? Who among us has not felt the pangs of reminiscence about what it was like when life was easier and less confusing? We too have awakened to find that we are in the Land of Oz. The changes that are occurring today in America are so pervasive and roll over us at such incredible speed, it is no wonder that we may find we long for Kansas in our hearts.

With so much evolving so fast, many of us experience a high level of uncertainty, especially when confronted with choices. In Kansas everything seemed so clear. But like Dorothy upon waking in Oz, we find that often our most basic assumptions are no longer valid. We are uncertain, sometimes to the point of paralysis.

The purchase of technology provides a good illustration. Our school district has embarked upon a project designed to put in place the technology and teacher training necessary to move our curriculum in the direction of information technologies. Ultimately we want our students capable of applying these new technologies in higher-level thinking and problem solving. The largest cost is equipment. But we all know that information technologies are evolving so quickly that whenever we buy equipment, it will be outdated very quickly, sometimes even before it is delivered.

As we were preparing to make a major purchase, one individual started questioning whether we should be buying any technology at all, since it would be obsolete as soon as we bought it. It did little good to argue that on the basis of this reasoning, we would never buy any equipment and the program's goals would not be met.

This is how many people are likely to respond—indeed do respond—in the face of major, continuous change. The boundaries of life become fuzzy, and some of us are not wired to handle such uncertain conditions.

Read through the following list and ask yourself, "How many times have I wrestled with one or more of these questions in the past year?"

Questions of Uncertainty	Faces of Uncertainty
What is true and what is not? Can I possibly know?	Uncertainty of Knowledge
Will there be a place for me? Or will I be replaced or displaced?	Uncertainty of Place
What is happening to my neighborhood?	Uncertainty of Community
What is happening to the family?	Uncertainty of Family
What is right and wrong?	Uncertainty of Morality
With so much changing, can I trust the basic tenets of my faith?	Uncertainty of Faith
If who I am depends upon what has been, will I become lost in what is coming?	Uncertainty of Identity

When one is so uncertain, what is the impact upon the psyche? Anxiety. None of us can experience so much uncertainty without feeling increasingly anxious. Peace of mind comes from stability and certainty. But with so much that is uncertain, that is destabilized by all of the crosscurrents, many of us feel that the world we know, or thought we knew, is threatened. And it is! The world we have known is changing. That will make us anxious to return to the Kansas we imagine we have known.[1]

But we will never go back. Kansas no longer exists except in our memories and personal myths. The Land of Oz has become our world. We must develop the ability to live in this strange new land as individ-

---

[1]It is important that we do not confuse nostalgia with reality. For large groups of people, especially minorities, the past was far from idyllic. In fact, we have created a myth of what America was like that has more to do with wishful thinking and childhood memories than with the hard realities of everyday life. Sometimes it is hard to distinguish between what we remember from shows like *Father Knows Best* and the realities of the past. Also, our childhood memories are just that—childhood memories in which there is no place for the problems and realities of the adult world of our childhood.

uals, as members of our communities, as participants in social institutions such as our public schools—even as members of the institutional church in America.

The profound and radical changes we face can be summarized in a few deceptively simple questions.

- What is the place and role of the institutional church in such a changing social and cultural environment?
- How are we to respond to the magnitude of changes and stresses we face, while remaining faithful to the Gospel?
- How will our churches look?

What are we to do?

THE FRENCHLICK ERROR

IN THE FALL OF 1979, I was invited to accompany Dr. Ray Stedman, formerly the pastor of Peninsula Bible Church, on a speaking trip. The gathering was a conference for the staff and leaders of Christian conference centers around the country. It was held that year at a big hotel in a small community called Frenchlick, in the southern tip of Indiana. The origin of the name remains a mystery to me, but the lesson I learned there became a central component of my theology and continues to influence every aspect of my thought and ministry.

Ray was only one of several speakers. One of the other speakers, who also happened to be a psychologist, was quite interesting and entertaining. I had the occasion to hear him several times. His messages consistently revolved around keys to living life to its fullest and being a truly happy Christian in successful ministry.

But each time he spoke, I was left with a measure of discomfort. After the second address, I turned to Ray and stated that there was something amiss in what he said. He agreed, but when asked what the problem was, he suggested that I think about it and try to figure it out on my own.

I wrestled with the question all day and into the next and finally approached Ray again. Realizing I was not going to figure it out on my own, he said simply, "There is no death in his message." The speaker painted a wonderful picture of an abundant Christian life and ministry filled with happiness and success, but he never once indicated that what it would take to get there included any kind of change in one's current lifestyle. His message was, "If you will simply do all of these things in

Central to book's focus

addition to the life you already live, you will be filled with all joy and your ministry will be fruitful."

But this is not the biblical Gospel, nor authentic Christianity in any sense. At the core of Jesus' message is the insistence that unless there is first a death, there can be no life. Unless we say no to our self-will, we cannot know the depth of God's will; unless we turn away from following our own way, we cannot know God's way; unless we confess our sin, we cannot know God's forgiveness and his gift of righteousness; unless we are willing to die to self, we cannot know our true selves; unless we die, we cannot discover the life of God.

> Then Jesus told his disciples, "If any want to become my followers, let them deny themselves and take up their cross and follow me. For those who want to save their life will lose it, and those who lose their life for my sake will find it. For what will it profit them if they gain the whole world but forfeit their life? Or what will they give in return for their life?" MATT. 16:24–26 NRSV

The fact that this popular speaker promised all of the positives without any exchange, without a death, is what I, ever since, have called the "Frenchlick error": The true Gospel calls us to die in order to live.

As humans, it is our natural propensity to build around our lives structures of self-dependence that give us a sense of security. This is true individually and collectively. Though we are loathe to admit it, we would rather trust ourselves and our own accomplishments than God or anyone else. This is the dark, broken side of our humanity.

There is often little difference between our behavior, as Christians, and the behavior of non-Christians. There is one difference, however. We find ways to fit God into our structures, whether they be our psychological defense systems or our institutional fortresses. Wrapping many of our thoughts and actions in "God talk," we nonetheless develop elaborate self-made systems and consume enormous amounts of personal and institutional energy to sustain them.

One of the great tragedies of our humanity is that in our blindness and presumption, we do not see that all of our self-made systems cannot save us from death. The law of diminishing returns eventually overwhelms our efforts. Those built upon such self-dependence ultimately fall. Yet for these to die is no real loss on the grand, eternal level—though it is usually a blow to our pride!

At the center of the Gospel, however, is the principle that there is no true life without a death. So what needs to die in our personal lives? Our sin and its attendant blindness that enslaves us to inevitable death.

The call of the Gospel is a call to die in order to beat death. Each of us is going to die, but we face a decision when confronted with the Gospel. We can reject its hope, stay on our current course, and die, period. Or we can embrace the truth about ourselves, allow our self-dependent systems to be put to death, and experience the power of God to bring life out of death. This is the hope of the Gospel!

THE DEFINING MOMENT

THE INSTITUTIONAL CHURCH in America finds itself in the same place. It has built up many structures of self-dependence upon which it relies and into which it pours great resources. Yet these structures are failing. Like the individual who faces the faltering of his or her structures of self-dependence, the church is moving rapidly toward a moment of decision, a *defining moment*. It is a moment of definition because, whether we like it or not, the church in American culture is being redefined. And our options are very limited.

What are the options? *Simply, we can die because of our hidebound resistance to change, or we can die in order to live.* As an institution, the American church must choose between these two. There are no other options. However, it is not as easy as merely examining the two options and choosing.

The reality is that the church is already on a direct course toward the first option. If the institutional church does nothing, which it is in fact good at doing, the choice has been made. Nothing short of an intentional act of collective choice on the part of the body of people who comprise the institutional church is required if we are to adopt the second option: to die in order to live.

Choosing the second option will not be easy. We will experience many forms of fear and discomfort. Anger and frustration will plague our efforts. Recalcitrance will thwart plans. Uncertainty will be a constant companion.

SIX COMMITMENTS

IT IS OUR HOPE and prayer that we will choose to die in order to live. But to do so will require six individual and collective commitments.

1. We must understand the dynamics of change that are at work today in our culture.

2. We must understand the various faces of change emerging as we prepare to step into the twenty-first century.

3. We must accept that the traditional place of the institutional church in American society is dying, and with it the institutional church itself.

4. We must be willing to let our traditional forms and structures that are the foundation of the institutional church die.

5. We must wrestle to forge new ways to proclaim the Gospel in this changing world.

6. We must do the work of revisioning the church for the twenty-first century—from the local congregation to the national denominational office.

It is the purpose of this book to address each of these commitments. The first one is dealt with at length in part 1, which deals with the dynamics of change. The second commitment is covered in part 2, which deals with the focal points of change. The other four commitments are discussed in part 3: commitments 3 and 4, in chapter 16; commitment 5, in chapter 18; and commitment 6, in chapter 19.

Our pilgrimage must begin with open, honest hearts seeking the wisdom of God. Without this wisdom, we will continue to swirl in our own ignorant ways, and the inevitable march toward death will continue unabated.

A decision is imminent, but it is only a decision about HOW the church will die. Death is inescapable. We cannot and will not avoid it. The institutional church will either choose to die or it will choose to die in order to live. We as Christians find ourselves in the shoes of Saint Augustine. Behind his queries into the nature of things was the assumption of "faith seeking understanding." Beginning with faith, we too must seek understanding if we are to meet the challenge.

PART ONE

Change

CHAPTER 2

Last One Out,
Turn Off the Lights!

*In this matter, as in so much else in our great country, why
cannot the status quo be the way forward?*

Speaker at the General Synod of the Church of England[1]

IN THE FIRST CHAPTER were outlined six commitments that we believe
are necessary if we are to make the wise choice as we enter our
defining moment. The first insists that we must understand the dynamics of change that are at work in our culture. Before we consider specific
changes and how they might affect us, *we must first understand change
itself as a force that is reshaping our world.* If we do not understand the
forces of change, we will be overwhelmed by them. They will push us
to the sidelines, leaving us to sit on the bench while the real action is
played without us.

This is no small challenge for the church and its leaders. The
church does not have a stellar track record of embracing and adapting
to cultural change. At various key moments in the church's history, it
tried to hold on tenaciously to the status quo.[2] Today the tendency to
withdraw into the status quo is stronger than ever, because change
today bears two characteristics that make it more unsettling than social
change of the recent past.

---

[1]Quoted in Charles Handy, *The Age of Unreason* (Boston: Harvard Business School
Press, 1989), 3.

[2]This is, of course, an oversimplification. The church has in fact adapted to cultural change ever since it began. But change usually occurred in spite of the innate tendency of the church—and of any religion—to equate its truths with the cultural forms
in which those truths are expressed. Change never came easily—witness the Reformation as a prime example.

First, it is global rather than local. In the past, social change happened in larger or smaller regional pockets. If you really wanted to escape it, you could always move![3] Today's social change occurs on a global scale. It is inescapable.

Second, the rate of social change moves at supersonic speed compared to the rate of change in the past. We have less and less time to reflect on the changes occurring around us. This is a luxury of the past. Any organization or institution that continues to behave as if we had all the time in the world to reflectively consider the full implications of modern change will be trampled by change and will cease to exist.

In business, the strategic planning systems of the late 1970s and 1980s are being abandoned because they are not responsive enough to the ever-changing business environment. Long-range planning has become increasingly meaningless. Today's planning systems promote the principle we call "PlanDo." In a rapidly changing environment, one can no longer separate planning from doing. There must be a seamless flow in and out of each other. Planning and doing have become one continuous action: input of information, reshaping information, making decisions to act, and responsive action.[4]

For much of human history, except in times of great social turmoil, people were relatively unaware that things were slowly evolving and changing. Within the scope and perspective of an individual's lifetime, it would be possible to conclude that nothing had changed. Those who wanted change usually left to go elsewhere. Knowledge was finite and relatively stable, and the wisdom of the past was held in high esteem. Testing and licensing systems were designed to ascertain whether or not the individual had mastered a particular body of knowledge.

This is no longer true. With the information explosion, there is simply too much content. Education now must teach students how to use information technologies to solve problems. The adult of the future will increasingly face a new situation that will require the ability to apply

---

[3]While it may actually have been more difficult to move in the past than it is today, it was possible to escape. We are more transient, but there is nowhere in the world to go today to escape the social changes that are reshaping our world. In the past, change affected segments of the world population; today it affects the entire population, although the specific changes may differ from group to group.

[4]In 1931 Alfred North Whitehead made an important observation about change as we were to experience it in the twentieth century: "In the past the time span of important change was considerably longer than that of a single human life. Thus mankind was trained to adapt itself to fixed conditions. But today our training must prepare individuals to face a novelty of conditions." This principle will be the norm of the twenty-first century.

thinking strategies to many different and changing conditions accurately and quickly—or fail to stay competitive. (This is a change from the recent past, in which doing rather than thinking became prominent.)

How do we respond to the pressures of change?

One option is denial. Some time ago we met with a committee of a Presbyterian church to assist them in their planning process. They were looking at the results of the community demographics, congregant survey, and other responses from the congregation.[5] Indicator after indicator clearly pointed to a changing environment. We insisted that they needed to deal more effectively with that change if they were to see the mission of their church reborn. In response, one elderly woman complained, "Why do we have to change? Why can't you just leave us alone until we all die, and then change the church if you want to?" As far as we know, she won the day. Her church is dying with her.

In 1970, Seattle was in the throes of one of the Boeing Company's downturns. With the abandonment of the supersonic transport, Boeing was laying off thousands of people. The mood of the time was reflected in a rather peculiar bumper sticker that read "Last one out, turn off the lights." This fits the attitude in many churches today, and too many are unwilling to address it. Consequently, we have literally thousands of churches standing as monuments of a former era.

It is time to stop the denial. It is time to stop minimizing the realities we face and avoiding what we must do. We cannot simply "let the status quo be the way forward." The defining moment is coming, and if we are to respond in faith, faithfully, we must prepare for it.

The first step is confession. *Our strategies have not worked!* We work with hundreds of church leaders across America. As we interact with them, we see women and men working harder and harder with fewer and fewer positive results. Meanwhile budgets are shrinking and more is being placed on their backs. And they are exhausted!

We must accept the fact that our world has changed, is changing, and will continue to change. The changes are so extensive that simply tinkering with our models of understanding how to assist and develop congregations will completely fail. We must admit this fact.

Second, we must learn how to do it differently. The beginning of that learning is understanding the chief force that has thwarted our efforts—change itself. We will not be able to adequately respond to our challenge if we do not understand how change is shaping our world today.

---

[5]This program is provided by Percept. It is called "Your Church and Its Mission: A Congregational Strategic Planning Program" (1988).

CHAPTER 3

Predictable Change I:
The Generational Cycle

Continuous change is comfortable change. The past is . . . the guide to the future.

Charles Handy[1]

W E ALL KNOW life must change. But we like our change to be comfortable and predictable. "Comfortable change" is the kind that moves forward in time with a continuous rhythm, in regular increments—it is continuous and incremental. Because of this incremental nature, we assume it is possible to predict where things are headed and approximately when they ought to get there. Indeed, predictability is a key characteristic of continuous, incremental change—it is simply a matter of drawing a straight line into the future, based upon the past. Continuous, incremental change is essentially static—that is, it is relatively unchanging in its predictability.

Predictability allows for control. If change comes in regular increments of cause and effect, it affords us the ability to maintain a high level of control over our lives and spheres of involvement. We control the unfolding of events such as our career paths, our family life and experience, and even how we go about being the church. If we are in control, change is not a significant force in our lives. Indeed, under such conditions, we control change; it does not control us. The future is simply an extension of the past.

When we look at the details of history, there doesn't seem to be much of a pattern, but when we look at the large picture, we can see broad, general patterns. Predictable, continuous change is like a river.

---

[1]Handy, *The Age of Unreason*, 3.

Each individual water molecule follows what appears to be an unpredictable path, but the river as a whole flows in a single direction.

One attempt to discern patterns in the flow of history is known as generation theory. Pioneered by a number of prominent European thinkers, North American interest in generation theory dates back to the emergence of the "baby boomers" as a distinct, identifiable group.[2] The most recent discussion of the generational cycle is found in the book *Generations* by William Strauss and Neil Howe.[3] Generation theory provides us a way to look at the world and historical events. We do not suggest that it is *the* way. It is only *a* way. That is, using generational theory as an interpretive framework, we are able to provide some measure of explanation for particular phenomena we observe in historical events, both in our culture and in the church. There are, of course, many different frameworks one can use. But we find generational theory to provide an unusually helpful one.

The patterns of the generational cycle can be observed not only in social and secular institutions but also in religious faith and religious institutions. An understanding of these patterns will help us understand the past, present, and future of the institutional church. The next few pages are rather theoretical, but we will come down to earth when talking about how these concepts fit in with our own recent history.

---

[2]Although "in recent years, generation theory has had few champions and many critics," this interdisciplinary approach to thinking about culture can provide a framework for comprehending patterns of change. See John C. Zimmerman, "Leadership Across the Generation Gap," *Crux* 31, no. 2 (June 1995).

[3]William Strauss and Neil Howe, *Generations: The History of America's Future, 1584 to 2069* (New York: William Morrow, 1991).

The Generational Cycle

Strauss and Howe suggest that when we look at the broad sweep of history, it appears that there is a regular and repeated cycle that is roughly eighty to ninety years in length. This cycle, in turn, can be divided into four periods of approximately equal length, hence four generations of twenty to twenty-two years each. We can visualize the generational cycle as an elliptic orbit around two pivotal points as is demonstrated in the following illustration.

Each pivotal point represents a significant moment in our collective social life and lasts about a decade, though its influence is felt before it occurs and for some time after it passes. Strauss and Howe call these two points a spiritual awakening and a secular crisis.

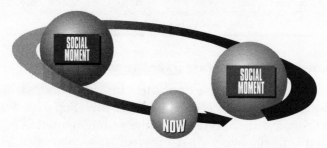

First Pivotal Point: Spiritual Awakening

During a spiritual awakening, society focuses on the inner life, on values and beliefs. Such consciousness-raising moments are provoked and fueled by a reaction against the secular values of the period preceding them. As society moves toward an awakening, signs of inner spiritual discontentedness begin surfacing in many places, reaching their highest intensity just as the cycle begins to swing around the awakening moment. At the point of highest intensity, a spiritual awakening of the soul breaks out and continues for around a decade.

Awakening moments call a society to renewed concern for the inner life of the spirit and to judge the facile and meaningless material values revolving around the creation of things. All of the great awakenings in U.S. history have occurred at the same point in the generational cycle.[4]

Strauss and Howe identify six awakenings, beginning with the Reformation and ending with the most recent consciousness-raising revolution of the late 1960s.

---

[4]Strauss and Howe, *Generations*.

Six Awakenings		
The Awakenings	**Years**	**Key Figures**
The Reformation Awakening	1517 - 1539	Martin Luther, John Calvin, John Knox
The Puritan Awakening	1621 - 1640	John Winthrop, John Cotton, Anne Hutchinson
The Great Awakening (1st Great)	1734 - 1743	Jonathan Edwards, George Whitefield, William Tennent
The Transcendental Awakening (2nd Great)	1822 - 1837	Ralph Waldo Emerson, Nat Turner, Charles Finney
The Missionary Awakening	1886 - 1903	William Jennings Bryan, Jane Addams, W. E. B. Du Bois
The Boom Awakening	1967 - 1980	Arlo Guthrie, Mark Rudd, Rap Brown

Source: *Generations* by William Strauss and Neil Howe

Second Pivotal Point: Secular Crisis

A secular crisis is just the opposite. This is a period when the troubles of the world reach a boiling point and then boil over. Just prior to a secular crisis, the social order becomes so fragmented in its individualism that it is finally overturned, provoking a secular crisis. In response to the crisis, society begins to feel its vulnerability to negative forces and in reaction halts its individualistic and fragmented momentum and begins to recoalesce around a common set of values—generally for survival reasons.

Strauss and Howe identify five secular crises.

Five Secular Crises		
The Secular Crisis	**Years**	**Key Figures**
The Armada Crisis	1580 - 1588	Sir Walter Raleigh, Francis Bacon
The Glorious Revolution Crisis	1675 - 1692	Cotton Mather, John Wise, Peter Schuyler
The American Revolution Crisis	1773 - 1789	Thomas Jefferson, James Madison, John Marshall
The Civil War Crisis	1857 - 1865	Ulysses S. Grant, Stonewall Jackson, Andrew Carnegie
The Great Depression - World War II Crisis	1932 - 1945	John Kennedy, Robert Oppenheimer, Walt Disney

Source: *Generations* by William Strauss and Neil Howe

To get a full picture, we provide an integrated table that demonstrates the regular rhythm of the generational cycle.

The Regular Rhythm of the Generational Cycle			
The Awakenings	Years	The Secular Crisis	Years
The Reformation Awakening	1517 - 1539	The Armada Crisis	1580 - 1588
The Puritan Awakening	1621 - 1640	The Glorious Revolution Crisis	1675 - 1692
The Great Awakening	1734 - 1743	The American Revolution Crisis	1773 - 1789
The Transcendental Awakening (also known as Second Great Awakening)	1822 - 1837	The Civil War Crisis	1857 - 1865
The Missionary Awakening	1886 - 1903	The Great Depression - World War II Crisis	1932 - 1945
The Boom Awakening	1967 - 1980	The next crisis	2015 - 2025???

Source: *Generations* by William Strauss and Neil Howe

The Four Eras of the Generational Cycle in the Twentieth Century

As the cycle moves back and forth around the two pivotal points, it moves in regular rhythm between the inner life of the soul and the outer structures of the world. Within the rhythm of the cycle are four distinct eras (which, as we shall see, coincide with the four generations in each cycle). Each era manifests a particular "mood" that reflects a prevailing social emphasis or mind-set.

Two of the eras are the *crisis era* and the *awakening era*—the periods when the spiritual awakening and the secular crisis take place. These are followed by an *outer-directed era* and an *inner-directed era,* respectively.

The diagram that follows presents the cycle again but with the addition of the eras and the dates proposed by Strauss and Howe for the current cycle. When considered with the "moods" of each era, one can begin to feel how the cycle flows.

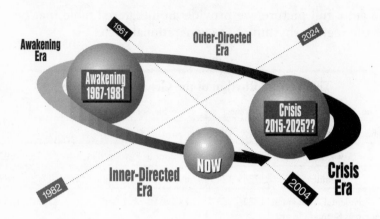

The last secular crisis occurred in the period preceding and through World War II. Exhausted from a period of excess and over-indulgence, American society collapsed into the depression of the 1930s. This crisis was deepened by the unsettling winds of war that began to blow across Europe and Asia in the late 1930s. In response, a social mood of community building and support began to emerge as the country struggled to pull itself together to face the threat that loomed before it. As the cycle moved toward the "apex" of its orbit, the world found itself embroiled in the worst, most extensive war in world history. Coalescing around a common threat and hope, Americans rallied and were victorious, though the world was in shambles.

Such a crisis era naturally evolves into an outer-directed era as the collective energy that was marshaled to defeat the enemy is rechanneled to rebuild the structures and institutions of society. The postwar economic boom stands as a prime example of the efforts of an outer-directed era. It is a period marked by the motto of the Three Musketeers: "One for all, and all for one." As American society moved through the end of the forties and into the fifties, there was a mood of unanimity of purpose and destiny. More great institutions were formed and/or grew larger, and an overarching spirit of conformity prevailed as cookie-cutter suburbs spread like wildfire around urban centers coast to coast. A singular model of the family was characterized by the Cleavers of the television show *Leave It to Beaver*. All of these phenomena are characteristic of an outer-directed era. It is a time of *secular building*.

However, such outer-directed periods do not last. As the culture expends its spiritual resources to build the external world, it finds itself increasingly depleted, and an inner hunger begins to form. It is at these moments in the cycle when an awakening era will begin to emerge. In reaction to the lack of attention to the concerns of the spirit during outer-directed eras, the social mood turns toward the inner person. This inner orientation rejects the high level of social conformity that had marked the preceding outer-directed era. The inevitable outcome gives birth to an awakening of the spirit.

The last time this occurred in U.S. history was the "spiritual awakening" of the late sixties through the seventies. As the current baby boomer generation came of age, it rejected the material values and social conformity of its parents and elders. Instead of building big institutions, this idealistic generation focused its attention on the flowering of the inner spirit. Under this banner, the young adult boomers experimented with drugs such as LSD and marijuana. They envisioned harmony with the natural and the spiritual, instead of slavery to the material. The antiestablishment mood and the so-called generation gap of the period really only reflected a massive gap in the value systems between the young boomers and their elders. Attending such revolutions of the spirit is an intensifying concern for the individual and an equal disregard for the community.

This same moment spawned the Jesus People movement, which was a spin-off of the "hip" antiestablishment culture. They were anti-institutional church as the larger hip movement was anti-establishment culture. The emergence of the New Age movement is directly attributable to this period of awakening to spiritual values.

However, such inner-directedness inevitably digresses into an overabundant concern for the self and the inner life. As this occurs, the awakening era evolves into the next era, an inner-directed era.

The social self-absorption of inner-directed eras causes social policy and beliefs to fragment into smaller and smaller interest groups and personal concerns, at the expense of the national collective life. As we close the twentieth century, we are in just one of those periods. One only needs to reflect upon the national mood revolving around the historic capture of both houses of Congress by the Republicans in 1994 to see it at work. Most rational people knew that it was more of a vote against the status quo than an affirmation of the Republican agenda. The mood of the country was distrustful and angry.

During such inner-directed periods, institutions lose favor and go into decline. Political life takes on an edge of meanness and moral corruption as the self-indulgent ethos unfolds. In the fragmentation, it becomes nearly impossible to build community consensus on anything of real substance.

Toward the end of this era, a new moralistic spirit begins to emerge as the generation of self-absorbed idealists emerges out of their period of narcissistic self-indulgence and, with idealistic fervor, begins to push its moral agenda on the already fragmented public—creating further hostility and fragmentation. An example is the two political platforms of Bill Clinton and Newt Gingrich (both boomers) midway through the 1990s. Though they appear worlds apart in their political positions, they share one feature in common: they both build on the assumption of the moral imperative. In other words, typical of idealists—and boomers are idealists—the issues are nothing less than the battle for right and wrong, good and evil. Under such conditions, compromise and collaboration are incompatible. Too much is at stake! Every position is an attempt to drive a stake on "high moral ground." As the twentieth century closes, we can all feel the strain that pulls at the seams of our cultural fabric. Many wonder if that fabric will tear and bring on national disaster. Yet the moral ideologues on both sides of the political aisle show no signs of abating their vicious and frenzied drive to shape national policy and culture around their moral ideal.[5]

Putting all this in chart form, we get the following:

The Generational Cycle			
Era **Outer-Directed Era**	**Awakening Era**	**Inner-Directed Era**	**Crisis Era**
Era Moods	Conformity and stability, triumphant ideals secularized, great institutions built	Cultural creativity, new ideals, old institutions/ values challenged or rejected	Individualism, fragmentation, and animosity over divergent ideals, confidence in institutions fades, secular problems increase, spirit of public meanness and distrust	Emerging communitarian spirit to face social problems, era culminates in secular crisis, single ideal prevails over others, new foundation for community building
Average Duration	20 to 22 years	20 to 22 years	20 to 22 years	20 to 22 years
Cum. Time	0 to 22 years	23 to 44 years	45 to 66 years	67 to 88 years

Sources: *Generations* by William Strauss and Neil Howe, and Percept Group, Inc.

---

[5]On a somewhat less ominous note, it is curious that during the last awakening–inner-directed period of the early 1900s—we had prohibition, and as we move through this era again toward the end of the century, the prohibition of the 1990s has emerged around the antismoking movement!

The Generational Cycle: Speculations on the Future

We have reviewed the cycle through the twentieth century up to the point in time in which this book was written. Based upon the cycle, what lies before us?

Historically, the edges fragment too far. We suspect the same is on our immediate horizon. On the world scene, the winds of discontent will again begin to blow, and as they do, the inner-directed era will evolve into an era of pending crisis. In response to a growing sense of social insecurity, the inner-directed values of self-indulgence will give way to a renewed communitarian spirit. Signs of this are already evident halfway through the decade of the nineties. Common moral values, once not even considered a legitimate topic of public discourse, have begun to emerge as an acceptable subject for discussion. In the midst of our overwhelming social and moral fragmentation, there are definite signs that we might in fact be able to congeal around some common moral ideals.

The current inner-directed era will most likely run out of steam around 2003 and set the stage for the next crisis era. Already, a growing sense of uncertainty hovers over our culture. As the next crisis era approaches, we will in fact see many of the structures that have been sagging fall apart. It is curious to us that Congress has projected 2004 as the year when the entitlement programs may finally consume the entire federal budget!

About a decade into the crisis era, a secular crisis will erupt of such magnitude that it will reorder the known world. It is projected to occur somewhere between 2015 and 2025. What will it be? Who knows? But we do know that in the period since the last secular crisis of World War II, we have become a global village.

Futurists make it their business to provide scenarios for the years ahead. Sometimes they are on target, sometimes not.[6] But they force us to face what will happen if, as Dickens put it, "these shadows remain unchanged." One futurist, Joseph F. Coates, released a report entitled "The Highly Probable Future: 83 Assumptions about the Year 2025." Under the heading "World Tensions," he suggests that "internal strife and border conflicts will peak between 1995 and 2010. . . . Widespread contamination by a nuclear device will have occurred either by accident or as an act of political/military violence. Epidemics and mass

---

[6]In the 1970s many of them were telling us that we would all have great amounts of leisure time on our hands in the 1990s. How wrong they were!

35

starvation will be common in World 3. Environmental degradation will be substantial."[7]

In response to the threat, the last vestiges of social fragmentation will give way to a majority commitment to the particular moral vision of a grand society. Around this vision our culture will rally, and if all goes well, we will survive the crisis and come out as victors, as we did from World War II.

Following the crisis—if we survive—the social emphasis will turn outward, and a new era of concern for secular social structure building will reemerge. In such outer-directed periods, large institutions of every kind are built—for example, businesses, unions, government, and religious denominations. This grand building continues until the next awakening era begins to emerge, moving the emphasis toward the inner life again, in reaction to the dominating but spiritually dead outer-directed secular emphasis.

Where does this leave us? There is a measure of comfort in the fact that predictable change allows us to say some things about the future with a small degree of confidence. The downside is that the things we can say about the future aren't exactly comforting. Is the church exempt from the changes that we know are coming? We think not—at least not any more than the church has been exempt in the past, as we will see in the next chapter.

---

[7]Joseph F. Coates, "The Highly Probable Future: 83 Assumptions about the Year 2025," *The Futurist* (January-February 1995), 35.

CHAPTER 4

Predictable Change II: The Church

The God of history is on our side—but history may not be.

Anonymous

W E BELIEVE THAT THE *invisible* church of Jesus Christ exists outside of and independent from culture. However, the *visible* church, which manifests itself in every era and place as a social institution, reflects the social norms and beliefs of its host culture. Indeed, it is unavoidable, for the visible church is comprised of people who live in cultures and reflect the assumptions of those cultures. Furthermore, if we accept the notion of the generational cycle, then the particular form the institutional church takes reflects where we are in the cycle at any given moment.

Let's look again at the cycle and the four eras. Each awakening era and the inner-directed era that follows it share common values and social emphases. Each crisis era and subsequent outer-directed era share different values and emphases. The awakening–inner-directed combination reflects a more experiential and personal orientation—it is an *experiencing faith period*. The crisis–outer-directed combination is more secular and institutional in orientation—it is a *doing faith period*.

THE EXPERIENCING FAITH PERIOD

IN AWAKENINGS, THE RELIGIOUS community turns its focus toward "matters of the heart" and one's spiritual relationship with God. Personal internal transformation becomes central as people pursue spiritual experiences. The avenues down which people travel in their pursuit

37

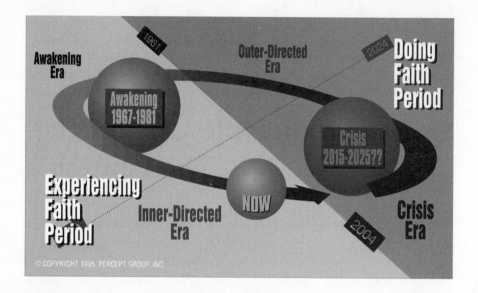

may or may not look like traditional spiritual quests, but they are quests nonetheless. The emergence of the New Age movement within our current cycle is one example. Even within the relatively loose bounds of traditional faith, such movements as the Jesus People and the Christian communes of the seventies illustrate how much concern there is for spiritual experiences in such times.

Also attending such awakening moments is a concern for the authentic. For many, the more traditional forms of the institutional church feel as though they have lost their way, and a longing for authentic and vital spirituality moves into the forefront. During such moments, discussions about the future of the institutional church revolve around its demise. At times, the language verges on the apocalyptic. The prevailing institutional forms of faith of the prior outer-directed era are branded as apostate and evil. Rhetoric about the soullessness of the establishment and its "godless religion" abounds from those leading the revolution. Indeed, religion—period—gets a bad rap as banners declaring that it is about "relationship, not religion" prevail.[1]

In the late seventies, I attended a church that had outgrown its sanctuary, and serious consideration was being given to designing and building a new one. Being a young, enthusiastic, and—I must confess—

---

[1]The particular descriptions used here to typify the end of "doing faith" periods in the cycle reflect my historical bias as an author. This is because this is the one I have lived through and am therefore most aware.

arrogant idealist, I accused the leaders of the church, in a letter, of having an "edifice complex," just because they wanted to build a newer, bigger church building. I insisted that the body of Christ was organic and that God's Spirit was within us. Therefore we did not need fancy "sanctuaries" to worship God. Indeed, religious space, I insisted, was an Old Testament concern that had been superseded by the new covenant. (There are few things worse than an inordinate amount of zeal and a dangerously minimal amount of biblical theology!) While I don't fully disagree with the ideas even in my older years and having passed through seminary twice, I am still amused and somewhat embarrassed by my youthful naïveté and presumption. Yet for all of that, my thoughts were completely consistent with what would be expected during the heights of experiencing faith periods. The emphasis is religion of the heart, not external structures of brick and mortar.

However, once the initial period of awakening passes, such concerns for spiritual revival subside, and attempts to generate revival in a fashion consistent with an awakening fail. Some years ago a pastor longed to see spiritual revival overtake his church. Toward that end, he studied Richard Lovelace's book *The Dynamics of Spiritual Life*. Lovelace outlined the factors that occasioned the great awakenings of the past. He also made the point that it was in focusing on the great themes of sin, justification, and sanctification that revival would erupt. In fact, Jonathan Edwards's great sermon that helped bring about the Great Awakening was "Sinners in the Hands of an Angry God." So this pastor preached sermon after sermon following Lovelace's outline. But little happened, except that many in the congregation became increasingly convinced that he was deeply angry with them. It was not long after this that he moved on to a different church.

Now, there was nothing wrong in his sermons. They were great models of theological reflection. But they were not preached in the same kind of era as when Jonathan Edwards preached. Edwards preached in an awakening era. This was the late 1980s. The awakening was over, and the inner-directed age of therapy was center stage. Sermons on the depth of one's moral and spiritual depravity simply did not feel very good. In inner-directed eras, people want to feel good about themselves. They want sermons that assist them in this quest.

As the awakening evolves into an inner-directed era, the programmatic concern of the church shifts subtly toward self-development and sometimes self-indulgence—even spiritual self-indulgence! It is curious that one of the countervailing criticisms of the past twenty years has been the increasing privatization of personal faith. Those who lodge this criticism suggest that faith becomes such a personalized issue that connection with the larger social environment is eclipsed, if not lost entirely. Consequently, while demonstrating deep concern for one's own personal spiritual growth, the world is allowed to "go to hell in a handbasket." A near obsession with personal growth within faith traditions is maintained under the banner of "getting to know God." We wonder if perhaps it is not just a way to justify another manifestation of self-indulgence, a behavior pattern completely consistent with the "mood" of the inner-directed era.

During experiential periods, religious traditions that emphasize the experiential side of faith are more likely to grow and thrive. Within our current cycle, there is significant evidence that this is the case. During the early years of the current experiential period (the early 1970s), the fastest-growing traditions in the Christian church were denominational groups such as the Assembly of God out of Springfield, Missouri, or the Calvary Chapel movement coming out of California. Likewise, the charismatic movement, which crossed over all denominational boundaries as a renewal movement within them, emerged during this same period. At one point, the eighties were even heralded by the media as the decade of the evangelical.

But it is not just within this cycle that this has been the case. The birth of the Pentecostal movement occurred during the last experiential period of the prior generational cycle. It was around the turn of the twentieth century in Los Angeles that the famous Azusa Street Church revivals occurred, giving birth to the modern Pentecostal movement. In such periods, those traditions with the greatest emphasis on the personal life and religious experience of the "believer" will thrive. It is also in these periods that new groups spin off from existing institutional structures, reflecting the overall tendency in such periods to reject the established structures. Conversely, during such inner-directed, experientially oriented periods, those traditions within the Christian church that place less emphasis on the personal experience of the believer will be pushed into the background, with growth curtailed or—as is actually being experienced currently—seriously declining.

THE DOING FAITH PERIOD

ON THE OTHER SIDE of the cycle is a doing faith period. During doing faith periods, the cultural ethos revolves around the development of social structures and institutions. Less emphasis is given to the devel-

This is, I believe where we are now; "let me see you walk the talk"

opment of one's personal spiritual life. It is a period wherein one is more concerned with doing faith than with experiencing faith. Consequently, traditions within the Christian church that emphasize social programs and institutional life move to center stage. Conversely, those traditions emphasizing the experiential move into the background throughout this period.

One primary thrust of the doing faith period is the development of the external forms of the institutional church. Within the current cycle, the membership and programmatic apex of the historic mainline denominations in America occurred within the bounds of the outer-directed era of the fifties. Indeed, these traditions saw significant membership growth every year until the mid-sixties. From then on, they all saw decline.

During such outer-directed, doing faith periods, the institutional life of the church is shaped, formed, and solidified. Many of the larger churches in the mainline traditions were built during this era. This is the era of the large, program-based church whose activities focus around doing the Gospel as a community. During the last doing faith period, we saw the development of ministry as community organizing. However, the emphasis on the development of institutions and the institutional form of the church is generally pushed too far. Some begin to feel that the institution is of greater import than the people. As the outer-directed era passes, an internal starvation begins to set in. Too much activism wears too many activists thin, and a longing for inner peace and renewal begins to surface. Predictably, these are the beginning notes of a new spiritual awakening.

Some years ago I served as an associate pastor in a nondenominational church in Southern California. At one point during the early seventies, it had been one of the fastest-growing churches in America, but what is of interest here is how and why this church was started. Several of the primary individuals who founded the church had been active lay members of a large, local Presbyterian church throughout the heyday of the doing faith era of the fifties and sixties. It was a time in which the clergy in the mainlines had the greatest power, and their concern was building the institutional church. The men and women who broke off were concerned that there was not enough emphasis on personal faith. They would even declare with an air of certainty that the pastor was not even a Christian! When did this occur? The late sixties, at the beginning of what was to become the next awakening!

41

THE LESSON FROM HISTORY

IT SHOULD NOT BE CONSTRUED from this discussion that *only* during inner-directed eras do the more experiencing faith traditions grow and *only* in outer-directed periods do doing faith traditions grow. This would be a simplistic conclusion and off the point. Social movements are seldom that tidy. Our point is simply that *traditions that are more inclined toward the experiential do better overall in inner-directed eras, because there is greater congruence between their theological tradition and the immediate spirit or "ethos" of the age. Conversely, those traditions that incline more toward the external and institutional do better in outer-directed eras for the same reasons.* Ironically, both emphases reflect key values within our Christian tradition. Biblically, we are a people of inner faith translated into external concern and work. While individual manifestations of such a balance can always be found, the larger social trend seems to reflect the dialectical shifts of the rhythmical inner-outer movement of the cycle.

In recent history, the inner-directed trend has translated into net losses for many of the mainline, doing faith, Protestant traditions. But it does not follow that traditions that are more experiential will necessarily decline in doing faith periods. Rather, the data suggest that their growth slows during these periods but accelerates during experiential periods.

To support our thesis, we provide the following graphs as examples. In the first graph, the membership totals for the Assemblies of God and Presbyterian Church (U.S.A.) are compared. Notice that the apex of the Presbyterian membership occurs toward the end of the outer-directed era. In contrast, notice where the membership curve begins to accelerate for the Assemblies of God. While relatively flat through the doing faith era, their growth rate spikes as the awakening and therefore experiencing faith era begins.

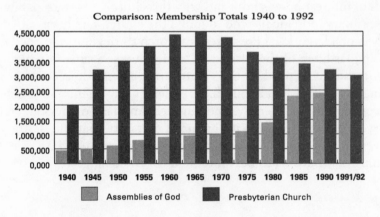

Comparison: Membership Totals 1940 to 1992

A similar pattern is illustrated by comparing the Episcopal Church and the Church of God, Cleveland, Tennessee.

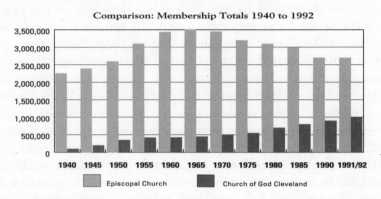

ON THE WAY TO WHERE?

THERE ARE SOME MORE subtle revelations if we examine what historically occurs in the American institutional church in each of the four eras. We present again the generational cycle table. Only this time, we have added dates to the eras. Note that as we enter the twenty-first century, we near the end of an inner-directed era. On the horizon looms the next crisis era.

The Church in the Generational Cycle				
	Outer-Directed Era 1943 - 60	Awakening Era 1961 - 1981	Inner-Directed Era 1982 - 2003	Crisis Era 2004 - 2025
Faith Emphasis	Doing Faith— Secularized Involvements	Experiencing Faith — Privatized Involvements		Doing Faith— Secularized Involvements
Ministry Focus	Building the Institution	Building the Believer		Building the Institution
Institutional Status and Trends	Rise of the Mainlines Decline of the Experiential	Rise of the Experiential Movements (e.g., Charismatic Churches) Decline of the Mainline Institutions	Rise of Independent/ Non-Denominational Churches Decline of the Experiential Denominations & Continued Decline of Mainlines	Uncertain
Structural Examples	Apex of Episcopal, Presbyterian, UMC, and Lutheran Denominations	Rise of A of G, Calvary Chapels, & Small Groups	Seeker Churches, Vineyards, and Cell Groups	
Mood in the Church	Collaboration Liberal Extending	Confrontation Reflection	Fragmentation Conservative Protecting	

Source: Percept Group, Inc. (1994)

What does this mean? Ironically, many of the models and strategies for developing congregations used by the mainlines were forged during the last doing faith period. Though we have been in the experiencing faith period for twenty years, many still hold to these strategies. Some do so with an air of indignation, viewing with disdain the movements and churches that have redirected their emphasis toward the experiential. Many even rationalized the decline in their congregations as evidence of their faithfulness to the prophetic Gospel as the culture rejected it. One of the great advantages of supposedly representing God is the additional opportunities for self-deception in the face of failure.

Understanding the rhythm of the generational cycle could avoid much of this frustration and sense of failure. It is a relatively predictable form of change. In fact, it is human to vacillate between extremes. The cycle actually works to create an overall balance. However, to the extent we fail to recognize this dynamic and in a particular moment in the cycle codify strategy, we are destined to wake up one day and find ourselves out of sync with the larger culture, sitting on the back burner and wondering what happened. Though we may feel some discomfort that social ebbs and cultural flows have a corollary in the ebb and flow of the church, the data do seem to support this notion. Like all other institutions, the church rides the cycle. And the cycle shapes the existential and institutional life of the church.

We believe that in each period, whether experiential or doing, the prevailing institution speaks and behaves with a relatively high level of hubris. To this day, many in the mainline traditions who have seen nothing but decline for the last quarter of the twentieth century seek to explain away this decline instead of facing and accepting it. Fortunately, many are beginning to accept it, and the generational cycle provides them some comfort in understanding what happened.

The traditions that stand on the experiential side (outside the mainlines) are now at the apex of their favored position in the cycle, and quite frankly, many are also rife with hubris. But these friends perhaps have even more to learn from this cycle than the mainlines. For if the cycle holds, they face an uncertain immediate future. Why? As the twenty-first century opens, we will move out of the current inner-directed, experiential period and into a crisis era. Doing faith may reemerge as the dominant cultural ethos.

This being the case, several critical questions ought to be considered. We pose the more significant and ultimately strategic.

- Some have insisted that the historic mainline denominations are dead. Is this true, or will the mainlines begin to recover as we move toward the next crisis–outer-directed era? Is their best strategy to "hunker down" and wait it out?

- Will the experientially inclined traditions begin to see their growth subside for the same reason?
- What will this mean for the strategies and tactics of the current "church growth" movement? Is it possible that many of these are really an expression of what works in an experiencing faith period?
- Will the independent-church movement continue to grow? Or is this simply a reflection of the anti-institutional bias of the era? Is it possible that the growth of the independent-church structure will begin to level off as the current inner-directed era runs out of steam?
- Will structural mission strategies such as cell groups and seeker-oriented programs continue to be the growth edge, or are they simply a logical extension of the level of structural fragmentation the church is currently experiencing in the generational cycle? Will they see their particular mission emphasis begin to trail off as the culture moves?

Honest persons of faith, regardless of where their particular tradition falls between the experiencing or doing faith emphases, must look carefully at these questions. Nothing short of their strategic future is at stake. It might be tempting for many to dismiss these questions by convincing themselves that their particular ministry is blessed by God and exists above this cycle. However, let us assure them that while that might be true, history is not on their side.

Those capable of transcending and going against the cycle are the exception, not the rule. The fact is that throughout most of American history, the nature and timing of church growth has been relatively predictable.

However, there is a trap in the generational cycle as well. One could easily justify a temptation to use the generational cycle as a basis for projection about the future. This is especially true if one's institutional tradition happens to be mainline Protestant. Most of these traditions fit the doing faith model, and the cycle is moving toward an era wherein that emphasis will move to the forefront. However, before anyone is too quick to draw conclusions, there is still another form of change at work, and it packs a mighty big punch—perhaps even big enough to shatter the normal predictability of the generational cycle!

We turn to it in the next chapter.

CHAPTER 5

Chaotic Change

Humanity faces a quantum leap forward. It faces the deepest social upheaval and creative restructuring of all time. Without clearly recognizing it, we are engaged in building a remarkable new civilization from the ground up.[1]

Alvin Toffler

WE HAVE TALKED AT some length about the predictable rhythm of continuous, incremental change and specifically how it is expressed on a grand scale in the generational cycle. We now turn to the other form of change that is also at work today: *chaotic change*. This second form of change occurs only occasionally, but when it happens, it is deeply discomforting.

The underlying dynamic of chaotic change is discontinuity. Unlike the more predictable and rhythmical nature of continuous change, discontinuous change does anything but flow with predictable continuity. It is not incremental. It is usually radical and transformative, as illustrated in the graphic.

---

[1] Alvin Toffler, *The Third Wave* (Bantam, 1980), 10.

An attendant phenomenon of discontinuous change is chaos. We are not in control. All of our assumptions break down. Our ability to predict and set forth clear courses often fails. Our discomfort peaks as we feel a profound threat to our values, lifestyles, and at times even our core belief systems. When we are threatened, our responses tend to be reactive. Rhetoric about the past and the way it used to be abounds. Many of the calls for a "return to our Judeo-Christian roots" in American life are merely the anxious responses to an uncertain, chaotic future. We long to restore "order" and return our personal world to continuous, rhythmic, predictable, and controllable change.

TRANSITIONAL AND TRANSFORMATIONAL PERIODS

DISCONTINUOUS CHANGE EMERGES during a period of social transition. *Transitional periods* occur when significant new movements emerge on the historical landscape and a culture goes through a transition that leaves a permanent imprint. Unlike the rhythmical form of change reflected in the generational cycle, this form of change alters the landscape permanently. The former condition never returns. History is filled with lesser and greater examples. From the vantage point of the church and salvation history, the first coming of Christ was *the* transition in all of history. Other historically significant transitional periods are the legalization of Christianity by Emperor Constantine, the invention of the printing press, and the Reformation (to name but a few).

A transitional period looks like an emerging wave preparing to break upon the beach. We live near the beaches of Southern California, and many times we have observed the impact on the shape and form of the beaches when a strong tropical storm comes onshore. Entire beaches can be wiped out or moved to other locations along the coast as a result of a single storm.

But there are waves, and then there are tidal waves. While a strong tropical storm can rearrange the beach, it generally only impacts the beach. A large tidal wave, on the other hand, can travel for miles inland, completely wiping out any form, structure, or boundary in its path. Transitional periods can be subtle, resulting in barely noticeable historical and cultural changes—or they can be so far-reaching and fundamental that the basic structures and forms of life are altered. When they are the latter, they constitute a very special and rare kind of transitional period: a *transformational period*.

A transformational period, like a tidal wave, builds up massive amounts of energy and releases it upon society. When it subsides, the boundaries of the former epoch are changed permanently, and all socio-cultural structures and institutions have been reshaped: family, religion, politics, economics, education, philosophical assumptions, and so on.

Two transformational periods in history were the transition from a hunter-gatherer economy to an agrarian-based socioeconomic structure, and the move from agrarian to industrial society.[2]

We are currently in the midst of another transformational period as we move from an industrial society built around nation-states to an information-based society built around the global village.[3] To be sure, wrapping our minds around such a notion is overwhelming. In fact, most of us cannot do it except in the abstract. So much of what we have known, what we have depended upon, and what we have done with our lives is in flux. There is a new world coming, and it is erupting with massive force, rising up out of the world that is passing.

How long this transformational period will take is unknown. We suspect not long, given the general rate of change that is driving it. But it is not so much the time it takes as the effects of the change that make it transformational. Once wandering hunters settled as established farmers, their lives were never the same. Once the farm was abandoned for the city, few would ever return to the former structure of life. Like-wise, once the current transformation is complete, no matter how hard people try to hold on to the passing modern era, it will not survive.

It is the transformation from one world to the next that is generating so much chaos and consequently social uncertainty as we prepare to step into the twenty-first century.

Crossing Waves of Change

We used the image of waves and tidal waves of change. What happens when two waves meet—whether they be water waves or, shifting

---

[2]These two transformational periods represent radical shifts in the economic base. If we use a noneconomic model, we could see the shift from oral culture to written culture, and the later shift from handwritten to printed text as transformational periods (although the effects were not as immediately observable).

An additional observation is that what may be a transitional period for one culture can represent a tranformational period for another. For example, the settling of North America by Europeans was transitional for the Western European culture—but trans-formational for the Native American cultures.

[3]We speak here from a Western perspective. Many Third World countries have not yet made the transition from agrarian to industrial. For a more detailed discussion of the major transformational periods in history see appendix A.

the metaphor slightly, seismic waves? When the crests of two waves meet at a given point, they amplify each other. In an earthquake, for example, the seismic waves can be destructive, but when two seismic waves meet, the results can be devastating. The destructive power of the converging force is magnified, often many times.

But if a crest and a trough pass through a point at the same time, the effect is the opposite. The force is actually dampened. This explains why, in an earthquake, two buildings in the same area can be affected very differently: one may be demolished, the other relatively unharmed.

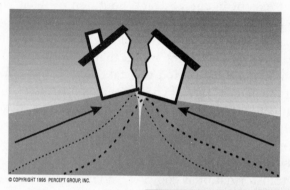

© COPYRIGHT 1995 PERCEPT GROUP, INC.

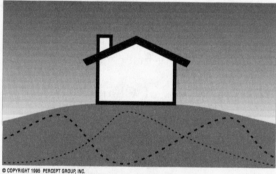

© COPYRIGHT 1995 PERCEPT GROUP, INC.

By analogy, as we step into the twenty-first century, we are experiencing a similar phenomenon. Two different forms of change are rolling through our lives like two seismic waves emanating from different sources but at times crossing each other. There is the normal rhythm of the generational cycle at work—the first seismic wave. While it has its good and bad moments, it is at least relatively predictable. Meanwhile, we are in one of those rare points in human history in which we are also going through a massive social and economic transformation— the second seismic wave.

Each alone creates its own challenges. But at various points, we find ourselves experiencing either the convergence of two crests that amplifies and intensifies the impact of the two forms of change, or we find ourselves in a moment when a crest and a trough cross and the impact momentarily dampens the two forces of change.

THE CHURCH'S RESPONSE TO CHANGE

WHAT DOES ALL THIS mean for the future of the current form of the institutional church? Unfortunately, too many, like the alcoholic, are living in denial. Others are immobilized, having done little positive mission or ministry in their communities for years. Governing bodies, while facing declining congregations and, consequently, falling budgets, fill their time making sure the ecclesiastical machinery doesn't skip a beat. At least we know that is stable and unchanging. In fear, many are cutting back on the very activity that is most needed: a renewed effort to develop healthy congregations while facing the stewardship issue raised by the growing number of dead ones.

Charles Handy tells a story about the Peruvian Indians that powerfully illustrates the present danger. As the Spanish invaders approached Peruvian Indian lands by ship, their sails were in clear view. Something was on the horizon that indicated a change. But the Peruvians dismissed it as a freak of nature and went on about their business. They had no concept of sailing ships within their limited experience, so they simply rejected it all. The rest is history.[4]

What about the church? It depends upon whether we mean the church of Jesus Christ or the institutional forms the church takes in any age and culture. Biblical and theological conviction assures us that the church of Jesus Christ will continue until God completes his purpose in salvation history. However, we must not dismiss the possibility that our human structures, our human institutions, may pass into history. If we choose to follow the status quo strategy, the church as we have known it will be crushed in the seismic waves of change that are rattling our lives.

Earlier we discussed the ebb and flow of faith between experiencing and doing. We are coming toward the end of the forty-year cycle of experiencing, and the era of doing is on the horizon. However, we believe this cycle will be interrupted to some degree, because of the

---

[4]Handy, *The Age of Unreason*, 9 ff.

51

overwhelming impact of the current transformation of our society. It is our suspicion that in some manner, the cycle will not work out quite as we might project. The confluence of the two forms of change are amplifying the effects of some of the changes, and it may simply be too late for some institutions.

To put it bluntly, we believe it would be foolish and irresponsible for those church traditions that do better in outer-directed eras, such as the historic mainline Protestant denominations, to think their time is about to return. Such a belief depends upon the central role of the church in society remaining the same through the generational ebbs and flows. It isn't! Let's be honest with ourselves. Within these traditions, there are literally thousands of churches across America that are old and dying. In many churches, the average age of its members is between sixty-five and seventy. More and more these churches can no longer financially support themselves, and they will not recover.

Likewise, we also believe the more experiential traditions—such as the evangelical churches of independent or nondenominational persuasion, or some of the denominations that place more emphasis on the experience of spirituality, such as the Assemblies of God—face an equally if not more daunting challenge. Not only is the generational cycle moving away from them, they too must deal with the reality of the shifting role of the church. Indeed, for these traditions, the future may be even more precarious than they think. Many of them are riding high currently, but a mighty institutional crash may be just around the turn of the century!

Both traditions are moving rapidly into a defining moment, and we would do well to heed Erich Hoffer's warning:

> In times of change, learners inherit the earth, while the learned find themselves beautifully equipped to deal with a world which no longer exists.

An Example: Restructuring the Family

All this may sound esoteric without an example. Therefore let's explore one social concern that is relatively common to all: the future of the family in America.

During outer-directed eras of the generational cycle, higher percentages of the adult population are likely to marry, and at a younger age. We saw this during the fifteen- to twenty-year period after World

War II. However, as the cycle evolves into an awakening and subsequent inner-directed era, the percentage drops, and the age of first marriage rises. Conversely, in outer-directed eras, the number of single adults is low but then rises during the inner-directed eras.

So how does the confluence of the two forms of change amplify the effects on the family? As we came out of the last outer-directed era in the early 1960s, there was a significant rise in the number of single people. Some of this can be attributed to the cycle as noted above. However, also as we were coming out of that era of conformity, two unexpected and unheard-of social developments occurred. First, there was the phenomenal increase in divorce. Never in American history had divorce been so widely pursued. Second, more people were choosing to live a single lifestyle. Marriage was not automatically considered to be the first goal of young adulthood.

During that same period, changes in thought and belief, more directly attributable to the transformational period, opened up a new level of social tolerance unknown in any prior time. What had been socially unacceptable was suddenly acceptable. For example, consider what has developed for women in the past thirty years. Women have gained remarkable status in our society, regardless of their marital status. Indeed, they now have the social and economic option of setting forth their own futures. They can determine whether or not a man will be included. Men have also found that their career ladder may no longer be thwarted by their marital status. As a corollary to this, there have emerged new and looser definitions of the family.

The de-emphasis of the family characteristic of an inner-directed era crested at the same moment as changing assumptions about life crested. The resulting confluence of both waves amplified the impact on the future of the family. One visible manifestation of this is the sheer speed of its transformation. In a short, thirty-year period, fundamental assumptions about the roles of women and men have been transformed. Regardless of what one personally thinks about this, it is an undeniable fact of late-twentieth-century life.

Now as we move back into a crisis and the subsequent outer-directed era, we suspect that more traditional notions of the family will attempt to again take center stage. This phenomenon coincides with the normal flow of the cycle. It also provides an illustration of the dampening effect. The more traditional era of the cycle will slow the progress of some of the more transformative social developments. This is already evident in public discourse. More and more people on both sides of the political and philosophical spectrum are voicing their concerns about the future of the family. This may well dampen the outward fragmentation of the family in America that has marked the past twenty-five years.

However, we think it is highly unlikely that divorce will drop to the negligible levels of the past. Women will never return home by force of moral and spiritual convention. If they do, it will be their choice. Marriage (and the image of the "family man") will never again be a precondition of career advancement. The force of transformation at work is the reason. We will never go back to the traditional family model that floats around in our minds. The structure of the family is being transformed, just as it was when we shifted from an agrarian to an industrial society.

Furthermore, many of the alternative family structures that have emerged in the latter half of the twentieth century are not likely to disappear either, though their presence may diminish somewhat with the more traditional swing of the cycle.

This is just one simple example of how the two forces of change amplify and dampen one another. The rhythmical inner-outer swings of the generational cycle encountering the forces of change pushed ahead by the current transformational period either heighten (amplify) or minimize (dampen) the impact of the changes on our culture.

PART TWO

Focal Points of Change

In chapter 1, we outlined six commitments that we believe are critical to the future of the institutional church. The first of these was addressed in part 1: the need to understand the dynamics of change at work today in our culture. Part 2 addresses the second commitment: *We must understand the various faces of change emerging as the twenty-first century unfolds before us.*

Our world is being reshaped by the twin seismic forces of the predictable rhythm of the generational cycle, and the discontinuous and chaotic changes driven by the social and economic transformation of our world. The resulting changes converge around a series of four interrelated focal points.

- Changing reality: our understanding of truth, knowledge, and what is real is being challenged.

- Changing structures: the frameworks that give shape and meaning to our place in the world are being turned inside out.

- Changing players: demographic changes are bringing new players onto the American scene.

- Changing faith: trends in religious faith and preferences reveal profound changes.

We do not presume to be all-inclusive. Our focus is driven by the primary question, *What impact are these changes having on the future of the church and the need to face our pending hour of decision?*

CHAPTER 6

Changing Reality I:
A Requiem for Modernity

> *It's a combination of perceptions that crime is getting worse and
> criminal defendants are being treated more leniently....
> Whether that is true is questionable, but the perception is there.
> Perceptions are all that matter in a democracy. That is our sys-
> tem. People vote on the basis of perceptions.*[1]

> Evan Lee

O NE OF THE MOST profoundly unsettling aspects of the transformational change that is pushing us into the twenty-first century
revolves around a cluster of significant questions: What is real? Can the
real world be truly known? Or is whatever we *think* is really out there
just a creation of our own minds?

Consider this. At the height of the O. J. Simpson preliminary hearing, *Time* magazine ran an altered picture of Simpson on the front cover
that made him look more sinister. A *USA Today* editorial by Michael
Gartner insisted that what *Time* had done was a blurring of the line
between news and art. This is how the editorial began:

Where is the line?
Where is the line between fact and fiction?
Where is the line between truth and drama?
Where is the line between news and entertainment?

---

[1]Hastings law professor Evan Lee to *Los Angeles Times* reporter, reflecting on the
O. J. Simpson case and the difficulty of getting good juries (July 7, 1994).

Moving.
And most of us don't know where.[2]

Where is the line indeed? Increasingly, it is wherever one wants to draw it. Reality is something we create with the help of a story line and, more and more, the assistance of digital computer enhancing. As we step into the twenty-first century, reality creation will increasingly challenge our sense of knowing the real.

We are becoming a "reality-creating" society. We can observe the phenomena in every area of our lives. We only need to look at our children's video game systems or MTV. We elect presidents based upon the created images of the "handlers" and "spin doctors." They fabricate a reality about the candidate which they want us to believe is the *real person*. Whether the real person is at all like the created image is immaterial. It is the created reality that is important to their ends.

How did we come to be a society that invents reality? Every major social change and economic transformation brings with it a change in how we perceive and understand the real world, truth, and the nature of knowledge. To understand the current transformation, it will be helpful to look at three ways of looking at reality: premodernity, modernity, and postmodernity. In the West, premodernity lasted until about the seventeenth century, when it was replaced by modernity, which is today being replaced by postmodernity.

It is important to realize that we speak here of the *mainstream* of Western culture. Premodernity is a thing of the past in the mainstream of Western culture, but there are regions and groups, even in North America, who still see the world through essentially premodern eyes. In the Third World, premodernity is alive and well in many areas. Thus we must look at premodernity, modernity, and postmodernity primarily as *ways of perceiving reality*, rather than as historical periods, even though in the West these three ways of perceiving reality coincide by and large with historical periods.

---

[2]Michael Gartner, "Why Risk 'Enhancing' the News?" *USA Today* (June 28, 1994), 13.

Premodernity

Premodern
Period
Knowledge Based
Upon Authoritative
Tradition

Religious Tradition

Quest for Truth and Knowledge

In premodern society, reality is singular and all-encompassing. There is only one central belief system. The official story, which gives meaning to and provides the justification for the society, is the truth, period. The notion of reflecting on the "truthfulness" of the central story is unheard of. Indeed, those in authority are commissioned to insure conformity to the prevailing demands of the belief system, since they are charged with maintaining the status quo. People are simply expected to conform. The untimely death of Socrates stands forever as the ultimate example of this principle. Socrates dared to question the fundamental belief system of Athens, and for his reflections was charged with subverting the minds of the young.

The Old Testament reflects a premodern society. The narratives about the war of conquest provide us with a focused example. In these stories, the young nation of Israel engages in battles to inhabit the Land of Promise. Yahweh commands the conquest of Canaan, and he goes before the people as their Mighty Warrior. The battles were his. The conquerors were to show no mercy:

> *When the LORD your God brings you into the land that you are about to enter and occupy, and he clears away many nations before you . . . and when the LORD your God gives them over to you and you defeat them, then you must utterly destroy them. Make no covenant with them and show them no mercy.* DEUTERONOMY 7:1–2

What was it they were destroying in the annihilation of whole peoples? Was it not their belief systems?

> *Do not intermarry with them, giving your daughters to their sons or tak-*
> *ing their daughters for your sons, for that would turn away your children*
> *from following me, to serve other gods. . . . But this is how you must deal*
> *with them: break down their altars, smash their pillars, hew down their*
> *sacred poles, and burn their idols with fire.* DEUTERONOMY 7:3–5

In that premodern society, there could be no conflicting belief system. It was Yahweh or Baal, period. Only one faith was allowed in the land. In other words, only one story that gave meaning and legitimacy to the social and political structures was acceptable. No choice of belief was offered. The tragic history of Israel is one of failure to fully expunge the land of the religions of the native peoples.[3]

In premodern society, there exists a direct and reciprocal relationship between religion and political power structures. The state religion legitimizes the state. Conversely, the state protects the place of the state's religion and its belief about reality. The religion of the land provides the basic belief structures around which society functions, and the state upholds these beliefs.

In the time of the early church, much of the conflict experienced by the early apostles and evangelists was the result of their new faith challenging the established belief system in Palestine or the established

---

[3]If we are honest, these stories cause us some discomfort. Part of our historic tradition assumes that into this ancient society, Yahweh spoke and called forth a people. A tenet of our faith is that through the Hebrews, God was carrying forward salvation history. In other words, through a people's particular history, special history was at work, a history that is still unfolding through God's people today. Without this assumption, our faith becomes meaningless, lacking a proper anchor and apologetic for our continued existence. (See Peter Craigie's *The Problem of War in the Old Testament* [Grand Rapids: Eerdmans, 1978], which wrestles with the modern person's dilemma of holding to a concept of biblical revelation that is able to address the repugnancy of holy war.)

Yet while we hold this assumption, we find our moral sensibilities troubled. Such behavior would not be tolerable today. A critical issue of the nineties is dealing with the moral implications of resurgent nationalism and the ethnic cleansing occurring around the world (in Bosnia, for example). If we remove the salvation history component of ancient Israel, we must admit that the Israelites' actions were, in effect, a form of ethnic cleansing. Perhaps our troubled consciousness will be somewhat appeased by at least understanding that in premodern society, such behaviors were normal. The choice to hold other views of reality was simply not on the menu of options for any society. (See Craigie's appendix, "War and Religion in the Ancient Near East," p. 115.)

belief system of other parts of the Roman Empire. In premodern societies, the concept of separation between church and state (or religion and state) was incomprehensible. So when it did happen, those who were swimming against the tide were subjected to no small amount of persecution. The early church was persecuted until Emperor Constantine made Christianity the official state religion in A.D. 313—which, some think, is the worst thing that could have happened. In terms of the relationship between church and state, there was no difference between Rome under paganism and the Holy Roman Empire under Christian emperors.

A more modern example is the story of Galileo. The astronomer Copernicus had theorized that the earth revolved around the sun, not the sun around the earth—a theory that challenged the long-held Ptolemaic system. Galileo publicly declared his agreement with Copernicus, using his telescopes to make his case. He twice ran into trouble with the official teaching of the church over his position. Under a premodern social structure, the church wielded total power over the acceptable worldview. Even the social and political structures of the day initially lined up with the church. Ultimately Galileo was pressured to recant his thesis and was sent into isolation—while the earth kept revolving around the sun.

Such is the relationship between church and state in premodern societies. This relationship between religion and political power structures continued until well after the period of the Reformation.[4]

---

[4]Many Western countries still have state religions. Germany, for example, has the Lutheran *Landeskirche*, which in the past served the premodern function of providing social and political stability but now has a relationship to the state that is largely administrative and formal.

Modernity

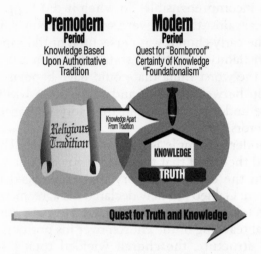

In medieval Western culture, truth was embodied in the teachings of the Catholic Church. Around the time of the Reformation and Renaissance, this all began to change. Questions about the foundation of knowledge started to arise, and alternative belief systems were emerging all over Europe. Galileo is only one example in a growing flood of thinkers who began to challenge the worldview posited by the church and supported by the state. This set the stage for the end of the premodern era and the birth of the modern.

> The bloodshed and chaos that followed upon seventeenth century differences of belief lent urgency to the quest for universal agreement. . . . So from Descartes' time, the idea of human knowledge focused on the general, the universal, the timeless, the theoretical . . . . Basing all knowledge claims on indubitable foundations would compel assent from all rational people. So certitude and universal persuasion were closely linked.[5]

But if truth and the nature of reality could be separated from the church, it could be separated from any "revealed" source. Human reason alone, through the careful observation of the sensible world, would

---

[5]Nancey Murphy, *Philosophical Resources for Postmodern Evangelical Theology*, 5–6. Her comments are a reflection on Stephen Toumin's book *Cosmopolis: The Hidden Agenda of Modernity* (New York: Macmillan, 1990), ch. 1.

establish one singular, universal story that would serve as the foundation of all reality, in a manner that was to be *unassailable.* Or as one of our colleagues put it, the goal was to develop "bombproof certainty" of knowledge that would provide meaning to all of the particulars and at the same time separate truth from the hegemony of the oftentimes warring religious traditions. In other words, the modernist goal was a story that was so bombproof that all alternative stories based upon religious tradition and religious "truth" would finally be neutralized. Thus, driven by the goal of bombproof certainty, the premodern world was transformed into the modern world.

With the new freedom to consider alternative ways of understanding the world and even faith came the powerful, dramatic social changes of the last four hundred years: Reformation, Inquisition and Counter-Reformation, Enlightenment, political and social revolution, industrial revolution, separation of church and state, human rights. All of these developed as people questioned the singular, Western, premodern view of reality that was controlled by the prevailing religious tradition.

The very religious foundation of America and the issues that drove the Puritans, among others, to seek life in a new land was an expression of early modern ideas. The Puritans purposed to establish the city on the hill, a light to the world of the rule of God in human life. They had a vision of reality that departed from the prevailing assumptions of seventeenth-century England. That they could even embark on such an adventure reflected emerging modernity. When one compares their endeavor to the world of Joshua or even Savonarola (the priest burned at the stake in Florence for heresy in the fifteenth century), we must admit the world had changed.

It is ironic that the Puritans envisioned the establishment of a political reality where their understanding of truth and the Bible would prevail unassailed. Their goal would have amounted to a return to a premodern social structure. That they were not successful in that respect is a testimony to the age in which they lived. They could not reenact the "conquest of the land of Israel."

Modernity and Religious Truth

An agenda as basic and all-encompassing as modernity could not avoid having an impact on the essence of religious truth and knowledge. In the spirit of the age, theologians within the church adopted the modernist goal of finding *an unassailable foundation of truth.* But there was an immediate problem. How does one verify religious knowledge as "truth," using the standard tools of empirical observation and logical reasoning? A foundation was needed as final authority upon which one could build. What was that foundation? One part of the church appealed to an inner-directed foundation: religious knowledge was based upon "a feeling of absolute dependency," an inner awareness or a personal experience of the divine.[6]

Others in the church sought the foundation in Scripture, which is more objective than one's inner religious feelings. But the modernist problem of externally verifiable knowledge did not go away by positing the Bible as the foundation for religious knowledge. If the Bible was to be the foundation, then in the spirit of modernity and its goal of unassailable certainty, the Bible could not escape scrutiny. Using modern critical theory, scholars sought to demonstrate the truth of the Bible's claims, just as modernity sought to demonstrate the veracity of all truth statements.[7]

Because bombproof certainty was the issue (that is, "independent rational judgment rather than dogmatic authority"), how could one meet that criterion and yet speak of things invisible, things not sensibly observable? The solution was the modern doctrine of revelation. The Bible was revealed by God. It was imbued with special knowledge that, given its source, superseded the conclusions of modern science and reflection. Therefore one could make objective, propositional statements about the nature of reality, both seen and unseen, based on the Bible. As a revealed source of truth, it provided the absolute foundation.

How was this modern view different from views of the Bible's inspiration under premodernism? As a general rule, the premodern person would not have questioned the "truthfulness" of the Bible. The inspiration of the Bible was an apriority. The authority of the Bible and biblical interpretation were tied to tradition and dogmas, and the Bible was to interpret itself, to authenticate itself. More obtuse passages were

---

[6]Frederich Schleiermacher, *On Religion: Speeches to Its Cultured Despisers* (Harper and Row, 1959), xvi. The problem, of course, with the theological tradition that extended from this early liberal tradition was twofold: How can we translate inner knowledge into objective, external, and sharable knowledge? How can this allow for the possibility of unassailable certainty?

[7]"The veracity of scripture would and should be attested by independent rational judgment rather than dogmatic authority." Hans W. Frei, *The Eclipse of Biblical Narrative: A Study of Eighteenth and Nineteenth Century Hermeneutics* (New Haven and London: Yale University Press, 1994), 17.

to be interpreted in light of the more clear and obvious. This was Luther's point of view as reflected in his comment, "... through itself most certain, most easily accessible, comprehensible, and interpreting itself, proving, judging all the words of all men."[8] Similarly, Calvin's doctrine of the Spirit's internal testimony to the truthfulness of the biblical message does not allow for the possibility of reason to sit in judgment over the Scriptures.

> Let this point therefore stand: that those whom the Holy Spirit has inwardly taught truly rest upon Scripture, and that Scripture indeed is self-authenticated; hence it is not right to subject it to proof and reasoning. And the certainty it deserves with us, it attains by the testimony of the Spirit.[9]

But with the advent of modernism, the Bible for the first time had to defend its truthfulness under the scrutiny of reason. In the pursuit of certainty of knowledge, the goal of interpretation was to establish (if possible) the truthfulness of Scripture by means of rational proofs.[10] This one subtle shift changed the cultural view of the Bible forever.

In the final analysis, the answer to the bombproof criterion was a "leap of faith" relative to the Bible's inspiration. Even the more conservative of us make this leap, and if we are honest, we admit it. Why is this necessary? Because of modernity's criterion of unassailability. If we accept the criterion of an absolute and unassailable rational foundation, we are destined to make a leap of faith—not because the Bible cannot stand up to rigorous scholarly reflection but because the apriority of modernity, that truth and knowledge of any kind can and must be tied to an unassailable foundation, is itself not founded on an unassailable foundation. If this criterion is jettisoned, then establishing the Bible as our foundation is not a "leap" in the sense of the irrational and subjective—it is just faith, period.

---

[8] Ibid., 19. Quote from Martin Luther, "Assertio Ominum Articulorum," *Werke*, vol. 7 (Weimare: Bohlau, 1883), 96 ff.

[9] John T. McNeill, *Library of Christian Classics*, vol. XX, *Calvin: Institutes of the Christian Religion*, book I, chapter vii, section five (Philadelphia: Westminster, 1960).

[10] There is much more detail involved in this tradition. For example, philosophy of language played a significant role. The conservative tradition subscribed to the "referential theory of language." True statements are propositional. Thus doctrines reflect absolute statements of reality.

The Breakdown of Modernity

The modern era began to break down as the twentieth century unfolded. The unassailability criterion simply was untenable, and the harder it was pressed, the more obvious that became. At least three factors contribute to its demise.

- Failure of epistemology to develop an unassailable (bombproof) certainty.
- Failure to develop a "grand narrative," the "super story" that gives meaning to all other stories.
- The emergence of the global village, which brought ideas from other places and belief systems together at the time modern epistemology began to fail.

1. The Failure of Epistemology to Develop Bombproof Certainty

For all of the grand expectations of modernity—that humankind would be able to create unassailable certainty of knowledge—as we step into the twenty-first century, most philosophers and scientists would agree that this quest has been a failure. Logical positivism was the zenith of modernism. As a movement, it purposed to allow as truth statements only those which could be demonstrated by evidence. Positivism stretched the modernist agenda as far as it would go. Under this pressure, it broke.

As the century passed its halfway mark, two books were published that hastened modernity's demise. First was Michael Polyani's *Personal Knowledge*. Polyani demonstrates that all knowledge has a personal element; it is impossible to completely remove the subject from the object being examined.[11] All knowledge has a "tacit" (implicit) aspect because each one of us brings something to the knowledge event. Therefore to assume we can even observe an object with perfect objectivity is false.

The second writer was Thomas Kuhn, whose *Structure of Scientific Revolutions*[12] showed how paradigms control what we see and what we

---

[11] Michael Polyani, *Personal Knowledge: Towards a Post-Critical Philosophy* (Harper Torchbooks, Harper and Row: New York, 1964). This is at best a super-simplistic statement about Polanyi's thesis. But for the purposes of the book, we only care to point out what he was trying to point out, not to provide an explanation of his argument.

[12] Thomas S. Kuhn, *The Structure of Scientific Revolutions*, 2d. ed, (Chicago: University of Chicago Press, 1970).

believe reality to be. Kuhn argues that one's paradigm predetermines the conclusions that will be drawn from a process of inquiry.

A paradigm represents a mental framework and a set of conventional or articulated rules that govern the process of inquiry. Kuhn suggests that at any given moment our perception of reality is a function of our perceptual paradigm. This is true even in scientific inquiry. Normal science involves training future scientists in the assumptions about reality that are implicitly part of the prevailing paradigm.

Kuhn, in other words, demonstrated that our paradigms are culturally determined. We believe reality to be what it is because of our paradigm, our mental framework through which we view the world. Were that to change, we would most likely draw different conclusions about the nature of things.

It did not take the larger intellectual community long to figure out that his argument was not just limited to scientific knowledge. He had articulated a fundamental problem of epistemological certainty for any area of knowledge. *Certain knowledge could not be bombproof if our perceptions of reality were conditioned by our received paradigm.*

2. The Failure to Develop a Grand Narrative

At the same time that the quest for bombproof certainty was failing in science, philosophers dealing with language and meaning also found themselves coming up short. Accompanying the quest for a foundation for the certainty of knowledge was the quest for "the story," the "grand narrative" that would tie all of the social and political structures of humanity together without the assistance of a particular religious tradition.[13] The late nineteenth century and a large portion of the twentieth century saw several attempts at this quest.

The grand narrative legitimized knowledge. In other words, why was it important to know something? What gave meaning to a particular intellectual pursuit? It is the role of the grand narrative to supply legitimacy. For example, one form of grand narrative, the "emancipation narrative," was to supply the primary reason for the pursuit of knowledge—namely, to liberate the human spirit.[14]

---

[13]Jean-Francois Lyotard, *Theory and History of Literature*, vol. 10, *The Postmodern Condition: A Report on Knowledge*, trans. Geoff Bennington and Brian Massumi (Minneapolis: University of Minnesota Press, 1984), x–xi. The term *postmodernism* originated with Lyotard.

[14]Ibid. See pages 32–37 for a discussion of the issue of the legitimation of knowledge and the role of the emancipation narrative in this respect.

Marxism/Leninism can only be understood as an attempt to write such a super story putting every detail and every person in a nice, neat, and tidy place. Likewise, the Third Reich was based on (or perhaps rationalized by) a grand narrative. That both have failed—communism and facism—is a testimony to the larger failure of establishing a grand narrative on the basis of human reason alone, regardless of the philosophical first principles.

John François Lyotard, who originated the term *postmodernism*, feels very strongly about this, especially as it relates to politics. He insists that we should not expect to formulate a story that finally fulfills the desire for the ultimate, transcendental story that will pull together all of the particular parts into a single, coherent, unified story. To accomplish this goal, Lyotard says, pointing to Kant, requires the kind of political and social power that leads to terror. Why? Because it takes a great effort to force a unified belief system on a society. The fascism and communism of the late nineteenth century and the first eighty years of the twentieth century have demonstrated the error of this goal. In deep seriousness he asserts these two centuries "have given us as much terror as we can take."[15]

In the final analysis, in a capitulation to total relativism, Lyotard insists that we must simply abandon all efforts to find the one grand narrative that gives meaning to all of the particular stories that are our lives and our culture. For Lyotard, there is no such narrative that can pull together all of the social, economic, and political particulars in a singular whole. In effect, he says we must accept the many and forget the one.

In the end, the search for the grand narrative has been superseded by deconstructionism and its radical abandonment of the possibility of any kind of story that provides cohesion.

3. The Emergence of the Global Village

Finally, the world shrank into the "global village." The world became very small, and ideas from other places and belief systems came close. Modern transportation, communications, and computers have set the stage for the formulation of the global economy. The much-ballyhooed information superhighway will tie it all together. National borders are increasingly becoming meaningless. We conduct business

---

[15]Ibid., 82.

literally all over the world, and people from literally all over the world are coming here, many as immigrants.

At the center of the emergent globalism is economics, not politics. John Nesbitt points out that "in the global economy, economic considerations almost always transcend political considerations."[16] In the modern era, politics and religion were in the center. People moved to new frontiers for political and/or religious reasons.

But political or religious freedom no longer drives the mobility of people. To be sure, there are those who come to the U.S. for political reasons. But in the final analysis, even this is often directly connected to the lack of economic freedom or opportunity in their country of origin. In other words, ideological reasons are not the primary drivers behind globalization. People no longer move to new lands in order to establish communities of *the* truth.

Yet as they come, they come with their own cultures and belief systems. This continual and increasing exchange of peoples and cultures and their divergent ideas about reality adds the third nail to the coffin of modernism. No longer are we, or can we be, isolated from the other belief systems of the world. Indeed, the emphasis on Western civilization that has been the staple of American education has been continually under attack in recent times for its supposed elitism. People from other, non-Western cultures settle within the boundaries of the U.S. and increasingly take offense at our Western chauvinism and ethnocentrism. In the global village, we must deal with alternative views of reality every day.

Epistemological Bungee Jumping

We propose another metaphor that will better assist us in understanding not only the demise of modernity but also what is happening as it fails. Bungee jumping has become quite a recreational pastime for many. People tied to large rubber bands jump off bridges, out of hot-air balloons, or over cliffs. The sheer force of the body in free fall stretches the bungee cord way beyond its normal, nonstressed state. As it stretches, the cord is actually storing up energy. The farther it is stretched, the more potential energy.

When the cord is stretched as far as the weight can pull it, Newton's third law comes into play: *For every action, there is an equal and opposite reaction.* All of that stored energy is released, yanking the

---

[16]John Nesbitt, *Megatrends 2000* (New York: William Morrow, 1990), 21.

jumper in the opposite direction until once again it expends all of its energy.

Modernism's quest for bombproof certainty is like the jumper leaping from a high bridge. All of the weight of the effort, all of the ideas and expectations (and often hubris) that were poured into the original goal, stretched the epistemological cord as far as it could stretch. And what happened then? The stored-up energy sent the discussion shooting back in the opposite direction.

The result was that the quest for absolute certainty was replaced by a tendency toward *radical relativism*. If knowledge and truth cannot be absolutely affirmed, then no truth is absolutely true. For much of the culture, that means nothing can be "true" in the sense of right versus wrong. All truth is relativized, and it becomes entirely impolitic to suggest that one's viewpoint on matters is more true than someone else's. Reality is what you make it. In reaction, we have become reality creators, not observers. It is this phenomenon that has governed much of popular thought and culture for most of the second half of the twentieth century.

CHAPTER 7

Changing Reality II:
A Reality for Every Occasion

Cold hearted orb that rules the night,
Removes the colors from our sight.
Red is gray and yellow white,
But we decide which is right. And which is an illusion?

Days of Future Past, The Moody Blues[1]

W E DECIDE WHICH IS RIGHT. And which is an illusion?" Welcome
to the postmodern world! As the twenty-first century opens,
we live in a world wherein so much has been relativized that reality
creation for whatever purpose has become quite acceptable. If nothing
can be absolutely demonstrated to be true, then nothing is true. There
is only argument and persuasion and power. Whereas under modernity
there was the quest for the foundation of all knowledge, in the postmodern world such a quest has been abandoned. In its most radically
relativistic form, the postmodern is about many stories, all competing to
be heard and embraced.

In a democratic society, this competition translates into political
agendas, spin doctoring, and power. In other words, which story is most
likely to provide an advantage? Whether the story is "true" or not is
meaningless. "Reality" is the spin you put on a story to meet a particular goal. The story must be told in a manner compelling enough to get
fifty-one percent of the population to "buy" it. Enter the marketing and

---

[1]The Moody Blues, *Days of Future Past* (Decca Records, 1967).

advertising world or the political-image-making industry. Or even some forms of modern religion.

CREATORS OF REALITY

WITH THE FAILURE OF the modernist goal of a single, true story about what is real (the grand narrative), we have adopted in its place the belief that "truth" is merely a cultural construction. Those in power are those who have been most successful in weaving a believable construction of reality. Presidential elections are not won on clarity of issue and policy today. They are won by those most successful in creating a story attractive to a majority of Americans at a moment in time.

Many freely develop stories supporting their particular belief systems. Instead of arguments over the truth, people discuss their belief systems as options in the marketplace of stories. I was speaking with one of my son's teachers one day. The particular subject completely escapes me. However, I clearly remember one specific comment. He said, "In my belief system, each life experience is part of working out your karma." I remember thinking, "Now what do I say?" He had not suggested that mine was wrong. He was only offering an alternative way of viewing the subject. From what I could tell, it did not matter to him whether one was more "right" than the other. They were simply alternative versions of "reality," intended to give meaning to one's life experience.

We are becoming a culture of creators and consumers of realities. There is a reality for everyone and every occasion. An extended browse through any super-bookstore today will provide ample evidence of this. A couple of examples may help make the point.

Example 1: Retelling Prehistory

One story, proposed by some radical feminists, suggests that the feminine goddess in prehistoric mythologies was the primary social force. Consequently, people in these ancient civilizations were peaceful, productive, and progressive. In *The Chalice and the Blade*, Riane Eisler retells the history of the early Minoan civilization. She insists that these early civilizations were under the influence of the goddess, a female-spirit religion. Governed by women, many of whom were the priestly class, these early civilizations were benign, creative, and peaceful as well as economically prosperous, though without unnecessary competition. This all lasted until around the eleventh century

B.C. Apparently, at that time wild macho-male barbarians from Europe and Asia came down from the hills, bringing a new culture of violence and male domination.[2]

She bases her thesis on a reassessment of prehistorical art and artifacts. In referring to this art, she notes,

> It tells us a great deal about how they thought, for in a very real sense Neolithic art is a kind of language or shorthand symbolically expressing how people in that time experienced and in turn shaped what we call reality. And if we let this language speak for itself, without projecting on it prevailing models of reality, it tells a fascinating—and in comparison to the stereotype, a far more hopeful—story of our cultural origins.[3]

To make her argument, she insists that the traditional interpretation of the prehistoric artifacts is based upon the male-dominator view of history, with all of its attendant assumptions about early civilizations. Now, she may be correct in this. The male-dominator model is an interpretive overlay that will influence how we see the data. However, she is inconsistent. She insists that "if we let this language speak for itself, without projecting on it prevailing models of reality, it tells a fascinating—and in comparison to the stereotype, a far more hopeful—story of our cultural origins." Really! She is not projecting upon it her prevailing model of reality? We think she is, and it is this very blindness that has attracted significant criticism of her methods and results.

Such reconstructions ultimately have noble ends. Ms. Eisler envisions a better life for us all. But her method blurs the line between fact and fiction. To anchor a new social model for our modern world on such a reconstruction seems most foolish. The reality question is always there, unless your view of the nature of reality is that you make it what you want. This, we believe, is what Ms. Eisler is attempting to do.

Now, we hasten to add that her vision of what could be is not troubling to us. We affirm the trends toward greater partnership between men and women—as well as between women and women, and men and men. Less emphasis on one dominating another is, we believe, a biblical vision. It is her methodology, the creation of reality to support her agenda, that we find troubling. She presupposes that

---

[2]Riane Eisler, *The Chalice and the Blade: Our History, Our Future* (San Francisco: Harper, 1988).

[3]Ibid., 17.

she can simply retell the story in language supportive of her vision and then appeal to it as an authority. This is reality creation.

A more troubling trend is the use of such feminine-goddess myths by women seeking to gain a sense of meaning within the Christian theological tradition. In the early nineties, most mainline denominations were embroiled in a controversy surrounding an ecumenical conference titled "Reimaging God." Congregations across the country were tangled in debate around reports of prayers to Sophia, goddess of wisdom, and a communion service using milk and honey. In the spirit of Riane Eisler, this was an exercise in reality creation. Even though we find these themes troubling, we still find the intent of assisting women to find a place in the church, with images they can relate to, a worthy task.

Example 2: The End of the World at Waco

Some reality creation, however, does not have any noble or redeeming intentions. The horrid story of David Koresh and the Branch Davidians serves as a stark example. A charismatic leader constructed a worldview in which he emerges as the Messiah. He claimed to be a prophet king and a warrior angel.[4] God told him to form a new house of David. Like David, he was to have many wives. Many of these "wives" were young teenage girls, some no older than twelve. Astoundingly, many of the girls' parents consented to and blessed the arrangement. Robin Bunds, one of Koresh's former wives, explained that they did it because "they [the parents] believed in his message." In 1989 Koresh announced that God told him he could have as many wives as he wanted, but he was the only one. All other marriages were annulled.

Newsweek wrote an article about Koresh's cult from the perspective of the children who were allowed to leave during the standoff. Therapists who worked with the children "described a twisted universe completely dominated by David Koresh."[5] Children were taught that there were two kinds of people: good and evil. Of course, all of the good people resided within the Branch Davidian compound. Everyone else in the world was evil. This is reality creation at its worst.

---

[4]"The Messiah of Waco," *Newsweek* (March 15, 1993), 56.
[5]"The Children of the Cult," *Newsweek* (May 17, 1993), 49.

These two examples are not equally problematic. Clearly, the feminist-goddess story purposes to provide a framework for greater peace and cooperation. This was not the objective of David Koresh. His objective was that of a self-indulgent maniac. He created a reality around himself to fulfill his own personal, consumptive obsessions. It was a dangerous and violent and fatal construction of reality.

Why construct a belief system about reality? Quite simply, to justify agendas and personal aspirations. And why not? If we have abandoned the goal of bombproof knowledge, and all truth stories have been relativized, then any story is valid. How do we judge the appropriateness of a particular created reality? In a postmodern world, who is to say who is wrong?

This is where we find ourselves as we step into the twenty-first century. Popular culture has lived under the cloud of radical relativism for decades. A primary arena for radical relativism has been moral values. If all stories are right, then no story is RIGHT. As modernity has failed, globalism has brought us into contact with many world cultures and their various belief systems. But are all aspects of every culture's beliefs morally upright and good for the social whole?

A third-grade teacher found herself having a very difficult time with a young Middle Eastern boy. He was disruptive and disrespectful. When she would try to guide or correct him, he insisted she had no authority over him. The teacher called for a conference with the boy's parents. When she explained to them the boy's comments, the father insisted his son's view was right. He proceeded to tell her that as a woman, she had less value than a cow. As a boy, his son *was* superior to her. That was what his culture believed. That was the way it would be.

Is this a story we can and should embrace as valid under the banner of cultural pluralism? Is it in fact true that in a postmodern world, we cannot make any statements about the nature of reality, of right and wrong? Is there no basis in a diversified culture to evaluate and judge one story against another? Or are we destined to drift with no recourse in such scenarios? Ultimately the question is, Is there no possibility of knowledge in a postmodern world?

KNOWLEDGE IN A POSTMODERN WORLD

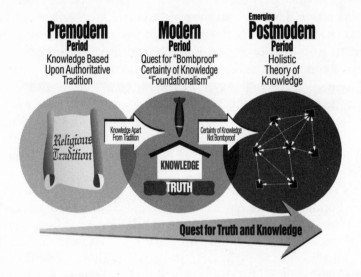

Writers such as Thomas Kuhn or Michael Polyani are not radical relativists, who insist reality is whatever you want it to be. Rather, their point—somewhat simplistically stated—is this: *Our knowledge of the external universe, of the real world, is always conditioned by our subjective mental framework (paradigm).* We are finite. Our knowledge is finite and partial. We cannot escape this. Therefore all our knowledge about reality is relative, and it is not possible to know anything absolutely, *within the definition of modernity.* But that does not mean it is a free-for-all!

Using the bungee cord metaphor again, modernity stretched the cord as far as it could go, and the rebound took us into radical relativism. But we are reaching the point where the cord has once again stretched as far as it can, and we are now rebounding from radical relativism. We know that we can't have bombproof certainty of knowledge, but we are also beginning to realize that this does not mean everything we know is strictly a creation of our own minds and has no connection whatsoever with the external, real world. How is this different from a modernist view?

Modernists assumed that an objective universe exists and that it can be known through logical reasoning and empirical data. Postmodernists fall along a continuum of belief about the reality of the objective universe. On one end is the *postmodern constructivist,* who believes that all reality is merely a construction of the mind. At the other end is the *postmodern objectivist,* who asserts relative certainty without the burden of absolute certitude.[6]

The postmodern constructivist believes that reality is fully a creation of the individual or group. "Whatever is out there . . . remains for all time out there, and all our systems of thought are stories we tell ourselves about something that remains essentially unknowable."[7] Reality is a "construction" of our own minds. We can create a reality for every occasion. Some do this consciously, some completely unconsciously.

On the relative certainty side stands the postmodern objectivist, whose goal is to have a solid understanding of reality. These people believe that the objective universe exists and is knowable in some relative fashion. For objectivists, things are the way they are because that is what they are, even if our understanding is relative. Changes in our understanding about the nature of reality are the result of better ways of viewing and interpreting what is really there. Thomas Kuhn has helped us recognize that our ability to properly perceive the world out there is in part a function of our limited ability to receive the data, and in part the models or paradigms we employ to derive meaning from the data.

Moreover, postmodern objectivists, unlike modernists, recognize that much of life is not black and white. A theory of knowledge must be able to account for this. Something may be not true in one setting but true in another. It is in the relationship that its validity is affirmed or denied. This principle applies in all arenas of study, from quantum physics to moral theology.[8]

Some who hold a postmodern epistemology will look as if they subscribe to the goal of modernity in its search for the real. The difference lies in the recognition that a truth statement can never be bombproof, not because reality isn't there but because our ability to perceive it is relative. The principles of logical reasoning still govern the pursuit of knowledge, but with one additional criterion: *unsurpassability.*

---

[6]Walter Truet Anderson, in *Reality Isn't What It Used to Be* (San Francisco: Harper, 1990), uses the terms *objectivist* and *constructivist,* but his *objectivist* means roughly the same as *modernist.*

[7]Ibid., 13.

[8]The theory of relativity is a good example. We realize that this discussion alone could encompass a whole book. Our intent is simply to make the contrast between the binary nature of absolutism and the holistic, interrelated nature of the postmodern objectivist.

Alasdair MacIntyre, writing on "truth as unsurpassability," says, "The test for truth in the present, therefore, is always to summon up as many questions and as many objections of the greatest strength possible; what can be justifiably claimed as true is what has sufficiently withstood such dialectical questioning and framing of objections."[9] *A truth statement passes the test of unsurpassability if, after rigorous testing, the statement stands unsurpassed in its explication of that portion of reality it purports to address.* In other words, a truth claim is posited as true until a better explanation surpasses it based upon sound method (that is, the principles of logical reasoning).

On this principle, the postmodern objectivist does not assume that all stories are equally valid. Some will simply not stand up to sound reasoning nor provide the best explanation of what is right and appropriate. On the basis of unsurpassability, we would insist that the cultural position that devalues women does not stand up against the biblical story that insists that God created all persons equal and imbued them with his own image. When the two stories are placed side by side, one surpasses the other as a moral foundation and framework for positive human relationships. Does this still sound relative? Yes. But whether the modernists like it or not, this is as good as it gets.

Reality and Choice

Having concluded that empiricism will not deliver the goods on reality, the door is again opened to the possibility that knowledge and truth cannot (and must not) be limited to "unassailable" empirical proofs and reason. Within this framework, religious tradition and belief can again have a significant role. We are not saying that the empirical method is rejected (at least, not by those of us on the objectivist side of the continuum), only that postmodernists recognize that all of reality cannot be captured by this method. It is this realization that opens the door for other traditions to be explored, including other belief systems, without the onerous burden of unassailability.

In this respect, postmodernism has more in common with premodernism than with modernism. Whereas the modernist ideal was unassailable certainty based upon empirical data and logical reasoning apart from religious tradition, postmodern thought recognizes an important role for historical tradition as a source of authentic knowl-

---

[9]Murphy, *Philosophical Resources,* 24.

edge. Why? Because a bombproof authority was not possible, and we need to connect to something for the sake of meaning. To put it another way, modernity failed to remove the untidiness of faith. It could not remove the necessity of assessing and subscribing to a story that gives life meaning.

How is this different from premodernism? *The most important distinction is that of choice.* This is what makes the epistemological issue different. Modernity released us from necessary submission to an authoritative tradition by elevating autonomous reason and the goal of absolute certainty. Once we insisted that we will only submit to that which is absolutely true, we opened the door to choice.

However, having recognized that absolute certainty is not reasonable nor possible has not removed from us the *awareness* of our ability to choose. Our eyes have been opened by more fruit from the Tree of Knowledge of Good and Evil. Now we must choose to submit to an idea as truth because we have become convinced it is the truth (or perhaps only because we think it is a clever idea!), not because of some absolute external certainty that says for all time, "This is the truth." Choice has been democratized! It is not optional.

> In the postmodern world, we are all required to make choices about our realities. You may select a life of experimentation, eternal shopping in the bazaar of culture and subculture. Or you may forego the giddy diversity of contemporary lifestyle swapping and fall into step with some ancient heritage: be an Orthodox Jew or a fundamentalist Muslim or a bible-toting Christian or a traditional native American. The range of such choices is enormous, but the choice is still a choice and requires an entirely different social consciousness from that of Jews, Muslims, Christians and native Americans who knew no alternatives. . . . We have to make choices from the range of different stories—stories about what the universe is like, about who the good guys and the bad guys are, about who we are—and also we have to make choices about how to make choices.[10]

The person today who subscribes to any traditional belief system, be it Judaism, Islam, Christianity, or Native American spiritualism, does so out of a choice that is very different from those who followed these faiths in the past. One may object by insisting in every age a person must choose his or her faith. Indeed, within the Christian tradition,

---

[10]Ibid., 7–8.

there is a strong emphasis on individual choice to become a disciple of Jesus. Yet the *level of choice* is determined by the context in which we live. How much choice was there really for a child born in a premodern society? While most faith traditions had some kind of confirmation process, the outcome was seldom in doubt. What were one's alternatives? One was a Catholic or Muslim or later even a Presbyterian for life, active or not. This is no longer true in American culture.

We have a choice, and we are aware of that choice. We cannot overemphasize this point. It explains a critical phenomenon within the church today. For years now we have listened to denominational pastors of mainline Protestant churches bemoan the loss of "brand loyalty" among boomers and the generation following them. There is a choice. People today choose the construction of reality they find most appealing. They look for the form of story that provides the greatest meaning for them. For many this is an interative process of embracing one new reality after another.

And where is the church in all of this? It is simply one more of the many alternative reality constructions available in the marketplace of beliefs, which is why it resorts increasingly to marketing techniques. *It has no premier position.*

As the institutional church faces the unfolding of the twenty-first century, it faces a great challenge. In the postmodern world, there is a "reality for every occasion." The church's message is simply one more voice in the cacophony of created realities competing to attract a following. This will not change. It is in engaging what this means that the church again comes face-to-face with its own death. However, it is also in this place of death that its greatest opportunity dwells, and nowhere else.

CHAPTER 8

Changing Structures I: The End of the Grand American Story

As truth has been relativised—absolutely relativised, so to speak—so has morality.

Gertrude Himmelfarb

WITH A REALITY FOR every occasion comes a story for every occasion. Unfortunately, this also means the end of THE story for ALL occasions. Radical relativism has relativised all stories. One victim is the story that for most of our national history gave meaning to our distinctly American experience.

America was formed around a great story. As a new nation, it saw itself as having a great calling, a calling that gave universal meaning to the American experience. Throughout our early history, one finds leaders who spoke with a clear sense of American destiny. We were to be a special people, a people from many places and traditions, cultures and religions, who found a place under the rule of democracy. We were to be "one nation under God, indivisible, with liberty and justice for all." Much of American history has been driven by this grand story. Indeed, in our greatest moments of infidelity to the nobility of the vision, we were still believers in the story. It was this belief that at key junctures gave us the moral courage to face our hypocrisy. How else could we have challenged the deplorable practice of slavery, or the social injustices that led to the civil rights movement?

E Pluribus Unum. Out of many, one.

This noble vision has a distinctively religious flavor and consequently a firmly moral mission. Many of the European founders of our

81

nation came here in pursuit of religious freedom. Faith and a particular moral vision of life were essential pieces of the incipient American story, which was rooted in both Western civilization's progress toward democracy and a biblical vision of the value of all humans as beings imprinted with the image of God. We were a people of destiny, and that destiny was somehow wrapped up with the divine. There was an underlying self-understanding that allowed for and was able to absorb the many different perspectives and tensions that were present.

Such a beginning definitively shaped our national character, in some ways more than the historical reality itself. In many Christian circles prevails the myth of America as a Christian nation, founded upon Christian principles. We would certainly agree that Western thought was shaped and formed by our Judeo-Christian tradition. But we dispute the notion that we were ever a "Christian" nation, even though a central belief of our national story insisted that God had blessed America as a nation in a very special way.

With that blessing came responsibility, *individual responsibility*. There was a summons to work, to build, to participate in something great and larger than oneself. America would shape culture the way it was supposed to be, and God would bless its efforts. While we were a nation of individuals unlike any other nation in human history, the thrust of the story provided a master framework, giving meaning to our individual pursuits. It was our grand narrative. It owned us. We owned it.

THE END OF THE GREAT STORY

BUT THE SINGULAR AMERICAN story is no more! There is no longer a distinctively American story that gives meaning to all of American life. The story that had its origin in a White, northern European, Protestant theo-culture has lost its primary position as the great story. We have diversity with little if any sense of unity. No replacement has emerged. Yet without this larger moral vision as the foundational story, the American dream is reduced to materialism and libertarian individualism—an apt characterization of American culture as we close the twentieth century.

Why has this happened? While we are quite suspicious of the simplistic analysis that attributes this to some secular humanist conspiracy, the continued emergence of secularism has been a contributing factor. Modern science has certainly contributed. Knowledge of the universe has been increasingly realigned by scientific discovery, and we have found that many of the tenets of the old story are no longer valid. Globalism contributes no small piece to the puzzle. As our world has become smaller, we have encountered many other great stories. In the process of integration with other peoples and cultures, we have become increasingly pluralistic.

But ultimately, the end of the great story came with the end of modernity. In the wake of modernity's failure to provide a single, unifying story, and with the impact of globalization, we have relativized all stories. Indeed, it is politically incorrect to suggest that any particular cultural story provides a superior moral vision. All stories are equally valid.

> It can no longer be taken for granted that Milton deserves to be more "privileged" than Micky Mouse, that high culture is higher, more elevating, than popular culture, and that some events in history are more momentous than others.[1]

All is leveled. Every story is equally valid; therefore no story is eminently valid. There is tremendous cultural resistance to *any* singular story, because a story bestows power and influence on some and takes them away from others. With the growing diversity of people and belief systems, it is easy to understand the stake that various smaller stories have in resisting a great story. Furthermore, we have opted for protecting the right of individuals to hold their own story, at the expense of our unified American story. Much of the cultural warring that has marked the end of the twentieth century reflects the tug-of-war between those who want to conserve the grand American story and those who want to finally break free of its "tyranny."

We must pause to make sure that our intent is not missed. Historically, as people from different places and cultures have come to America, they have consistently been treated poorly. As a nation, we have decided that a higher level of respect of people as humans ought to be shown newcomers. (Though as of this writing that ethos is turning ugly again.) Part of demonstrating respect includes showing deference to their cultural and religious beliefs, even if they are contrary to our own. We believe this to be a positive accomplishment. But at the same time, this respect, when coupled with a rejection of a singular grand story, has compromised our ability to become one as a nation. Instead of *E Pluribus Unum*, we have become *E Pluribus Pluribus*. Out of many, we have many. We have many stories but no STORY.

---

[1] Gertrude Himmelfarb, *On Looking Into the Abyss: Untimely Thoughts on Culture and Society*, (New York: Alfred A. Knopf, 1994), 40.

THE LOSS OF THE GRAND-STORY TELLERS

FOR A GRAND STORY to hold its power, there must be a "grand-story teller." Throughout the industrial-modern age, three institutions fulfilled this task: the public schools, the church, and the family. The demise of the grand story has had a major impact on the role and importance of these three grand-story tellers.[2]

The Public Schools

In American culture, the public school system has been the primary storyteller of the American grand narrative. The classrooms of America were the formative centers for inculcating in the young what it meant to be a good American. The public schools taught those values that were essential to the common good, the distinctively American values.

In the late 1960s this began to change. The role of grand-story teller was taken away from the public school. Many factors contributed to this shift, but the central factor, we believe, was the loss of the grand American story. We no longer insisted on a single story. America ceased to be the melting pot of many diverse cultures and values. America now was many, not one.

Nowhere was the impact of this shift felt more than in the traditional role of teaching children moral values. Teachers were no longer supposed to teach children right and wrong. They were only to assist them in "clarifying" their own values. (Assuming, of course, that they had moral values that could be clarified!) The effect of this policy plagues us now, twenty-five years later.

The Church

The American church also played the part of grand-story teller. During the Industrial Age, the role of the church was to assist the family and the school. It was to prepare people for heaven in the future and instill within them moral qualities of good citizenship for the here and now. This was possible, of course, because the overwhelming majority of the population was at least nominally Christian. Therefore the

---

[2]It is entirely likely that a changing role for the storytellers also contributed to the demise of the grand story. We are not attempting to suggest the influence moved in one direction only. In reality, it probably was very dialectical.

moral-religious elements of the grand American story were consistent with the baseline elements of the Christian story. Each supported the other. They were so interwoven that for many being American meant being Christian.

But this traditional role of the church is collapsing. Within the American church itself a serious battle has raged for much of this century over what the baseline elements of the Christian message are. The essence of the Christian story has fallen victim to the relativism that has entered the church. As America equivocated around its grand narrative, the church did the same around the Gospel. So while theologians battled one another, local congregations stagnated.

Meanwhile as the church fought its internal battles, the external culture turned away from the church and rejected it as a grand-story teller. This rejection can be based either on the church's insistence that not all stories are created equal and that its story, the story of Christ, takes precedence over other stories or, conversely, because other segments of the church have surrendered the distinctive Christian story and have become irrelevant because they have nothing to say. Their traditional cultural role diminished and their evangelical role confused or forgotten, many churches have done nothing for the past thirty years and today are on the brink of extinction.

The Family

The family is the third and perhaps the most important grand-story teller. Working in conjunction with the school and the church, the family provided the most fundamental element of the story. It taught the child what place his or her particular family had in the grand American narrative. One was proud to be an American. The opportunity to participate in the dream that was America, including the freedom to worship God, was a high calling. Children were taught that this was a land where faith and hard work filled the soul with a sense of accomplishment.

This too has changed. In the past, the family itself was an integral part of the grand story. But the family as an institution is disintegrating. The out-of-wedlock birthrate has skyrocketed since the late sixties. As the family has broken down, there has been an attendant increase in child abuse, crime (especially among youth), welfare dependency, poor educational performance, and so on. William Bennett, former secretary of education, noted that during the past thirty years, "violent crime has risen 560%, [out-of-wedlock births³] have increased 400%, divorce rates have quadrupled, teenage suicide has risen 200%."⁴

The third grand-story teller is on the edge—and in too many places falling!

So there is no great story, and our grand-story tellers have been silenced or muted. There are only stories and storytellers of stories. As we step into the twenty-first century, we live in a culture of competing stories, each vying for place, power, and recognition. There is the

African-American story
Liberationist story
Religious-cultural conservatist story
Feminist story
Libertarian story
Traditionalist story
Fundamentalist story
Native American story
White supremacist story
Hispanic-Latino story
Vietnamese story
Poor White male story
    and so forth . . .

Story upon story upon story. Every group and subgroup has its story and its storytellers. But we have lost the grand story and silenced the grand-story tellers.

---

³Bennett refers to out-of-wedlock as illegitimate births. We take exception to this designation. No human being who is born is illegitimate, and it is time we stopped calling them that.

⁴*Los Angeles Times* (September 4, 1993), B13.

CHAPTER 9

Changing Structures II: When the Grand Story Fails

Politics is about perception, not reality.

City councilman and active Christian,
subsequently convicted of forgery

EVERY STORY TAKES CONCRETE shape in three key areas: morality, institutions, and leadership. **Morality** provides the principles of right and wrong that govern our behavior, the standards by which we live. **Institutions** provide the context through which we become a collective body—family, church, school, and so forth. We form institutions to give concrete form to our values and to sustain them over time. **Leaders**, tied to the grand story in their hearts, rise up to point the way forward and, setting out before us, call us to follow toward the fulfillment of the grand vision. Leadership and institutions, founded on moral principles, are inextricable extensions of any grand story. Without them a story remains only a story. With them the story takes shape as a community and perhaps ultimately as a culture.

What happens when a grand story fails? Morality, leadership, and institutions begin to languish. In the confusion created by the failure of the moral vision to which the collective whole subscribes, frustration and even hostility toward leaders and institutions increase. Leaders, and the institutions they assist us in developing, are a means to the envisioned end. When the vision is unclear, their reason for existence also becomes vague.

It doesn't take great perception to see that at every level morality, institutions, and leadership in America are languishing. Apart from where we are in the generational cycle, the reason is directly tied to the absence of a compelling central story. Public schools are struggling to redefine their role. Political parties are in ideological disarray. Joining these ranks is the church.

MORALITY

Moral Devolution

How has this loss of a singular moral vision manifested itself? For the past thirty years, we have been on a binge of self-centered indulgence. Having been freed from the grand narrative, we have pursued unlimited personal freedom coupled with an unabashed chase after material things. Commercials have shamelessly told us that whatever we want, we deserve. In an age of therapy, thousands have sought personal solace in protracted periods of self-reflective psychotherapy. The moral values of the community and even the family have been subordinated to the desires of the individual. Culturally, we have lived through a thirty-year period of narcissism.

Three popular phrases epitomize the devolution through three decades of our obsessive individualistic binge. They follow on schedule the moods of the generational cycle.

- In the sixties, we insisted that you should "Do your own thing!" It was a naïve call to break free of the expected and constraining conformity of the outer-directed, civic-building era of the generational cycle. "Do your own thing" meant turn inward to the self.
- This was followed in the seventies by "You can have it all."
- By the eighties, the devolution of morality had reached an unprecedented low captured for all time in the phrase "Greed is good." We were fully into the inner-directed era with its narcissistic bent. Amplifying the effects of the cycle was the radical relativism sweeping the country as the certainty of modernity came to an end.

Choices Without Consequences

The inner-directed emphasis coupled with the rampant relativism gave rise to a modern myth. *People began to behave as if the relationship between behavioral choice and consequences had been detached.*[1]

---

[1]Fred Siegel, a Cooper Union social historian, says, "We have conducted a 30-year experiment in desublimation, everyone gets to act out. There are no consequences." By desublimation he means that instead of rechanneling (sublimation) sexual energy, for example, into constructive expressions, we simply let our desires have their way with us. "Whose Values?" *Newsweek* (June 8, 1992), 19.

Nowhere was this assumption more prevalent than in the "sexual revolution." When the pill was introduced, the primary external deterrent to nonmarital sex, the threat of pregnancy, was removed. Men and women were free. And of course, we ushered in the era of "free love." Young men and women explored their sexuality without restraint, assuming that pleasure alone made it right—as long as no one got hurt. We assumed that no one was getting hurt.

Our young people provide us with a powerful mirror of ourselves. What they think and believe reflects what we have taught and modeled. Two studies should give us pause.

1. Declining Moral Values and Attitudes

Dr. Fred Schab of the University of Georgia has conducted a longitudinal study of the ethical behavior of high school students since 1969.[2] The following tables provide a glimpse of the moral slippage that is occurring among high school students.

Comparative study of high school behavior covering three decades			
CONDUCT - Percentage who have:	1969	1979	1989
Lied to parents about school.	55%	60%	70%
Signed parent's name to an excuse.	26%	42%	48%
Taken books from a library without checking them out.	8%	18%	19%
ATTITUDES - Percentage who believe:			
Honesty is always the best policy.	82%	73%	60%
Crime does not pay.	89%	57%	65%
To succeed in business requires some dishonesty.	32%	42%	45%
Source: Dr. Fred Schab of the University of Georgia			

The devolution of moral values is obvious.

---

[2]Fred Schab, "Schooling Without Learning: Thirty Years of Cheating in High School," *Adolescence* 26 (Winter 1991), 104, as reported by Michael Josephson, *Ethics, Values, Attitudes, and Behavior in American Schools: A Report by the Josephson Institute of Ethics* (1992), 29–30.

2. Ethics, Values, Attitudes, and Behavior

In 1991 and 1992 the Josephson Institute of Ethics conducted an extensive national survey on ethical attitudes and behaviors of over eight thousand high school students, college students, and young adults. The findings were presented in a report entitled *Ethics, Values, Attitudes, and Behavior in American Schools.*[3]

Some of the key findings:

- *Prevalent Dishonesty:* While "honesty" is viewed as a fundamental characteristic of the ethical person, today's young are likely to define honesty so narrowly as to preclude such behaviors as explicit misrepresentations yet condone other forms of deceit.
- *Value Priorities:* Young people do value honesty and integrity; they just value other things more, as is evident in the following table.

Rank	High School	Essential	Rank	College	Essential
1	Getting a job you enjoy	77%	1	Getting a job you enjoy	78%
2	Getting into college	73%	2	Imparting firm ethical values to your children	71%
3	Getting a well-paying job	66%	3	Having trusting personal relationships	67%
4	Having trusting personal relationships	66%	4	Being honest and trustworthy	63%
5	Being respected for your integrity	55%	5	Being respected for your integrity	58%
6	Being honest and trustworthy	54%	6	Being kind and caring	52%
			Source: The Josephson Institute (1992)		

- *Theft and Fraud:* One in three high school students, and one in seven college students (16%), admit to stealing something from a store within the last twelve months. A startling 69% of high school students and 61% of college students confess that they had lied to a teacher at least once in the past year.
- *Cheating:* Among high school students, 61% cheated on an exam in the past year. Among college students, this drops to only one-third (32%)!

---

[3]Michael Josephson, *Ethics, Values, Attitudes, and Behavior in American Schools, A Report by the Josephson Institute of Ethics* (1992). A copy of the report can be obtained by contacting the Josephson Institute.

- *Lying:* One out of three high school and college students indicate that they would lie on a résumé to get a job. Sixty percent
of high school students indicate they frequently lied (four or five
times) to their parents during the last year.

Among the current young adult generation (birth years 1960 to
1981), cynicism prevails. The most neglected generation since the turn
of the century finds it difficult to hold to a grand moral vision. And
their selfishness is different from that of the two generations who par-
ented them. *They have had nothing else modeled for them.* Today's
twenty-year-olds were coming of age at the height of the "Greed is
good" eighties. Moreover, they have figured out that the same economic
rush will not fall within their experience. The more savvy realize
already that they will inherit the massive debt that is the legacy of that
period. That even those with the best intentions would struggle with
selfishness and cynicism is understandable.

But the moral decline is not merely the province of the young. It
affects young and old. None of the items on the following list particularly shock us anymore—they are too familiar.

- Young men who find significance in their sexual conquests.
- A national debt that will most likely bury the aspirations of aging
boomers and rising young adults.
- Young women, barely teenagers, who are sexually active yet confess that they wish they had never started.
- Communities that are more concerned with greenbelts than
funding education for our youth.
- An older generation that is more concerned for its own welfare
than the welfare of our young.
- Parents who provide drugs or alcohol and a room at the Marriott
for graduation parties.
- A society whose greatest heroes are Hollywood celebrities and
sports figures.
- An abdication of individual moral responsibility, and a belief that
"if it is legal, it is ethical; if it is permissible, it is proper."
- Rising membership in racist groups such as the White suprema-
cists.
- African-American communities where 80% of babies born are
to unwed mothers.
- Churches more concerned with their survival than with their
neighbors.

And the list goes on. Without a grand story filled with moral passion and a vision of what ought to be for all, we are left morally adrift and uncertain of where to go.

A New Moral Vision — A New Story

The good news is that there is a change in the air. At the height of the binge, the question "Whose values?" was considered to kill a discussion on the grounds of intolerance; today there are concerted efforts across America and around the world to develop a set of "core moral values."

This trend is evidence that the more sensible epistemology of the postmodern objectivist is supplanting postmodern radical relativism. While the objectivist does not affirm with absolute certainty the "rightness" of a particular story, he or she *does* insist that not all stories are of equal validity and importance. Moreover, the objectivist believes it is reasonable to support a single story above other stories when that story provides the best possible explanation. Asserting a story is true based upon the principle of unsurpassability is defensible.

In the search for core moral values, the objectivist seeks those moral values to which all civilizations subscribe and of which all recognize that without, no civilization will survive. On what basis are these core moral values to be judged? Again, the principle of unsurpassability. Those most likely to support human life will pass; those that do not, fail.

Therefore when the father from the Middle East insists that his son does not have to obey his third-grade teacher because she is a woman and, according to his culture, a woman is lower than a cow, we can say, "No! That is not acceptable, and it is not just an American value that says so. It is a fundamentally human value." A story that follows a belief system that denigrates women is destined to fail. It does not pass the test of unsurpassability. Indeed, it is easily surpassed by a moral code that affirms the equality of all persons and their right to mutual respect.

However, this return to moral values and stories that support them does not reflect a return of the grand old American story. While the new concern for moral values is on schedule with our current place in the generational cycle, this alone does not account for the reemergence of a central story. It is a new story, based on finding common ground across cultures and belief systems.

The grand American narrative was heavily rooted in Western religious theo-culture. The new story that is emerging has been divorced from this historic religious foundation, which is gone and will not return.

The new story will have a distinctly global perspective with a high level of cultural inclusiveness. The rise of globalism will make this inevitable.[4]

LEADERSHIP

AS WE STAND ON the edge of the twenty-first century, every sector of life, whether government, politics, corporate America, or the church, shares the same concern: where are the leaders that are equal to the task? There is no dearth of people to fill positions of leadership. The dearth is of leaders who have the kind of qualities necessary to provide the type of leadership that will be required.

What Kind of Leadership Do We Have?

Leadership in America in general could be described as either well-meaning but directionless managers or power-hungry consumers driven by selfish ambition. What they have in common is a disconnection with a grand cultural story and the moral vision implicit therein.

Well-Meaning Managers

Back in the late sixties, my friend Cal was lead guitarist in a band. I was impressed with how easily Cal could move up and down the neck of his guitar—he could even pick with his teeth! But my appreciation was tempered when another friend, who unlike me was a musician, observed that Cal had great technique but lacked passion. *He had developed tremendous technical capabilities, but he lacked the spark that transformed his technique into art.*

This is precisely one of the weaknesses of many current leaders. They know management technique but don't have that passion of leadership rooted in a moral vision. We have an abundance of middle managers. Many of these persons are faithful, hardworking people and need to be recognized for their faithfulness. But the issues facing our culture and even the church will in the long run require more than good management technicians.

---

[4]We must point out that though the new story is not one based upon our Christian theological tradition, at its core it is not incompatible with it. Indeed, we believe that whether culture recognizes it or not, when it affirms certain core moral values, it is simply affirming that which is true—whether or not they are aware of its source. We have a great opportunity as the church to participate in these formative discussions of the new story, but only if we are willing to let go of our insistence that we were once founded upon Judeo-Christian principles and must return to these.

A less pleasant variant of the well-meaning manager is the "duck-and-cover" manager. Impotent to provide true leadership, such a person takes no risks. The challenges of the information world pressing down on us require clear-sightedness and decisiveness. Duck-and-cover leaders provide neither. Rather, when their performance is under scrutiny, they give all the reasons why they did not or could not do something. The parable of the talents comes to mind.[5]

Power-Hungry Consumers

The second characteristic of modern leadership is far more troubling. Without moral passion, raw ambition replaces vision and imagination. Too many leaders demonstrate little more than a lust for power. They never have enough. Their appetite is insatiable. Unchecked, they would consume everything in sight.

Few symbolize better the consumptive lust for power than the Ivan Boeskys of the world. There was absolutely no moral vision at all behind his actions. He was driven solely by ambition and unrestrained greed. Like many, he was not driven by a vision of what ought to be but by ambition for what he personally wanted to accomplish.

At the center of ambition, we too often find a lust for power, fame, money, or all three. What is needed instead of leaders with ambition is leaders with moral passion. Ambition is self-serving. Passion is a response to a hope larger than oneself that compels a person to give oneself to the cause.[6]

---

[5]"Then the man who had received the one talent came. 'Master,' he said, 'I knew that you are a hard man, harvesting where you have not sown and gathering where you have not scattered seed. So I was afraid and went out and hid your talent in the ground. See, here is what belongs to you'" (Matt. 25:24–25).

[6]Ambition is a drive to advance oneself. It is just this phenomenon that Paul the apostle points to in Philippians 2:3: "Do nothing from selfish ambition [eriqeia] or conceit, but in humility regard others as better than yourselves" (NRSV).

The Theological Dictionary of the New Testament, vol. 2 (Gerhard Kittel, Grand Rapids: Eerdmans, 1978), 660, defines *eriqeia* as "the attitude of self-seekers ... i.e., those who, demeaning themselves and their cause, are busy and active in their own interests, seeking their own gain or advantage." On its use in the New Testament: "We do best to see a reference to the despicable nature of those who do not strive after glory, honor and immortality by perseverance in good works, but who think only of immediate gain.... It is best to understand eriqeia as 'base self-seeking' ... the nature of those who cannot lift their gaze to higher things."

It was an ancient, stock word in catalogs of vices. The image is exactly that of

What Kind of Leadership Do We Need?

The leader of the future will need to handle a world far more complex than any leader has ever had to face in the past. Indeed, this is one of the causes of the failure of leadership—complexity. But at a more basic level, we need leaders who are driven by moral vision.

A visionary leader is a leader who is driven by a clear image of an ideal condition, a condition that does not satisfactorily exist. It is a vision of what ought to be in the lives of people, in contrast to what is. It imagines people living free and wholly alive in a world where peace and justice prevail for all persons, not just the self or a privileged class. The disparity between "what is" and "what ought to be" generates passion in the heart of the leader. A passion in the soul compels him or her to transform this vision into reality. Such passion has a distinctly moral quality to it.

The core of the historic grand American dream generated this kind of passion, for it was indeed a high moral vision. Nowhere is it better articulated than in our own Declaration of Independence: "We hold these truths to be self-evident; that all men are created equal; that they are endowed by their creator with certain unalienable rights; that among these are life, liberty and the pursuit of happiness. . . ."

An example of a truly visionary leader was Dr. Martin Luther King Jr. His was a vision of what ought to be for African-American people. All Americans are created equal and ought to have the same protection and rights under the law. In other words, he was captured by the

---

many in leadership today, whether in business or public political life or, too often, in the church.

In contrast, Paul uses the word *filotimeomai*—also unfortunately translated *ambition* in Romans 15:20 (NRSV)—more in accordance with our concept of passion. "Thus I make it my ambition [*filotimeomai*] to proclaim the Good News where Christ has not already been named, so that I do not build on someone else's foundation."

Filotimeomai is a compound of *filia*, love, and *timh*, honor—that is, loving honor. It is just the opposite drive of *eriqeia*. Paul's motivation in proclaiming the Good News meant a love of proper honor. He wanted to be known for his commitment to carry the Gospel where no one else had gone before. And for what reason? To advance not himself but the Gospel.

In the Philippians passage, what concerns Paul is not the energy that drives the action; it is the fact that the energy is expended to advance one's own agenda in a totally self-serving manner with questionable motives. In the second passage, the energy—what we would prefer to call passion—is expended to proclaim the Gospel. In other words, it was energy generated by a passion for a high moral vision—the salvation of the world.

grand American story. However, what ought to be did not exist for his people. All of his efforts were directed at closing the gap between what was and what ought to be. Dr. King was a moral-visionary leader. Of course, societies do not always embrace leaders with moral conviction. It cost Dr. King his life.

Twenty-First Century Church Leadership

The same shortage of moral-visionary leadership exists within the structures of the church. While most of the men and women we work with through Percept are highly moral people, we have been concerned with the overall lack of vision. Too often there is more concern for the survival of denominational structures and one's position within them than for faithfulness to the mission of the church. We find many middle managers, some well-meaning and some duck-and-cover bureaucrats. But we wonder where the visionaries are.

While we have great appreciation for the efforts of the church growth movement, we contend that it too often emphasizes technique. Too little emphasis has been given to the larger issues of vision and the development of visionary leaders; too much emphasis has been placed on gimmicks to fill churches and Sunday school classes.

The issue of moral-visionary leadership must be explored by the church if it hopes to survive in the twenty-first century. Many institutional church structures, especially those deeply influenced by the radical relativism of the past three decades, do not like visionary leadership driven by moral passion. Indeed, in some mainline denominations, persons who demonstrate too much visionary leadership are often cut off at the knees. Our institutions have been immunized against this kind of leadership.

Take a simple tour of mainline seminaries. Where are the strong, visionary leaders? Where are those in training who are moved by a passion for the kingdom of God? In which classroom do we tell theological students that the church of the twenty-first century needs visionary leadership able to think big and bold? Where do we instill in them the level of courage necessary to face a world that is antagonistic to the church? We have taken Jesus' model of servant leadership and reduced it to insipid peonage.

These are hard words, written out of love and concern for the future mission of the church. One of the greatest challenges facing the church in America today is, Will we let real leaders lead? Or will we drive them out of our systems? Under the rubric of accountability, too many visionary leaders are driven out of a denominational tradition by denominational gatekeepers. Gatekeepers do not drive them away out of concern for true moral accountability to the Gospel. They drive them out for fear of true leadership! People will follow true leaders. In too many cases that is exactly what the gatekeepers fear.

Many unaffiliated churches evidence leadership that seems more consistent with vision, but we wonder if in many cases these visionary leaders are not driven more by consumptive ambition than moral passion. When they insist that they alone do significant work for the "kingdom," it would seem no more than self-indulgent ambition masquerading as passion for God.

INSTITUTIONS

Struggling for Legitimacy

With directionless leaders, we will also find our institutions directionless. Ralph Waldo Emerson observed that "an institution is the lengthened shadow of one man."[7] We would add "or of one woman," but otherwise the statement is quite profound. Without good leadership, institutions languish.

Institutions, which serve to structure our collective efforts, inevitably emerge when leaders work to translate vision into reality. It is through institutions that the many can become one. But the prerequisite is that there be a grand story and that there be leaders who, moved by the grand story, call us together as one in its pursuit. It is through the formation of institutions that visionary leaders work to close the gap between what is and what ought to be.

The Role of Institutions

Once institutions are formed, they in turn give shape to collective and individual experience.

> Institutions form individuals by making possible or impossible certain ways of behaving and relating to others. They shape character by assigning responsibility, demanding accountability and providing the standards in terms of which each person recognizes the excellence of his or her achievements.[8]

---

[7]Quoted in John Bartlett, *Bartlett's Familiar Quotations*, 15th ed. rev. (Boston: Little, Brown, 1980).

[8]Robert Bellah et al., *The Good Society* (New York: Vintage, 1992), 40.

We may fail to recognize the ongoing role institutions play in our lives, because it is such a part of inner-directed common culture to be suspicious of our historic institutions.[9] Like them or not, trust them or not, institutions are key forces in shaping us, for good or for bad.

Institutions in Crisis

Institutions, like visionary leaders, need a grand story. If they lose this, two dynamics set in: (1) they struggle to maintain a reason to exist, and (2) they activate self-survival tactics.[10]

IBM has struggled with this since the advent of the personal computer. Their paradigm of an information processor was based upon an Industrial Age paradigm of centralized control and processing. As the personal computer evolved and became more powerful, the need for centralized processing horsepower diminished. Local-area computer networks further aggravated the problem, and at one point it looked like IBM might go under.

However, not all institutions are willing, like IBM, to make adjustments for the sake of survival. They use the alternative strategy of activating self-survival tactics and developing strong immunological systems to fight off any effort to dismantle them. Many government bureaucracies are so entrenched in our system that even though their original reason for being has long since passed, they continue unabated.

This principle is well illustrated by our government's inability to shut down its helium stockpiling program, which was started during the pre–World War II era to provide a constant supply of helium for the nation's fleet of dirigibles. These airships continuously floated above naval fleets, looking for evidence of enemy submarines. The fleet of dirigibles became obsolete several decades ago. Yet the stockpiling program continues, costing taxpayers millions every year. Why? Because it has developed a powerful immunological system to defend it.

In 1995 the Republicans of the House pushed through their "Contract with America." It was supposed to clean up government spending

---

[9]Consider the role of the family. The community in which I live conducted a study of the reasons for violence and gang affiliation among youth. Expert testimony informed us that kids join gangs in order to feel attached to a group. Why? Because they are not getting such close affiliation from their families. The family is one of our social institutions. So also is the gang.

[10]Obviously, if the grand story provides the reason for existence, its failure supplants it. Not all American institutions face the loss of the grand American story. Some simply find they exist to provide a product or service the world no longer needs. But the principle is the same.

and cut costs. Yet a freshman Republican congressman from Amarillo, Texas, lobbied Newt Gingrich not to cut the helium program, even though another high-ranking congressman, under Gingrich's tutelage, was working to dismantle it. Last we checked, we are still stockpiling helium!

It doesn't take too many such revelations before the general public grows suspicious and angry. Abraham Lincoln once said,

> This country, with its institutions belongs to the people who inhabit it. Whenever they shall grow weary of the existing government, they can exercise their constitutional right of amending it, or their revolutionary right to dismember or overthrow it.[11]

Ultimately, institutions no longer connected to a grand story will succumb to dismantling forces. They must, for they only exist to serve a story. As we enter the twenty-first century, we wonder about the future of many of our institutions, since so many of our stories are in question.

The Institutional Church?

What about the church? How does it fare as an institution? The very idea of the church as a shaping institution is being reshaped as the culture becomes increasingly suspicious of the role and motives of the church, whether conservative or liberal. The main reason is that the church suffers from a lack of a strong central story. This takes two forms, as we have already indicated.

The first reflects the impact of radical relativism: when all stories are valid, no single story is valid. When we stand for everything religious, we stand for nothing. When Jesus and Sophia are put on the same level, the level is low and the substance weak. Many historic Protestant traditions are struggling with just this issue. This modern form of syncretism threatens to neutralize what makes these traditions in any way distinctive. If this trend is allowed to proceed unchecked, the very reason for being an institution will be compromised. Because there is really very little to offer the larger world, the perception will increasingly be that the church exists only for itself and its own needs.

The second form still holds to a story, but the story is no longer cogent for the twenty-first-century person. Across more than a dozen different focus groups, respondents consistently voiced frustration that

---

[11]Abraham Lincoln, First Inaugural Speech (March 4, 1861).

the church too often preaches simplistic answers to complex moral and ethical issues. And in most cases it is not even willing to discuss the issues. *They perceive the church to be a telling institution, not a listening one*.

Anytime there is a perception that an official position is simplistic, lacking in sensitivity and openness, a credibility problem will develop. From inside the tradition, this will not appear to be problematic—in fact, the institution may take pride in the simplicity of its answers. As the population becomes more sophisticated and educated, and the world clearly more complex, the answers of the church to life's questions appear increasingly simplistic. For most of these people, stories that would have us hearken back to some prior theological "golden era" are completely untenable and unacceptable. They vote by their absence.

The struggles within the American Roman Catholic Church provide a prime example. American Catholics are fighting hard for the right to birth control, ordination of women, and marriage for the clergy. Yet they perceive that the church only tells. It does not listen. And so the gap between the hierarchy and the regular folks grows daily.

In C. S. Lewis's final book in the *Chronicles of Narnia* series, *The Last Battle*,[12] we see a similar failure of leadership and basic institutions. The dwarves, who had a checkered history of either supporting Aslan (the Christ figure) or falling in with someone who led them astray, finally found themselves at a point where they would no longer trust anybody, including Aslan. Their new rallying cry was amazingly similar to what can be heard from various groups today: "The Dwarves are for the Dwarves." Translated, "We don't trust any of you. We will gather around ourselves and care only for ourselves." The uncertainty grows, and with it social fragmentation.

If, as we suggested in an earlier chapter, a new American story is indeed beginning to emerge, we can expect our leadership and institutions to recalibrate themselves around the new vision. But what about the church? If we are right in suggesting that the American institutional church will no longer find a central place in the American story, it cannot expect a renewal to occur along with other institutions. As it moves closer to its moment of definition, it must demand of itself that it redefine or rediscover the essential pieces of its central story in terms that make sense to twenty-first-century people and in terms that are faithful to the core message.

---

[12]C. S. Lewis, *The Last Battle* (New York: Collier Books, 1970).

CHAPTER 10

Changing Players I:
E Pluribus Pluribus

FOR MOST OF AMERICA'S history, the face of the nation has been predominately White. Immigration policies perpetuated this. Within the power structures, the face was not only White but male. In the future, we will look very different. The next three chapters examine the demographic changes that are reshaping the face of America. On the surface, demographics seem far from interesting. But the changes represented here are so fundamental, and their implications so far-reaching for the church, that the time used thinking through these demographic changes is time well spent. Without an understanding of these changes, we will not be able to fully understand the challenges that face the institutional church in America. This is especially true for mainline Protestant denominations.

Behind the numbers reside the factors contributing to much of the anxiety and uncertainty that grip many Americans. We see our neighborhoods changing. We see people who look and speak differently winning job opportunities, accomplishing academic excellence, or creating new levels of community disruption. We become fearful as anxieties increase. Will there be a place for us? The human response is to circumscribe our world and to remove the threatening forces. Ironically, at a time of globalization, parochialism is being revived.

A LAND WITH NO MAJORITY

FOR MOST OF AMERICA'S history, Whites have been in the majority, while African-Americans were the second-largest ethnic group. Over the next fifty or more years, this picture will change dramatically.

101

Growth projections show that America has entered a period in which the population *as a whole* is barely replacing itself. We are projected to increase by less than 1% per year between now and the middle of the next century—from 249 million in 1990 to around 392 million by 2050. This is not a large increase.[1]

But this 1%-per-year growth is true only of the *population as a whole*. The net growth rate (that is, number of births minus number of deaths) for each ethnic group within the total population varies greatly, and that is one of the reasons why the face of America will look radically different.

The percentage of the White (non-Hispanic) population is projected to *decrease* by 30%, while the other racial-ethnic groups will *increase* by 92%. As a result, *by the middle of the next century, no single ethnic group will constitute a majority,* as the following graph shows.

Racial/Ethnic Population Projections: 1990–2050

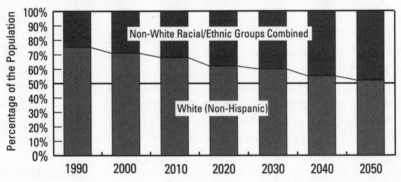

---

[1]While our growth is incremental, in many countries growth is exponential. Note the comparative growth rates in the following table.

World Population and Average Annual Rates of Growth, by Region
and Development Category: 1950 to 2020

	1950	1960	1970	1990	2000	2010
World	1.70	2.00	1.80	1.50	1.30	1.00
Developing Countries	1.90	2.40	2.20	1.80	1.50	1.00
Developed Countries	1.30	1.00	0.80	0.50	0.40	0.30
North America	1.80	1.30	1.10	1.00	0.80	0.80
Europe	0.80	0.80	0.50	0.30	0.20	0.00

Source: U.S. Bureau of the Census, International Data

The two primary factors behind this shift are (1) the ratio of births to deaths for each racial-ethnic group, and (2) immigration patterns.

1. Patterns of Birth and Death

The growth or decrease of a population segment, apart from immigration and emigration, is determined by the number of births less the number of deaths per year. For the four main racial-ethnic groups in the United States, projections for the first half of the twenty-first century show the following:

- **Hispanic-Latinos** are projected to see an ever-growing net annual population as births continue to increase faster than deaths. By 2010 the Hispanic population will be the second-largest racial-ethnic group in America.
- **Asian-Pacific Islanders** are projected to continue being the fastest-growing segment of the population. This group will see a continual increase in births over deaths until around 2030, at which point the ratio will stabilize.
- **African-Americans** are projected to remain fairly stable from year to year, with births and deaths maintaining almost the same ratio. The African-American population will increase from 12% to 14.4% of the total population by 2050.
- In the **White** (non-Hispanic) segment, on the other hand, *deaths actually are projected to outnumber births beginning around 2027!*

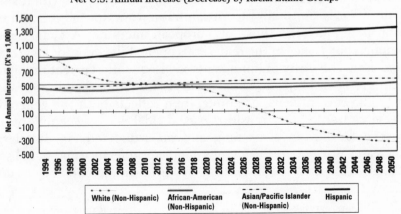

Net U.S. Annual Increase (Decrease) by Racial-Ethnic Groups

The net result will be a nation without a racial-ethnic majority.

2. Immigration

The second factor in the changing of the racial-ethnic face of America is immigration. We are in the third major period of immigration since the beginning of the nineteenth century. With ten million immigrants (legal and illegal) entering the U.S. during the eighties, and another ten million projected for the nineties, it makes this the largest period of immigration in our history. The following graph shows the decade-by-decade history of immigration since 1820. Note the wavelike ebb and flow of the pattern.

U.S. Immigration by Decade: 1830–1990

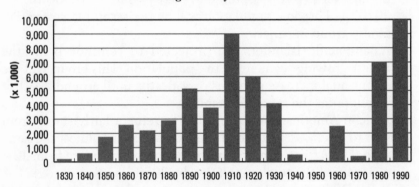

But it is not just the magnitude of the current immigration that makes this period distinctive. The last major period of immigration was mostly a northern European movement, which carried with it a nominally (that is, culturally) Christian framework. Indeed, U.S. immigration policy favored those of European ancestry.[2] A change in U.S. immigration policy in the mid-1960s opened the door for greater racial and ethnic diversity of immigrants. Consequently, current immigration patterns favor Hispanic-Latinos and Asians rather than Europeans.

The current wave of immigration reflects both the generational cycle as well as the transformational tidal wave sweeping over our world. During an awakening and inner-directed era, immigration increases, due in part to an ethos of greater tolerance and pluralism. As the clouds of crisis begin to form, however, immigration begins to look

---

[2]U.S. immigration policy up to 1965 effectively barred much immigration from nations other than those of Europe. The Nationality Act of 1965 replaced the national quota system with a standard twenty thousand immigrants per country for all nations outside the Western Hemisphere. The result was to open the door to non-European countries.

less promising, and the cultural ethos becomes markedly less friendly to outsiders. The current influx of immigrants matches what one would expect. As we close the twentieth century, we are at the end of a period of inner orientation. If the cycle continues according to form, we should see a leveling off of immigration within the first ten to twenty years of the new century.

However, the transformational component of the current immigration is reflected in its global reach. People are coming here from literally all over the world. This very dynamic has contributed to the demise of the American story. Having broken from our preference for European immigrants, we opened the door to peoples and cultures very different from those who historically reflected our Western, Judeo-Christian culture. People are pouring into America with very different cultural and religious stories. So at the very moment in which radical relativism demoted the grand American story, many stories emerged on the American scene. Again we have stories, no story.

THE GRAYING OF AMERICA

WE ARE GROWING OLDER. Given the large size of the baby boom generation, this "graying" should come as no surprise. However, this graying is not balanced across all racial-ethnic groups. In the graph below, the "All" line shows the average age of the entire American population. Above that line, at times significantly so, is the White (non-Hispanic) average age. All other racial-ethnic groups fall significantly below even the average age for all.[3]

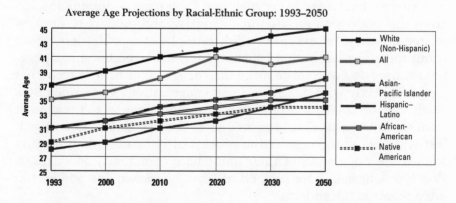

Average Age Projections by Racial-Ethnic Group: 1993–2050

---

[3]There are various reasons for this disparity, among them, for example, the age of persons when they traditionally immigrate and the fact that Hispanic families are typically larger.

The actual graying is a graying of the Anglo population. This trend foreshadows a potential trouble spot. The changing population dynamics will create a racial stratification based upon age! The gray American of the future is more likely to be White, and ultimately female. The young are more likely to be of some other racial-ethnic group. One wonders what the implications of this are, when realizing that the older group will sit in the seats of power and money while the other racial-ethnic groups will hold the youth?

The Face of the Church

In fifty years, the typical American will look very different from his or her counterpart in 1995. We will have come through a radical demographic transformation. Already these forces have changed pockets of America. Neighborhoods have been in transition for years, and the reshaping continues at a rapid rate. There are neighborhoods in major cities today that were White in the sixties, Black in the seventies, and became Hispanic in the eighties. When neighborhoods can change so quickly, individual people begin to wonder if there will be a place for them somewhere in the future. This in turn creates the uncertainty of community. How can one develop community stability in an environment that is so transitional?

How is the church doing with this change? Generally, not well! In these same communities sit thousands of churches, most of which never made the first transition. As a result, many have become White religious ghettos in the midst of racially diverse communities. For the past twenty-five years, every mainline Protestant denomination has given top priority to racial-ethnic diversity, and funding to develop related ministry. Yet except in a few rare places, most leaders would admit the effort has been a failure at the local level. Local congregations simply do not want to make the changes. Our firm, Percept, has worked directly with dozens of small congregations surrounded by a neighborhood totally unlike themselves. Most drive in to the church from the communities they moved to as the neighborhood changed. But when asked to consider the process of refocusing their mission toward the population of their immediate community, most resist. Words of affirmation for such efforts may be spoken, but actions too often sabotage the efforts.

So where do we find ourselves? If the birth-to-death ratio for all racial-ethnic groups was the same as that of the White population, aging alone would be the demographic dynamic to watch. The population as a whole would then reach a point where deaths would out-number births, and America's net population would actually decrease. Given enough time, we would become extinct.

We know that this is not the scenario that we will see happen in the country as a whole. *But this scenario is exactly what is happening in the institutional church in America.* While the face of America is chang-ing, for the most part the face of most large historic Protestant denom-inations is not, except for the color of members' hair! Our research (1993 data) shows the following:

- Persons seventy years of age and up are significantly above the national average for the United Methodist Church, the Presby-terian Church (U.S.A.), and the Evangelical Lutheran Church in America. However, they are essentially at the national average for the Episcopal Church, the Roman Catholic Church, and the Southern Baptists.
- Persons between fifty-two and sixty-nine are above the national average in each of the denominations.
- Persons between thirty-four and fifty-one (boomers) are below the national average for the United Methodist Church, the Pres-byterian Church (U.S.A.), the Evangelical Lutheran Church in America, and the Southern Baptists. The greatest underrepre-sentation is among United Methodists and Presbyterians. How-ever, this age group is represented at the national average among Episcopalians and Roman Catholics.
- Persons between thirteen and thirty-three are significantly below the national average among every denominational group but the Southern Baptists. Yet even there they are still below the national average.

What do we conclude from this?

- Across all denominations, there is a failure to reach the youngest generation.
- Methodists and Presbyterians are also failing to reach boomers.
- In contrast, Methodists, Presbyterians, and Evangelical Luther-ans are overwhelmingly slanted toward the elderly population.

In other words, while the overall U.S. population is graying, *the his-toric Protestant institutions are graying faster!* Of all of the denomina-tions, the Roman Catholics and the Southern Baptists are the most balanced across the generations.

The following graph summarizes the findings.

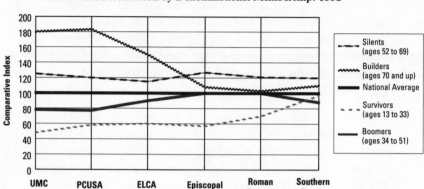

Generational Distribution by Denominational Membership: 1993

What about the racial-ethnic balance and representation in the mainline churches? The findings are relatively disastrous for the historic institutional church in America. Except for the Episcopal Church, which has a significantly above average representation of African-Americans, all major denominations are mostly White (non-Hispanic).

So while the general U.S. population is backfilling its declining Anglo-European population with diverse peoples and cultures from around the world, the church is choking on the change. Most of our mainline Protestant systems are based upon our European cultural roots. While most of us find it difficult to see the difference between the Gospel and our Presbyterianism, other cultures can! How frustrating it is for so many Episcopalians that younger generations of Ameri-

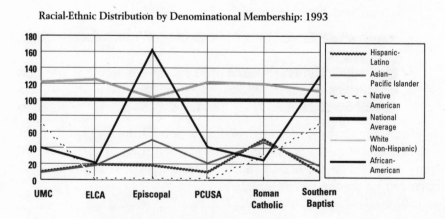

Racial-Ethnic Distribution by Denominational Membership: 1993

cans have lost the significant value of "high tea." What a tragedy it is for so many Baptists that many in America today cannot wrap their faith in the American flag. And so it goes.

As long as we insist on these matters of culture and ideology rather than focus on the Gospel, we will die. We can live in false security, because the population is still predominantly White. But the increase in cultural diversity is accelerating, and young people in the next century will be predominantly non-White. Based on demographics alone, the future of the church is grim. Unfortunately, the story gets grimmer still.

CHAPTER 11

Changing Players II:
The Passing Actors—
Builders and Silents

*By the year 2004, spending on Social Security and Medicare
will nearly double and will be closing in on the $1 trillion mark,
dwarfing the projected $669 billion discretionary budget for the
operation of the federal government.*

Los Angeles Times, October 25, 1994

E VERY STORY HAS ITS actors. The American story and the institutional church's story are no exception. We have seen that the face
of America is changing, that there are new actors from new or different
racial and ethnic groups who are currently working their way into the
emerging American story.

But the changing racial-ethnic face of America covers only one
dimension of this new story. An equally significant factor in the evolving American story is the various generations within the generational
cycle. While the changing racial-ethnic face addresses longer-term
national change, a focus on the existing generations within the current
generational cycle addresses more immediate issues. It is at the generational level that we can actually see who has been and who will be the
key actors in the American drama as we enter the twenty-first century.

GENERATIONAL TYPES

IN ORDER TO UNDERSTAND what is happening on the generational level,
we must first look again at the roughly eighty-year cycle of four eras
(awakening, inner-directed, crisis, outer-directed) that was outlined in
chapter 3.

111

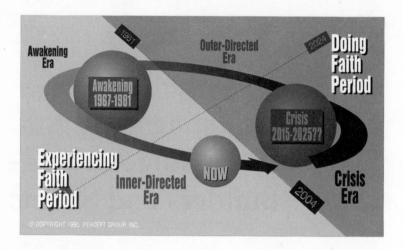

Each of these four eras has its own dominant mood and ethos.

Crisis Era	Outer-Directed Era	Awakening Era	Inner-Directed Era
Emerging communitarian spirit to face social problems, era culminates in secular crisis, single ideal prevails over others, new foundation for community building	Conformity and stability, triumphant ideals secularized, great institutions built	Cultural creativity, new ideals, old institutions/values challenged or rejected	Individualism, fragmentation and animosity over divergent ideals, confidence in institutions fades, secular problems increase, spirit of public meanness and distrust

The mood and ethos of each era has a profound impact on the generation that is born and comes of age during that era. The generation that grows up during a crisis era will be different in its ethos and outlook than a generation that grows up in an awakening era: the World War II generation and the sixties generation produced GIs and hippies respectively.[1]

The four generational types that come of age in the four eras can be labeled adaptive, idealist, reactive, and civic.[2]

Crisis Era	Outer-Directed Era	Awakening Era	Inner-Directed Era
ADAPTIVE	IDEALIST	REACTIVE	CIVIC

---

[1]Keep in mind that when we talk about generational types and characteristics, we are of necessity dealing with generalizations. There are many details that seemingly don't fit, yet the overall picture is coherent.

[2]Condensed from William Strauss and Neil Howe, *Generations: The History of America's Future, 1584 to 2069* (New York: Morrow, 1992).

It is critical to remember that the "personality" of each generation will typically demonstrate a particular ethos as it moves through its phases of life. In other words, each generation will reflect its own set of ideals, beliefs, or standards. This ethos pervades everything they think and do as a group. The following table shows how each of the four types functions in society as it moves through the four eras.

	Awakening Era		Inner-Directed Era		Crisis Era		Outer-Directed Era	
Youth (0–21)	*Reactive*	Criticized	*Civic*	Protected	*Adaptive*	Suffocated	*Idealist*	Indulged
Rising (22–43)	*Idealist*	Narcissistic	*Reactive*	Alienated	*Civic*	Heroic	*Adaptive*	Conformist
Midlife (44–65)	*Adaptive*	Indecisive	*Idealist*	Moralistic	*Reactive*	Pragmatic	*Civic*	Powerful
Elder (65+)	*Civic*	Busy	*Adaptive*	Sensitive	*Idealist*	Visionary	*Reactive*	Reclusive

To follow a generational group through its phases, start with the first generational type on the left and move right and down one row. In this manner, a type can be followed through its four phases. The table has been gray-scaled to assist in this.

Sources: Strauss and Howe, *Generations*, and Percept Group, Inc.

GENERATIONAL TYPES IN THE TWENTIETH CENTURY

WHILE THE TABLE REFLECTS the idealized generational model, our concern is for the particular living generations who will play key roles as we transition into the new century, and shape life for the first twenty-five years of the 2000s. Our purpose, therefore, will best be served by gaining insight into the five living generations. Who are they? What do they value? What has shaped their worldview, and how will that shaping affect their outlook and role as actors in the American drama circa 2000?

First, who are they? When we place the twentieth-century eras and the generational types on a timeline, we get the following:

1883–1900	1901–1924	1925–1942	1943–1960	1961–1981	1982–2003	(2003–2025)
Awakening	Inner-Directed	Crisis	Outer-Directed	Awakening	Inner-Directed	(Crisis)
Reactive	*Civic*	*Adaptive*	*Idealist*	*Reactive*	*Civic*	*(Adaptive)*

The first generation to have a name of its own was the generation that came of age at the end of the nineteenth century and was the rising generation in the first part of the twentieth century: the lost generation.

113

Today, the most widely used generational label is "boomers," for the generation born between 1943 and 1960. To facilitate discussion, we have given a name to each of the twentieth-century generations.[3]

1883–1900	1901–1924	1925–1942	1943–1960	1961–1981	1982–2003	(2003–2025)
Awakening	Inner-Directed	Crisis	Outer-Directed	Awakening	Inner-Directed	(Crisis)
Reactive	*Civic*	*Adaptive*	*Idealist*	*Reactive*	*Civic*	*(Adaptive)*
Lost	Builders	Silents	Boomers	Survivors	Millennials	?

In the remainder of this chapter, we will describe the face of the first two living generations. These are the generations who have been adults and in power collectively since the end of World War II. Of course, our primary purpose concerns the future of the institutional church in America. Therefore the relationship of each living generation to the church is critical and will cap each discussion.

The chart below combines the general overview of the four types as they move through the four eras on the more specific timeline.

	1901–1924 Inner-Directed	1925–1942 Crisis	1943–1960 Outer-Directed	1961–1981 Awakening	1982–2003 Inner-Directed
Youth (0–21)	*Builders:* Protected	*Silents:* Suffocated	*Boomers:* Indulged	*Survivors:* Criticized	*Millennials:* Protected
Rising (22–43)	*Lost:* Alienated	*Builders:* Heroic	*Silents:* Conforming	*Boomers:* Narcissistic	*Survivors:* Alienated
Midlife (44–65)		*Lost:* Pragmatic	*Builders:* Powerful	*Silents:* Indecisive	*Boomers:* Moralistic
Elder (65+)			*Lost:* Reclusive	*Builders:* Busy	*Silents:* Sensitive

Source: Strauss and Howe, *Generations*, and Percept Group, Inc.

---

[3]These labels reflect a key characteristic of each of the four types. Our labels are a modification of those used by Strauss and Howe.

Generational Type	Strauss and Howe Names	Percept Names
Civics	GIs	Builders
Adaptives	Silents	Silents
Idealists	Boom	Boomers
Reactives	13th	Survivors
Civics	Millennial	Millenial

THE BUILDERS

As a generation of civics, builders reflect the optimism of young adults who came out of the last social crisis as heroes. The victory of World War II provided them this status. They are called "GIs" by Strauss and Howe; we prefer the name "builder," because it better describes the actual full-life experience of this generation.

Civics always receive the best a society has to offer at every stage of their life. This is the builders' story. Unlike the reactive generation before them (the "lost" generation of the Roaring Twenties), they were protected as youths. Following this pattern, in 1909, while the first of the young builders were nine years of age or less, the first White House Conference on Children was called.[4] Following the expected cycle of benefit, in their busy elder years they worked to convene the first White House Conference on Aging in 1961 (a program that would benefit whom? the builders). The AARP (American Association of Retired Persons) is one of the wealthiest and most activistic special interest associations in America. With its ranks filled with these busy elder civics, they will insure that the entitlements this generation put in place for themselves continue to care for them (at the expense of other age segments) until they pass away.

As the twentieth century closes, these busy elders create so much fear in the hearts of politicians that both parties are afraid to even mention what everyone knows: Social Security and Medicare are killing the federal budget, and unless something is done, they will collapse sometime early in the new century.[5] Of course, there is a point out there when politicians will have to take action, but it will most likely occur after the busy builders are no longer a political force.

---

[4]Strauss and Howe, *Generations*, 266.

[5]In the mid-nineties a front-page article appeared in the *Los Angeles Times* addressing this very issue: "Afraid to touch 'the third rail of politics'—the sacrosanct benefits of America's elderly—both the Clinton White House and congressional Republicans have been forced to deny the other's campaign charges that they plan to slash Social Security and Medicare. . . . The latest controversy shows that Americans and their political leaders are still in denial about the need to face up to the painful choices that will have to be made in coming years to put the nation's economic house in order" (James Risen, "Cuts to Elderly Benefits Seen as Political Poison," *Los Angeles Times* [October 25, 1994]).

The Builders Birth Years: 1901 to 1924 Projected Builder Population: 1993 to 2050 (In thousands)						
	1993	2000	2010	2020	2030	2050
Total U.S. Population	257,935	276,243	300,442	325,900	349,993	392,031
Builders	22,138	15,120	5,102	928	0	0
Percentage of Total Population	8.6%	5.5%	1.7%	0.3%	0.0%	0.0%

Source: Census Bureau Middle Series Projections (1993)

Builders — The Ozzy and Harriet Generation

Ozzy and Harriet immortalize the vision of the builders. As powerful midlifers, the builders created the image of father and mother (in that order!) and smiling, accommodating children. A generation of groups, not individuals, the builders are known for their insistence on conformity. They expected the same camaraderie they felt as youth and as fighting young adults at war to continue as they built their families. Builder families epitomized the best of the now failing grand American story—the way it was supposed to be.

During their powerful midlife years, the builders built everything big that we now see crumbling as we pass out of the twentieth century. They built the big businesses, the big unions, and the big government. Moreover, they built the big cold war—the forty-year standoff between the two big empires—that fueled much of their other big accomplishments (that is, businesses, unions, and government).

They built one other "big" institution. Remember that during outer-directed eras, religious traditions that focus on cooperative "doing faith" emphases prosper. Consistent with this thesis, the builders were responsible for building up the big denominations and their big agencies through the fifties and early sixties. Builder pastors built big, "tall-steeple," mainline churches. They managed the largest expansion of mainline denominational churches in the twentieth century. "Build it and build it BIG" was the motto of this generation that provided the collective infantry of the last BIG war.

But such heroic and magnanimous efforts were not without pain. As a generation, they suffered hurt and confusion over the past twenty-five years as the idealistic boomers consistently showed no appreciation for what they built. But even worse, these young upstarts have militantly rejected their accomplishments on moral grounds! The image of Richard Nixon sneaking out in the early morning to meet with the protesters at the Lincoln Memorial symbolized forever builder confusion. He wanted to "tell" them what was right. Yet he never had a clue about the real issues being questioned. The image of him surrounded by protesters and looking absolutely nonplused captures the essence of the dissension between the two generations—the "generation gap."

How much was the out-of-touch characterization of former President Bush really a fundamental misunderstanding of the idealistic values of the boomers? Builders envision one great society, strong and patriotic. This vision precludes such notions as questioning authority and the integrity of the government in its affairs, especially foreign. This "noble" vision was the driving force behind the campaign to discredit Bill Clinton's actions during the Vietnam War and his brief foray into the world of drug experimentation (though, of course, we all know he never inhaled!). For builders, it is incomprehensible that solid, trustworthy American citizens would do such things. Yet this generation (at least the Republican side of the aisle) lined up behind Oliver North, who was convicted of lying to Congress. Why? Because his action was patriotic. He was supposedly acting as a good, faithful son of the system.

With the youngest builder seventy-six years of age by the year 2000, their future is one of retirement—though, in keeping with their generational ethos, a busy one. With the election of Bill Clinton to the White House in 1992, the era of political domination by the builders has seemingly passed—though as of this writing Bob Dole is taking one last run at the presidency.

Given the increasing life expectancy, however, the builders will be around in large enough numbers to see the formation of the next civic generational type, the millennials, whose initial birth year was 1982. Most likely they will see in these young people shadows of their own past. If they can see their way to notice the awful plight of the current reactive generation, perhaps they will participate in the process of redirecting the entitlements that have followed them through life back toward the generation that is closest to them in ethos. Who knows?

We do know, however, that this is a voting generation. Whatever political direction the nation follows into the twenty-first century will be impacted by the builders until the last of them depart. Inevitably, their voting will protect what they have built. And equally inevitable, they will continue to be a sore spot for those whose elder years will not turn out quite so well because of them.

The Church and the Builders

"Stable" is the word that best depicts the builder and his or her faith. Almost two out of three builders indicate that their faith has remained stable over the previous ten-year period. From our point of view, this would be the expected profile. Builders have struggled since the late sixties with the more experiential side of faith. Faith is what one does, not what one feels. Real faith is faithfulness in doing the work of building the church. Not surprisingly then, it is the mainline Protestant denominations where they are most likely to be found. The following graph demonstrates builder preferences relative to the national average. Every tradition that extends above the line is above the national average in its representation by builders. Those below the line are underrepresented by builders.

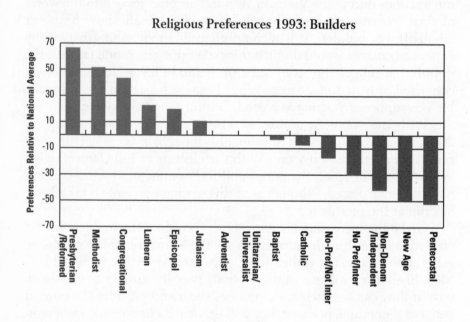

Religious Preferences 1993: Builders

The Last Industrial Age Generation

The builders are more than just the current elder representatives of a civic generation. They hold an additionally important role in the transformation reshaping our world. They are the last full generation of the Industrial Age. Indeed, their generational personality and ethos was amplified by its final thrust. No prior civic generation had accomplished as much. Conformity, bigness, top-down management, and massification, all characteristic of industrialism, reached their apex in builders' programs. Yet ironically, most of their accomplishments have been short-lived. These efforts were simply the last burst of the end of what was fading away. The younger builders witnessed the beginning of the end, but it is the next generation that has lived the transition. Remember, it was the year 1955 that supposedly marked the beginning of the Information Age—the year service workers outnumbered blue-collar workers. But it wasn't until the 1960s that the new force really began to build momentum. Enter the silents.

THE SILENT GENERATION

The distinctive trait of this adaptive generation is that they are facilitators. Unlike the builders before them and the boomers after them, both of whom (each in their own way) push for everything, this generation quietly facilitates life—or at least tries to. Strauss and Howe call them silents. Our experience and reflection finds this an apt description.

Silents: The Equivocal Generation

The silent generation was fittingly captured in the movie *The Dead Poets' Society*. The movie is set in a private boarding school for high-school-aged young men in the mid-fifties. It opens with Robin Williams, the new poetry teacher (most likely an elder silent), in the midst of an introductory discussion about the very nature of poetry. A student reads the textbook (most likely written by a builder), which provides a highly structured and scientific analysis of poetry. Meanwhile Williams is at the chalkboard, mimicking the author's model by drawing a great graph. Good poetry is that which gets the highest score along both axes. Good poetry is that which displays the appropriate form and order according to the author's rules. When the student has finished reading, Williams, using a rather colorful expletive, debunks the author's methodology and subsequently entreats the students to tear the introduction out of the book.

The drama is the internal tension this dissonance creates for these young men. They attended this school because it built the best foundation for the future. A private prep school taught all of the right rules of conformity necessary to become the next generation of doctors,

The Silent Generation **Birth Years: 1925 to 1942**						
Projected Silent Population: 1993 to 2050 (In thousands)						
	1993	2000	2010	2020	2030	2050
Total U.S. Population	257,935	276,243	300,442	325,900	349,993	392,031
Silent	40,714	35,504	27,264	15,368	5,468	0
Percentage of Total Population	15.8%	12.9%	9.1%	4.7%	1.6%	0.0%
Source: Census Bureau Middle Series Projections (1993)						

lawyers, and corporate giants. They were good boys, well trained to listen to the rules and follow them. Now they encountered a teacher who brought all of this into question.

Their response makes this picture a symbol of their generation. Builders would have rejected it all as nonsense and gone off to play football. But these sensitive boys, nearly suffocated as children during the Great War, felt something resonating within them. They felt a call to freedom, a call to break free of the rigors of their protected childhood. It was a call to risk, to walk outside the lines, if even for a moment. And they did. In doing so, they set the stage for the kind of experimentation and wholesale rejection of the rules by the generation that followed them—the boomers.

Many silents to this day feel a nagging guilt for stepping outside the boundaries of their elders. In their coming-of-age and young-adult years, their lives were marked primarily by conformity. Young silents followed the rules and did what they were supposed to do without question.

As a generation, the silents reached a Y in the road sometime during their midlife phase. Some of them chose to continue down the conformist road set before them by their elders, the builders. Since they had prospered as a generation, why mess with success? To this day, many silents do not understand the questioning of authority that has characterized the idealists who followed them—many of whom are their children. These silents still stand in awe of the accomplishments of their elders. To the silents, change seems strange, foreign, and scary. Having been raised in a safe, protective environment, silents want this same security to continue. Consequently, throughout their adult lives, they have pursued safe lifestyles, being careful to always do the right thing as defined by the builders.

120

This very propensity to pursue the safe has also become the silents' greatest challenge. It is the silents who have faithfully worked in the institutions built by the builders. Many in middle-management positions have waited for their opportunity to step into the top jobs. But just as they expected to make the jump, many institutions collapsed or were reorganized. The pressures of competition have forced corporate America to focus on profitability while decreasing expenses. The information revolution continues to change the face of the workplace, and the faces that are dropping out are middle management—silents.

What is worse, the people being brought in to make these changes are the boomers. A close colleague at Percept, Peter Wernett, is a silent. We asked him one day to reflect on his generation. His words tell the story the best.

> My generation has always lacked creative ideas. We have worked long and hard, and we can't be faulted for lack of loyalty. But the world is changing, and for survival, corporations are looking past us to the creative energy so typical of boomers. And we resent it. We feel caught between the builders who built and the boomers who insist on rebuilding it. I notice among many within my generation an anger and a growing stubbornness. We are becoming blockers. Out of fear that the systems we have faithfully served will pass us by, we have begun digging in our heels and using our skill as processors, stopping forward progress. Ironically, we rode the system the longest and received the most from it. Now we are afraid the ride is over, and we don't know what to do. So we block. Change is the enemy.

Only a member of the silents could say it so clearly.

When we look back on the nineties, we will all remember with anger the level of policy gridlock that gripped the nation. Who was in power? Silents. As the twentieth century closes, the anxiety of the silents—that they will be left behind—will increase. Unless things change, they will most likely assist in the creation of the very thing they fear—a world that will pass them by and forget them except as a filibustering bunch of indecisive blockers.

Earlier we had said this generation reached a Y. We have just described one side. But there was another. Though the two are not mutually exclusive, the themes are very different. Several silents, feeling the internal angst of having spent the first half of their life marching to the drumbeat of the builders, took a decidedly internal turn and began to explore their feelings and the experiential side of life. We cannot understand the heavy emphasis on the therapeutic over the last twenty-five years of the twentieth century apart from the soul search led by the silents.

Curiously, it was this decision to pursue the matters of the soul that sparked the most recent awakening. The silent generation was in its rising adult phase of life when the new idealist generation—the boomers—were coming of age. The silents' search for the inner world of values and meaning became the clarion call of the new generation. The always dutiful silents proceeded to mentor the young idealists in their spiritual pilgrimage.

Sensitivity groups came into vogue, and young boomers flocked to hear and—even more—experience the depth of their souls under the spiritual or psychic tutelage of their sensitive silent mentors. As the civil rights movement emerged in the sixties, many of its key drivers were silents whose sensitivity to the plight of others, and their expectation of fair play and justice, deplored the treatment of the Black American.

During this time in the life of the church, such organizations as Faith at Work arose, emphasizing the relational side of life. Faith wasn't just about doing, it was about relating! One of the direct results of this cause was the birth of the small-group movement.

Increasingly, a concern for the spiritual formation of the soul worked its way into even the more traditional denominational traditions—all led initially by silents.

The silents in their elder years will find themselves watching the activity from the sidelines, as if the world simply forgot they were here. Already, before the end of the twentieth century, they were skipped over for the presidency.[6] However, they will not live in poverty. They will continue to be the most affluent generation of the twentieth century. Their retirement will certainly not be one of economic hardship. Yet in their hearts will smolder the flame of hurt that comes from feeling forgotten and unappreciated.

The Church and The Silent

Following the lead of the builders, the silents are also characterized overall as stable. While still leaning toward mainline Protestant

---

[6]Of course, it is possible that neither Dole (a builder) nor Clinton (a boomer) will capture the White House for the final presidential term of the twentieth century.

traditions, silents do show signs of a shift away, as the following graph indicates.

We believe the shifting religious preference profile reflects the two divergent trajectories taken by this generation halfway through its life. Those who stayed on the builder path continued in the more socially acceptable religious traditions. Those who departed from the path began to explore new avenues of spirituality, a trend inherited by the next generation.

Religious Preferences 1993: Silents

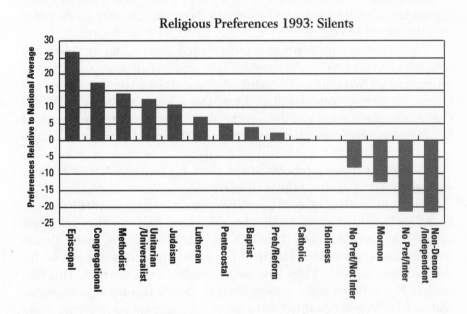

The Squeezed Generation

If the builders are the last Industrial Age generation, the silents are the in-between generation, caught in the squeeze between the end of the industrial-based world and the birth of the information-based world. While key players from both of these older generations helped develop the platform upon which the Information Age would be built, they could not make the jump.

For example, in a short, fifteen-year period, the personal computer has become the central and most important office tool in America. Yet on average, how many silent-generation persons have really been able to embrace it? This is the generation that looked forward to receiving, as its first sign of success, a Dictaphone through which one could dictate letters for the secretary to type and send. Yet the prevailing model for younger executives, especially in the world of downsizing, is to type one's own work in real time, using a computer with word processing capability. Such innovations cut out the need for the interim, expensive, and inefficient step. But they also cut out the need for one ornament of success—the personal secretary. Immediately, at management-level occupations, there was a disadvantage. Silents did not know how to type! Typing was something future clerical people took in high school. Those on the "academic track" in the thirties and forties did not take typing. It was considered a low-level task. Now the primary access point into the world of computers was a silly QWERTY keyboard!

Furthermore, the computer represented abstraction on a level to which most were not accustomed. Paper and pencil were solid. Computer screens were initially unfriendly and unlike the normal media with which they were familiar. Even the advent of the WYSIWYG ("what you see is what you get") technology did not completely remove the problem. For now the screen became a virtual emulation of the typewritten page, but it was still an emulation. The problem was learning to live in a super-symbolic world. It's a big jump to learn to live in such abstraction midway through one's life.

The builders had created a concrete world, and the silents had been raised to faithfully serve in that world. Then, halfway through their careers, that world changed. At the end of their careers, many silents feel lost and disoriented. The world they began with is not the world they are ending with. They have been caught in the squeeze. This factor has exacerbated their generational tendency toward equivocation, and as Mr. Wernett pointed out earlier, an anger and a growing stubbornness is resulting in progress-blocking behaviors.

Our firm is forced to address this issue on a daily basis. What we provide is super-symbolic information for decision making. Consistently we must deal with silent-generation leadership that is clearly overwhelmed by a world spinning out of control around them. In response, they shut down forward momentum. They are caught in the squeeze and are more comfortable doing nothing than moving forward into a foreign land of abstraction and information, where the old models and methods no longer work.

When the new century dawns, the youngest builder will be seventy-six and, except for a few exceptions, will have passed from the active scene. Among the silents, the youngest will be fifty-eight, and while many will still be active, more will not. We suspect that a larger number of silents will slip quietly into retirement at an earlier age than the generation on either side of them. The pressures of the changing world will simply be too much for them, and with their relatively high affluence, they will simply choose to step aside.

Who will take the reins? The boomers! And queuing up behind them, the elder survivors. While the position of the builders and silents is passing, their position as key actors is imminent.

CHAPTER 12

Changing Players III:
The Imminent Actors—
Boomers, Survivors,
Millennials

A S THE TWENTY-FIRST CENTURY opens, two new generations of leadership will have taken center stage: the boomers and the survivors. Throughout the nineties, this transition was in full swing. Halfway through the decade, a boomer sat in the White House and in the Speaker's chair in the House of Representatives. At that point the Senate was still controlled by the failing builders and the frustrated silents. Everyone knew, however, that their days of power were numbered. Most likely, the leaders of the Senate as well will be boomers as the new century begins.

The world these two generations are to lead will look very different. While it is the generational cycle that moves them into power, it is the chaotic changes transforming our world that will determine what they must do. However, the generational cycle will provide them its own set of challenges as well. Immediately facing them is the dawning of a new crisis era.

THE BOOMERS

There is no generation that has received more attention, or at least so it seems. For many reasons, beginning with the sheer numbers, the baby boom generation has been a dominant force during the last half of the twentieth century. Boomers were the children born beginning in

The Boomers						
Birth Years: 1943 to 1960						
Projected Boomer Population: 1993 to 2050 (In thousands)						
	1993	2000	2010	2020	2030	2050
Total U.S. Population	257,935	276,243	300,442	325,900	349,993	392,031
Boomer	67,645	66,984	63,961	57,571	44,577	9,610
Percentage of Total Population	26.2%	24.2%	21.3%	17.7%	12.7%	2.5%

Source: Census Bureau Middle Series Projections (1993)

the early forties to the parents of the end of the builder and the beginning of the silent generations. Their generation extends to the early sixties. Demographically, the boomers' birth years begin in 1946 and end in 1964. This was based upon the incredible postwar baby boom. Demographers consider this boom to have ended in 1964 because it was the last year the annual birth level surpassed the four million mark. Beginning in 1965 there was a significant drop in the number of births.

However, we continue to take clues from Strauss and Howe. In their scheme, the generational boundaries shift down a few years, from 1943 to 1960. While they would affirm the purely demographic phenomenon as spanning 1946 to 1964, they also contend that the pyschosocial forces that gave the boomers their generational identity began a few years earlier and likewise ended a few years sooner.

Boomers: A Generation of Idealists

Boomers are idealists in the generational cycle. As children, they were indulged. This is an important factor in understanding them. In part because of a reaction against their own overprotected childhood, the parents of boomers were not as strong in setting boundaries. In short, boomers were able to get away with much more than would have been possible for the two earlier generations.

This indulgence manifested itself in various ways. The late sixties saw an explosion of experimentation: drugs, alcohol, sex, and so forth. However, the experiments were not without cost. Many of us lost friends to these experiments through overdose or calamity resulting from pushing the edges too far. At my twentieth high school reunion, we reminisced about the summer of 1969, when Jack, my best friend

128

from eighth grade through eleventh grade, was killed in a car wreck—the seventh teenager from my high school in a one-year period. Reflecting back on that period, one woman observed, "It was a strange and dark period. It seemed that we all pursued destructive behaviors." I agree and would add, with abandon!

Like most idealist generations, we came of age in the midst of a spiritual awakening. I remember too well the period. For me, like so many young boomers, it was a period filled with high expectations and buckets full of pain. Everything was questioned, everything was tried. Nothing was sacred. We were long on declarations and short on respect. We had an idealized image of what the world should be, and in our arrogance, we assumed we would realize that image.

Nowhere was this more apparent than in the church. Part of the consciousness revolution included a spiritual awakening. But it was not within the mainstream religious traditions. It was in this period, as we observed earlier, that the mainline Protestant churches began their decline. These churches put a heavy emphasis on "doing faith," and the young boomers found hearts that were cold and without the fire of real spiritual life. Seemingly coming from nowhere, youth movements like the Jesus People's Army arose. Of course, we discovered later that these movements had their origins in the Pentecostal traditions with a "hip" face.

We were all captured by a grand vision, whether in the church or out. It was a spiritual vision of wholeness and authenticity wherein all found their true selves and peace. Noble images abounded, and love was in the air. But it stood in stark contrast to the brokenness and fragmentation that our pursuits actually created. Prior values of the builders and silents, such as duty and propriety, seemed dull and restrictive—choking the spirit of life. And within the church, as new, young, and zealous visionaries, we started pointing out everything that was wrong and inauthentic. The real church would look more like the church in Acts, a collective of believers besieged by the culture, not one with and in the mainstream of the culture. Images of the church as an organic body instead of a hierarchical organization prevailed in our hearts and minds. These same images scared and confused the builder pastors of the churches we invaded.

As we boomers moved into our rising adult years, however, we adopted much of the "plastic" materialism and establishment values we had so boldly condemned. And we did so with the same vigorous zeal with which we had pursued our spiritual revolution. Whereas the builders had formed great secular institutions for the good of the whole,

we turned completely inward and with narcissistic ardor took materialism to a new low. We pursued self-indulgence with the passion of a
true believer.

Of course, that is what we have always been—true believers!
Whatever we believe in is the TRUTH—not just our opinion! During
our young adult years, we did not involve ourselves in the larger community. We let those who cared about the material matters of the world
handle all such unimportant concerns. Others would care for our public schools, local, regional, and national government. It was a cocooning period for us. But in our cocooning, idealistic frameworks were
constructed, frameworks that would soon emerge as banners around
which we would rally.

In 1987 the older cohort of the boomers entered their midlife
years, and the rest will follow into this phase of life until the last of us
turns forty-four in 2005. We believe this is a critical period for America. Strauss and Howe make the point that idealists in their midlife
years come out of their period of narcissistic self-indulgence as raving
moralists. With the zeal of a warrior, midlife idealists cast every issue in
moral terms. Where silents are more likely to see the subtlety of issues
and demonstrate sensitivity to the feelings of others, boomers in their
moralistic zeal see no such areas of gray. As the decade of indulgence
faded, we came forth in fury, waving our ideological-moral banners.

If we look at the issues being debated, we find proponents of arguments on both sides. But always the topic is debated as a moral issue.
For example, consider the abortion debate. If you are a "pro-choice" person, it is a moral issue of a woman's right (rights are always moral issues
for idealists) to choose what happens with and to her body. However,
if you are a "pro-lifer," it is a moral issue of murdering a living being.
Both positions are completely polarized around their "absolute truth"
stance. Generally, no one in the public debate is allowed to construct a
moderate position without becoming the target of the righteous zeal
of both parties.

The last idealist generation gave us prohibition. The current, the
boomer idealists, will give us prohibition of the nineties—the eradica-
tion of smoking from every environment.

As we enter the new century, boomers will still be in our midlife
phase, and our moralistic zeal will have been rampaging for over a
decade. Our greatest strength and gift to our society is our idealism.
Society needs those who call it to a higher vision. But our greatest liability is our idealism as well. For as we march forward making our

moralistic declarations, we generally leave a path of destruction in our wake. This is the dark side of the boomer. Left unchecked, we could yet do grave harm to all.

The Church and the Boomer

The cover of the November 1994 issue of *Newsweek* announced, "In Search of the Sacred: America's Quest for Spiritual Meaning." It seems that suddenly this has again become an acceptable topic of reflection. Further reading revealed that the real thrust of the article, like so many other "trend" discussions, really revolved around boomers. The subtitle made this very clear. "Whether it's middle age or the coming millennium or a bad case of the blues, many Americans are on a quest for spiritual meaning." [1]

Great! Are the boomers finally going to come to their senses and return to the church? Don't hold your breath. This group will not be the salvation of the institutional church. As idealists, boomers have always been driven by spiritual issues. More recently they have even couched their discussions in spiritual language. During the mid-nineties, they were on an "In Search of Angels" quest.

While there may be a rising spiritual concern among boomers, it is not in the traditional institutional church. More likely, boomers—being the self-determining lot that we are—will pick and choose our religion. We like boutique faith, not superstores. In an interview with one woman, *Newsweek* found that after a difficult divorce, she decided it was time to look again into spirituality. But did she return to the church of her youth? No. She created a potpourri with a sprinkling of Unity thought, a smidgen of Native American spiritual practices, a touch of Buddhism, a Hebrew prayer, and an overlay of feminist-goddess religion. Not exactly your standard, orthodox religious fare. [2]

Unlike the builders and silents before them, the faith involvement of the boomers is anything but stable. Boomers are increasing their faith involvement. According to our Ethos II survey, close to 25% indicated having greater involvement in 1993 than ten years earlier. But the increase did not translate into involvement in mainline Protestant churches. We made two discoveries as we analyzed the data.

---

[1] Barbara Kantrowitz, "In Search of the Sacred: America's Quest for Spiritual Meaning," *Newsweek* (November 28, 1994).

[2] Ibid.

- There is no single mainline Protestant denomination in which boomers have an above-average preference.
- The span of preferences is much greater than for either the builders or the silents before them.

Both of these points are illustrated in the following graph of boomer religious preferences.

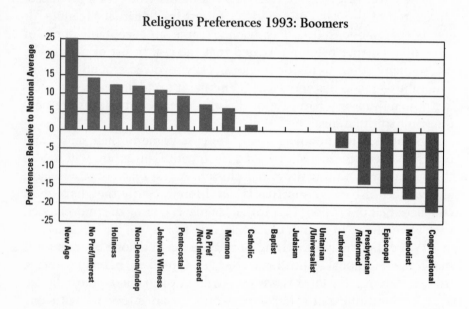

Religious Preferences 1993: Boomers

The First Information-Postmodern Generation

The builders were the last Industrial Age generation. The silents have been caught in a squeeze between the end of the Industrial Age and the advent of the Information Age. Boomers are the first generation of the Information Age. It's not easy being first, however. As this new era emerged, older boomers have in many ways experienced a disorientation similar to that of the silents. But whereas the silents faced the technological revolution at mid-career, most boomers entered the world of work already dealing with it. Even the oldest boomer knew of the computer. Most of us first experienced it as punch cards.

For boomers, the computer has always been a part of the world. Even though the personal computer revolution did not begin until the early eighties, the impact of computers and the changes they were forcing have been reshaping our world since the beginning of this generation. Consequently, boomers were better prepared conceptually for the implications of the information revolution. Even in elementary school, boomers were introduced to the concepts that were foundational to data processing and the complex computations possible only because of these amazing machines.

Therefore while it is true that many boomers do not always use the computer themselves in the work environment, they know that computers are essential to accomplish their goals, and will insure that they have people in their circle who do use them. As a result, the animosity and uncertainty that the information revolution causes for many silents is absent among boomers. This is a subtle but crucial distinction.

There is an additional distinction that is important and that is directly tied to this generational type. Being the first information generation and idealists provides boomers with an extraordinary place that other generational idealists have not enjoyed. The gift of an idealist is vision. That is, idealists are predisposed to see the big picture or to shape a big picture and point the way forward. Any visionary will be able to imagine a future and how to get there based upon the technology extant at his or her moment in time. So as visionaries standing on the threshold of the Information Age, boomers have a rare role to play: namely, we can set a trajectory that will influence generations yet to come. This can be positive or it can be negative. It depends upon what we as boomers collectively envision. This is a story yet untold.

THE SURVIVORS

The Survivors Birth Years: 1961 to 1981						
Projected Survivor Population: 1993 to 2050 (In thousands)						
	1993	2000	2010	2020	2030	2050
Total U.S. Population	257,935	276,243	300,442	325,900	349,993	392,031
Survivor	81,030	82,974	84,636	83,899	80,239	55,278
Percentage of Total Population	31.4%	30.0%	28.2%	25.7%	22.9%	14.1%
Source: Census Bureau Middle Series Projections (1993)						

A few years back, when my eldest son turned fifteen, he made a great discovery. A review of his wardrobe indicated that he had very little clothing that was not black. Upon reflection, he decided that perhaps he needed to consider some other colors—maybe some grays!

If colorful, even kaleidoscopic, is the mark of the boomer, black is a no less powerful symbol of the generation that follows them. Recently my wife and I were having a mocha coffee at one of the new local coffee bars. I commented that it was quite easy to identify the younger generation from the boomers. Simply look at their clothing. The survivors all wore either black or some other dark and drab color. In contrast, I said, look at us. We wore colors. Further observation confirmed this. We immediately noticed another couple around our age. They too wore colors—and the wisps of gray above their ears confirmed the assumption.

Survivors: Generation in Search of a Name

Without venturing too far into the esoteric, it would be our contention that the color is indicative of something deeper within the psyche of this (currently) young generation. These are the children born in the early sixties to the parents of the end of the silent and the beginning of the boomer generations. Their generation extends to the early eighties, with many ending the generational group in 1981. This generation will be in the last half of its youth and first half of its rising adult phases of life until the turn of the century. The pressures of young adulthood press upon the older end, while the youngest are in the upheaval of puberty.

It seems everyone has struggled to come up with a name for this generation. Because they are the thirteenth generation of America, Strauss and Howe call them the thirteeners—a name that does not adequately describe the experience of this next reactive generation. Names such as "baby busters" or "post-boomers" are not only unfair, they are indicative of the arrogance of the boomers. The idealism of the boomers tends to encourage an inflated sense of self. By calling this generation names based upon the boomers, this pretense is carried forward and imposed upon another. It is to suggest that this generation has no identity outside of the boomers. Our discussions with the young adults in this group indicate a level of bitterness at such an association.

They have been variously referred to as "generation X" or just "Xers" (a self-designation indicating their own sense of alienation) or the "MTV generation." For most of us, each name carries with it either an overt (or at least covert) repudiation and judgment. (It is us—that is, the adults—who do the naming, by the way.) We contend that many of us, especially boomers, hold negative images of this generation. Even though many of us have children within it, we view their generational ethos as dangerous and something from which we must protect them.

The last generation of reactives was called the "lost generation." Does this image strike a familiar chord? It does for me. In my school district, we had our first drive-by shooting. We felt as if our innocence had been lost (and some of our boomer idealism with it), and we have been forced to see the tragic side of this generation firsthand. I must confess that part of the image I have developed of this generation does provoke an image of lostness. Ironically, the response to all of this by the older generations is one of criticism and rejection. We look down our long, lofty moral noses at a generation that has, in a real sense, simply followed our lead. As a generational group, they will need to survive a world that has always been and most likely always will be hostile toward them. Therefore we call them "the survivors."

I am privileged to observe another side of this generation. While many boomers approached their teens and young adulthood with idealistic zeal and a commitment to reject and change the "system," many young people within this generation have chosen a more pragmatic approach. They study.

Few things have provoked a sense of holy gratitude in me more than watching my sons (my girls as of this writing are only in elementary school) embrace middle school and/or high school. When I was their age, the last thing I did was study. I placed very little if any value on the activity. In contrast, my boys will come home and spend two or three hours a night on schoolwork. And for all of boomer idealist loftiness, many young people of this generation have much clearer personal goals. My eldest son wants to be an engineer who designs and builds rockets. He has had this goal for several years, and there are many like him.

Yet we have criticized and rebuked this generation its entire life. One particularly odious manifestation of our arrogance is the constantly repeated statement that this generation is stupid, that we have dumbed down the curriculum, that it is nowhere near as rigorous as when we went through, and that SAT scores are in free fall. Let me address this in no uncertain terms: IT IS BUNK! SAT scores are remaining stable at the same time that a higher and higher percentage of total students are taking the test! When boomers were coming out of high school, maybe 10 to 20% took SATs. Now the level is closer to 70%. And the curricu-

135

lum? How can a generation that got credit in college for basket weaving be critical of a generation that takes trigonometry before leaving high school?

In my travels, I came across a book about this generation, written by one of their own. In his introduction, we can see how our views have impacted them.

> I've had it. For most of my life, my generation has been eclipsed by the 72 million omnipresent baby boomers. Like a pig in the python, because there are so many of them, the baby boomers have defined every era through which they have passed. Even relatively small subspecies of them, such as the roughly 4 million young urban professionals, have made social waves. And now that my peers and I are beginning to receive a bit of attention, we are getting clobbered.[3]

This book is fascinating in that it is a dialogue with real people across the U.S. One cannot read it without noticing the distinctive characteristics of the generation but also their continuity with what is valued by others. In other words, they have received a predictably bad rap.

What is common between these two different pictures of this generation? Again, I think we can best capture that difference by a comparison to boomers. Boomers, as idealists, have an overall generational ethos of entitlement. Between the nurturing experience of boomers and our sheer size, life has tended to revolve around our needs and desires. This younger generation has had just the opposite experience. Nothing has revolved around them. They do not expect to be taken care of. Rather, there is a streetwise pragmatism that teaches that if they are to survive, they must make it on their own.

Why has this happened to this generation? When the survivors were born and in their early years, their parents were pursuing the "self," living in communes, looking to the other world for life meaning, setting and pursuing super-careers, and so on. Their minds were not on the more mundane activities of life, such as nurturing children. The result? The latchkey generation. Thousands went home every day to an empty house. While dad and mom have been pursuing their own selves, these young people have been left alone. Adult self-fulfillment, an idealistic goal, has been at the expense of our children.

---

[3]Michael Lee Cohen, *The Twentysomething American Dream: A Cross-Country Quest for a Generation*, (New York: Penguin, 1993), 1.

For example, take one demographic phenomenon, the divorce rate. Between 1960 and 1985, the rate of divorce in the U.S. doubled. In 1960 seven out of a thousand children experienced divorce. By 1970 it had risen to twenty out of a thousand, an increase of 186%! In the twenty-year period between 1964 and 1984, one-third to two-fifths of this generation experienced divorce as a child.[4]

The story of abandonment does not stop at the front door. As a society, we have in the past twenty years consistently adopted policies that have marginalized the children. It has been noted by many demographers that twenty-five years ago the poorest among us were seniors. This is no longer true. The safety net for our aging population has never been greater. But while the seniors (read the builders) were making headway in their combat against poverty, poverty did not go away. It simply shifted onto the backs of our young. Removed from one place, it simply showed up somewhere else.

Even within the church, the one environment where one would expect greater concern for children, the emphasis has been on the adults and their spiritual development more than on children.

So how did we come to call this generation survivors? We realized that any name will generally fail, except for names such as the boomers, which only describe a demographic phenomenon. Our hearts would like to propose "the neglected." The name would not be intended as a negative judgment on this young generation. Rather, its intent would be a prophetic message to the older generations to take note and address the issues surrounding this generation on two fronts. First, for the generation of children born following the neglected. Unless we confess and repent our individual and collective acts of neglect, we may well carry these abandonment behaviors on into the next generation.

The second part of the prophetic message is for the neglected themselves. If Strauss and Howe are correct, we as a society are likely to continue to neglect this generation as they move through the stages of life. If this is carried out sixty years, the poor will again be the seniors. Only the poverty will have not moved. It will have remained focused on the same group of people from cradle to grave. Isn't it curious that at the moment when this generation will be in their midlife working years, providing the primary support, we as a nation will have the largest group of senior adults, as a percentage of the total population, in our history? Who is going to carry the burden of these people?

---

[4]Isobel Osius, "A Day Late and a Dollar Short," *American Demographics* (Ithaca, NY: 1991).

However, "the neglected" will not work as a name. First of all, it would be interpreted not in the prophetic sense but indeed as a negative declaration. We fear that in naming them the neglected, the result may be to encourage the very behavior we believe we need to correct, as if in the naming we justify the actions. Secondly, I watched the face of a dear friend from this generation when the name was introduced to her. There was pain in her eyes. Pain because of its truth, and it was being thrown in her face. For she had been neglected, indeed abandoned, by a father who simply left her and her mother to pursue a new life. They have never met, though she found out one day who he was and where he lived. My heart broke as I heard her tell us how she went and sat in the park across from his house and watched her father work in his yard, the father who wanted nothing to do with her.

So though neglect and criticism has been society's overall behavior toward this generation, it is their response that must govern how we think of them. They are a generation of survivors.

As we move toward the year 2000, when boomers will almost have completely moved into their midlife, moralistic years, the survivors will have fully moved into their young adult phase of life. What will fill their time during this period? Let's allow one of them to put it in his words.

> Most of them are not striving to be oh-so-boho in SoHo. Most of them are not hiding from the world by escaping to the California desert, whiling away the days by telling tales and boozing. Most of them are not paralyzed by a crushing sense of "futurelessness," fretting about the likelihood that they will be forgotten by History. Rather, most of them are striving to carve out lives for themselves and, in some cases, their families, even though they face some daunting obstacles—apparently diminishing economic opportunities and increasingly fierce international economic competition, a spiraling national debt, environmental degradation, a faltering public education system, AIDS. Yet if one were to judge today's young adults by the articles, books, and movies about them, one would likely label them the "dis ..." generation—disenchanted, dissatisfied, disenfranchised, disgruntled, disillusioned, discomfited, and disconnected.[5]

What should be clear when speaking of survivors is this: there is the contingent, often characterized by their popular musicians, that

---

[5]Cohen, *The Twentysomething American Dream*, 3.

does feel alienated and discarded. Indeed, many feel this. But not all are following this darkness into complete debauchery. While they do not share the more lofty ideals of the boomers, many are taking their place in our society as it is, with a whole lot less whining than is true of boomers still! This is not to say that there should not be grave concerns for this generation. For it is also true that they must learn to survive in a world far more violent than when we were growing up. But they will survive the battle and be shaped by it into very practical and effective midlife adults and respected, if reclusive, elders.

What can we expect from survivors as we approach the twenty-first century? Because they suffered as children from neglect, they will become the more conservative and protective parents of the young millennial generation. While they are more likely to have materialistic aspirations, they will do what is necessary to provide for their families. There will be a day, according to Strauss and Howe, when all of us will look to this generation to help us survive.

The Church and the Survivor

Whereas the boomers were more likely to have increased their faith involvement, survivors are more likely to have decreased it—but also increased. In other words, where survivors are least likely to fall is in the stable range. The largest percentage (38%) have decreased. But three in ten have also increased. We will find later that this generation is on the move.

A review of their religious preferences reveals two traits, one that they share with boomers and one that makes them distinct from boomers. What they share is diversity. Like the boomers, survivors are spread across many different traditions, and none of their above-average preferences are mainline Protestant. But unlike the boomers, survivors are more likely to prefer traditions that are more theologically conservative. So while 8% of boomers have a nondenominational preference, over 10% of survivors do. And while boomers are more likely to have New Age or Eastern preferences, survivors are not. Instead, they will prefer more conservative traditions such as the Adventist, Mormon, or Pentecostal.

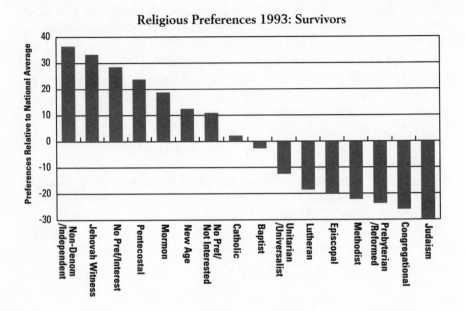

Religious Preferences 1993: Survivors

The Cyberspace Generation

While boomers are the first Information Age generation, there has always been some distance between the boomer and the machines of information technology. This is not the case with survivors. They have been raised in an information-rich environment—though not all of it positive. Interactive video games have been common fare for them. As a result, they do not feel intimidated by technology the way the older generations do. Most are introduced to personal computers in kindergarten, and computer lab is a regular component of each school week. This is different from the boomers' experience. While we were told about computers and what they could do, most younger survivors have actually used computers.

Consequently, life in cyberspace is not foreign to this generation. Conceptually they have little trouble imagining a world "in the wires" connecting house to house, business to business, and so forth. Moreover, television programs directed at this generation increasingly explore such concepts as "virtual reality" and life on the "Net" (short for Internet). *Tech Wars*, a popular program, toyed with a most intriguing concept. What could be more addictive than drugs? "Tech!" In the cyberspace world of the twenty-first century, power is not located in political nation-states, it is vested in "tech lords" who control the minds of the population in a manner analogous to how the drug lord of the twentieth century controlled the streets of our inner cities. All of these programs target the imagination of the young, technically sophisticated survivor. In fact, most computer hackers are survivors, as are those most adept at finding these pirates of the twenty-first century.

If boomers are the initial visionaries of the Information Age, survivors are the technical geniuses who will wire the vision and make it work. Boomers will employ the power of information technologies from the outside looking in. Survivors will be inside! Whether this is good for them or not remains to be seen.

THE MILLENNIALS

The Millennials Birth Years: 1982 to 2003						
Projected Millennial Population: 1993 to 2050 (In thousands)						
	1993	2000	2010	2020	2030	2050
Total U.S. Population	257,935	276,243	300,442	325,900	349,993	392,031
Millennial	46,040	75,661	91,562	94,702	96,274	93,528
Percentage of Total Population	17.8%	27.4%	30.5%	29.1%	27.5%	23.9%

Source: Census Bureau Middle Series Projections (1993)

In 1982 a new generation of civics had its first birth year. Called millennials by Strauss and Howe, this is the generation in its youth as we move toward the twenty-first century. No particular generational personality has yet emerged. It is too soon. We can, however, make note of social developments that are to be expected within the generational cycle that will most likely impact them.

Perhaps the most obvious is the plight of children. If public debate precedes public policy and social practice, then we are right on schedule within the rhythm of the generational cycle. A central discussion in the public arena in this last decade of the century is the plight of children. It has been brought to our awareness that one in five lives in poverty. We know that single adult households are growing. And finally we are admitting that this is probably not the best for the full, healthy

141

development of the person. The reemergence of the discussion about family values is part of this. Dollars per student spent for education is hotly debated, and there has been a growing popularity of preventive programs on behalf of small children.

We have all become painfully aware of how at risk so many kids are. As the first cohort groups of new millennials were born in the early eighties, the government released the revolutionary report "A Nation at Risk." This document became the moral vision for school reform for years to come. Who will benefit from all of this public debate? The survivors? No! The millennials.

If the generational cycle prevails, we will enter some kind of world crisis between 2015 and 2025. In 2015 the oldest millennial will be thirty-three, and the youngest somewhere around eleven. Like the builders before them, they will be at just the right age to fill the ranks necessary to defeat the rising threat. Not a happy thought!

We now have all of the generational actors on the stage as we step into the twenty-first century. In the background will be the remaining vestiges of the builders and the retired silents. In the foreground will be the boomers, who by 2000 will be in full control of all institutions, and the survivors, who (hopefully) will be emerging out of their period of darkness, ready to give themselves to the challenges rising on the horizon.

CHAPTER 13

Changing Faith I:
The Insiders

R ELIGIOUS FAITH IN AMERICA is dying!
Based upon the responses of over eighteen thousand Americans, what has been a foundational component of American culture is failing rapidly. Indeed, if the current decline in faith involvement continues, as indicated on Percept's last Ethos survey, around the year 2013 less than half of all Americans will still hold to some level of active faith.

As we have shared these findings with people, immediately we are hit with a torrent of "What abouts." What about all of the churches that are growing? What about the megachurches? What about the Holy Spirit? What about the Scriptures that teach that even the gates of hell will not prevail against the church?

Clearly, there are pockets of growth around the country and some mighty large churches, which for the most part causes us to rejoice. But let's put things in perspective. Consider the Willow Creek phenomenon. As of this writing it was drawing fifteen thousand people in the suburbs of Chicago. But in the mid-nineties, there were 6.5 million people in the larger Chicago metro area! And does Willow Creek come close to representing the diversity of the population that is projected for the greater Chicago area?

We do not intend to rain on any parades. Moreover, we are certainly not suggesting that the Holy Spirit will not do something wonderful. And we do not believe the "gates of hell" will prevail. But cultural change will prevail against the institutional church. The bubbles of good news are wonderful, but they are only bubbles. When we are forced to deal with the real, hard numbers, the institutional deterioration is overwhelming.

Ultimately, for this conclusion to be helpful, we need more information. Typically, we play the "winners-and-losers" game. If people are declining in religious faith, who is taking the hit? Which, of course, is an insidious way of seeing how my tradition is doing relative to yours.

Well, the winners-and-losers game is one of interest, if the priority question is, Which religious institutions are the winners and which the losers? But what if we recast the discussion and ask it from the point of view of people? In other words, instead of assessing our relative institutional success or failure (which is most likely only an ego issue), what if we look at the question from the perspective of people and how their religious preferences may or may not be changing? Is it possible to discern why there is a trend toward no faith involvement? Our findings would say yes. By examining the trends in religious preference, we can obtain a very real and powerful picture of what is occurring in America.[1]

The broad picture supports the claim that faith in America is indeed declining. Using our Ethos survey data, we created groups by their religious preference in 1983 over and against 1993. First, all respondents were separated into two groups: (a) those with a preference, and (b) those without a preference. The former we call the insiders; the latter, the outsiders.

Trend in Religous Preference		
	1983 Percentage	1993 Percentage	Net Gain or (Loss)
Preference—Insiders	87.0	83.0	-4
No Preference—Outsiders	13.0	17.0	4

Nationally, people are moving from sustaining to abandoning a religious preference. But the survey data enable us to create a much more detailed, nuanced picture. Six different types emerged and were named based upon the pattern of their preferences.

---

[1]The religious preference analysis is based upon Percept's 1993 national Ethos survey. The survey was sent to 30,000 households across America. The sample was regionally and demographically balanced to match the U.S. population. Over 18,500 completed responses were returned. This sample was adjusted to maintain the appropriate balance.

	% of Total Ethos	Survey Median Age	Size of Profile	Margin of Error	Definitions
Types					

The Shape of Religious Preference in America

THE INSIDERS: Those who do have a preference: 83.4% in 1993

Types	% of Total Ethos	Survey Median Age	Size of Profile	Margin of Error	Definitions
The Loyalist	72.2	49.0	11,224.0	0.8%	Preference now same as 10 years ago
The Switcher	9.4	41.0	1,467.0	2.3%	Preference now different than 10 years ago, but still have a preference
The Newcomer	1.8	36.0	275.0	5.3%	Did not have a preference 10 years ago, but do now

THE OUTSIDERS: Those who do not have a preference: 16.6% in 1993

Types	% of Total Ethos	Survey Median Age	Size of Profile	Margin of Error	Definitions
The Floating	5.9	42.0	854.0	3.0%	Some did have a preference, some did not, 10 years ago but do not now
The Disillusioned	2.8	40.0	412.0	4.3%	Had a preference 10 years ago but do so no longer
The Indifferent	7.9	45.0	1152.0	0.6%	Did not have a preference 10 years ago, and still don't

Source: Percept Group, Inc., Ethos II Survey (1993)

In this chapter and the next, we will briefly examine each of these six types.[2] The result will provide a powerful if uncomfortable picture of why traditional religious faith in America is dying.

We devote this chapter to the insiders, those who still maintain a religious preference. The largest group, and by far the most influential for that reason, is the loyalists. The switchers and newcomers are smaller groups, though important because they have found a new reason for hope. In the next chapter, we deal with the outsiders, those who for whatever reason have no preference. The three types are called the floaters, the disillusioned, and the indifferent.

Many of us will not like what this information reveals. But there must be a death before a resurrection. What follows puts a real face on our death.

---

[2]For a more thorough analysis of the types, see appendix A titled "Generations."

THE LOYALIST

"I WAS BORN AND BAPTIZED a Presbyterian, I was raised a Presbyterian, I married a Presbyterian and was married by a Presbyterian, I have been an active Presbyterian, and I shall die a Presbyterian. The Presbyterian Church is my church, and I am proud of it and proud to be a part of it."

Such are the sentiments of the denominational loyalist. It is just this predisposition upon which most denominations in America have depended for much of their history. Church growth was calculated just as the Census Bureau calculates net population growth. Annual new births less annual deaths equals net "church growth."

Seven out of ten persons in America are loyalists. They represent the historic and faithful mainstream of religious America. Tirelessly they have served their traditions, passing on to subsequent generations the values of their religious and theological heritage. Every denominational tradition assumes their loyalty. Of course, that assumption includes two factors: that they will always be there and that they are a constant group of people.

Unfortunately, the dear Presbyterian who reflected her strong commitment to the Presbyterian Church confesses as well to a significant level of frustration. This same commitment has not been realized in her boomer children. While one attends a Presbyterian church on occasion, the rest do not. One attends nowhere, and another attends the neighborhood's local independent church, where he "feels more comfortable." This same story has been repeated time and again within every denominational tradition in America throughout the final quarter of the twentieth century.

While the loyalist has been the stable backbone of American religion, as a religious preference type it is changing. And given the sheer numbers, no other group can and will have a greater impact upon the shape of religion in America. As goes the loyalist, so goes the denominational traditions in this country.

THE LOYALIST PROFILE

LOYALISTS ARE GENERALLY WHITE (90%) and on the older side, with an average age of forty-seven. They are likely to be married and relatively educated. While both boomers and survivors are underrepresented, both silents and builders are overrepresented.

146

Loyalist by Generation

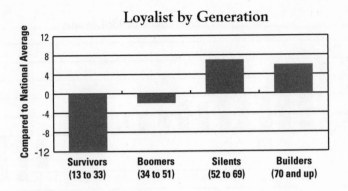

Loyalists indicate a growing dissatisfaction with their current faith environment—both their spirituality and the church itself. One must wonder how long they will remain loyal to their traditions. The number of loyalists will decrease in the years to come as they finally abandon their loyalty in search of a church with which they feel comfortable. Many who still count themselves among the faithful are hanging on by a thread. This growing ambivalence to their traditional loyalty places a serious burden on those traditions that rely on their faithfulness. If not addressed effectively, many loyalists will become switchers or worse in the near future.

Spiritual Satisfaction Indicator: Loyalist

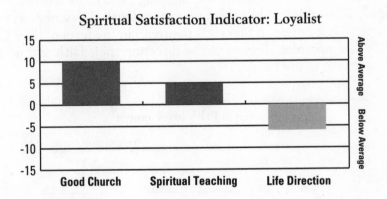

The religious preference of the loyalist provides insight into the futures of several faith traditions. Not surprisingly, most loyalists locate their preferences among the larger religious and denominational traditions.

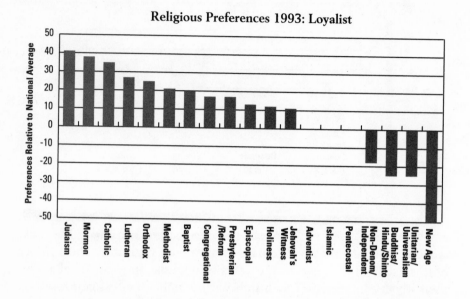

Religious Preferences 1993: Loyalist

Loyalists though they be, a large body of them are decreasing their faith involvement. An examination of the change in the level of faith activity of the loyalist provides a deeply sobering picture. For every two loyalists who have increased their activity, three have decreased.

Those whose faith involvement has increased we call the "ascending"; those who have decreased, the "slipping"; and those who have not changed, the "stable."[3] While the designation "loyalist" describes a group of people at a moment in time, it is the trend in the level of their faith activity that provides clues as to the direction their faith and preferences will take in the future.

Change in Faith Involvement	
	Percentage of Loyalists
The Slipping Loyalist (Decreased)	29.3
The Stable Loyalist (Same)	51.1
The Ascending Loyalist (Increased)	19.7
Source: Percept Group, Inc., Ethos II Survey, 1993	

[3]These names are used consistently as a way to discuss the dynamic of change within each of the preferential types.

THE SLIPPING LOYALIST

REPRESENTING ONE IN THREE loyalists, the slipping are younger than the average loyalist. Among the loyalists, it is the survivors and the boomers whose faith involvement evidences decline.

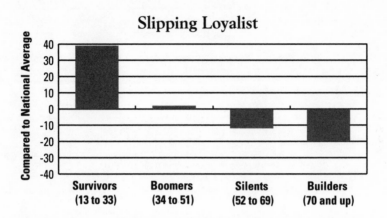

We must assume the slipping represent a distressing trend. Consequently, the greater the percentage of a religious tradition to be represented, the worse the news. The news spells calamity for *all* of the historic Protestant denominations. Slipping loyalty is a Protestant problem.

So where can we project the slipping loyalists are headed? Earlier we had noted that as a group, loyalists seek both "spiritual teaching" and a "good church." This emphasis does not prevail among the slipping loyalists. Both spiritual teaching and a good church fall quite low on a list of concerns for the slipping loyalist. However, the desire to find meaning in life is a concern.

This fact may be both condemnation of and a chance for the church. Condemnation because for whatever reason, these persons have not found in the church's presentation of the Gospel a story that answers their ultimate quest for meaning. Yet it also offers the church a chance, if it will do the work of telling the story of the Gospel. But the telling must make sense to the modern person. We will see this theme emerge again and again.

Religious Preference: The Slipping Loyalist		
	Percentage of Preference Among Slipping Loyalists	Percentage of Preference Among All Loyalists
Episcopal	4.0	3.4
Adventist	0.7	0.6z
Unitarian/Universalist	0.7	0.6
Methodist	13.5	12
Lutheran	10.0	8.9
Congregational	2.9	2.7
Baptist	18.9	17.7
Presbyterian/Reformed	5.2	4.9

Source: Percept Group, Inc., Ethos II Survey (1993)

THE ASCENDING LOYALIST

THERE IS, OF COURSE, the other side of the story. Almost 20% of all loyalists' faith involvement is ascending. Though a smaller group than the slipping loyalist, the ascending are the hope of the loyalists. They have the energy and the motivation to become positive contributors. Of course, we assume they are found in large numbers within historic church traditions. This is a false assumption.

Like the slipping, they are on the younger side, but they are not as young.

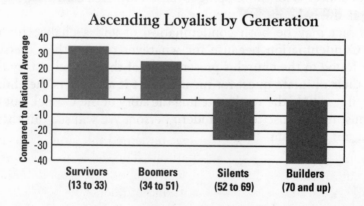

Ascending Loyalist by Generation

Representation of survivors and boomers is again above average relative to all loyalists. How can this be? How can these two generations be both the slipping and the ascending? Religious preference tells the story. Let's view this group from the "winners-and-losers" perspective. Who benefited from their new faith enthusiasm?

Religious Preferences 1993: Ascending Loyalist

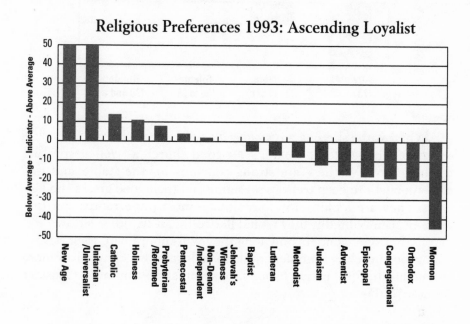

The more marginal Christian traditions or non-Christian movements are the clear winners. Unlike the slipping loyalist, the ascending loyalist does not form a historic mainline Protestant profile. With the exception of the Presbyterian and Reformed tradition, no other large Protestant body is found above the loyalist average. This is not good news for Protestants of any flavor, especially given that the ascenders reflect a younger profile.

THE STABLE LOYALIST

AT 51%, THE STABLE LOYALISTS constitute the largest of the three loyalist groups. Their faith involvement has remained the same. Their preference is mainline Protestant and Catholic. The stable are older. While the slipping and ascenders are more likely to be survivors and boomers, the stable are more likely to be silents and builders.

The Stable Loyalists by Generation

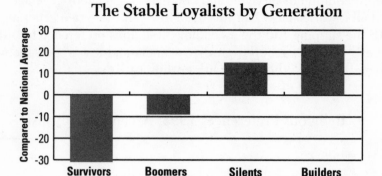

Whereas the slipping are *moving away* from the church, the stable are more inclined to be *looking for* a good church as well as spiritual teaching. Both of these are strong concerns for the stable, and this strength ought to keep us from presuming on their good graces and loyalties. They are looking for something—most importantly, spiritual teaching. Undoubtedly, they would like to find it within their own traditions. But one wonders how long they will subordinate their desires for a good church to their denominational loyalty, which revolves more around institutional maintenance than spiritual development. Consider the story of Debra.

Mini-Profile: The Stable Loyalist

Debra, age 40

Generation: Boomer

Preference: Presbyterian Church (USA)

Are you currently happy with your preference? Would you ever consider changing churches? If so, would you remain in the same tradition?

I am generally happy with my preference, although I think it is my particular church that keeps me in the Presbyterian tradition. Currently I am pleased with the quality of the youth ministry for my teenage boys, and the children's ministry for my younger girls. The worship service is the biggest plus for me personally. Also, it is within my community.

Any consideration of change would come from a distinct sense of lack of community or closer relationships within the church. I am concerned with certain behaviors that I feel are contrary to what the Christian life is about.

If I were to leave, I am not convinced I would stay in the Presbyterian tradition, as many other of their churches are considered "cold and dead."

Has your faith involvement increased, decreased, or remained the same?

While it has increased, some factors are pushing toward a decrease. I guess overall it is stable.

Please explain.

It is hard to measure the growth of one's faith. Looking back over the past ten years, I see the incredible faithfulness of God and how he has worked in my life to provide for and sustain me. I cannot be just the "same" as I ponder and reflect on the beauty and wonder of that reality.

However, I do feel I have become more pessimistic and disillusioned with church and the people who are involved in ministry (lay and professional). This, then, does affect my faith or desire to participate in church ministry.

While the loyalists' religious preference did not change, the trend relative to this large portion of the American population does not bode well for the institutional church. Having become disenchanted with the church and not having found answers to the meaning of life within the church, the slipping loyalist is moving away from the church. The ascenders long for spiritual teaching but are not looking for a good church. Indeed, they are less likely to be found in any historic Protestant traditions.

Perhaps the most disconcerting story is the stable loyalist. While they have been the backbone of most denominational traditions, as we prepare to enter the twenty-first century, they long for spiritual teaching *and* a good church. Are the stable about to make a change?

Complacently assuming they will always be sitting in our pews is an egregious error.

Church leaders dare not presume on the loyalties of any loyalists any longer!

THE SWITCHER

"I BECAME SPIRITUALLY DEPRESSED and no longer had enthusiasm for church or my spiritual walk with God. After we searched for a new church for several months, the Methodist church we now attend has provided a friendly, comfortable place to worship."

This man would have been classified as a loyal parishioner had the survey been conducted two years earlier. But his frustration with his former Presbyterian congregation simply became acute. He could no longer bear it, so he and his wife switched. There is a point out there where most loyalists will make a change. One direction will be that of the switcher who, having switched traditions, finds hope reborn.

Switchers are far more racially and ethnically diverse than loyalists. They are a well-educated and affluent group. Unlike loyalists, switchers represent the two younger generations. Kids are a hallmark of this segment. Loyalty is less important than the desire for something that meets their needs.

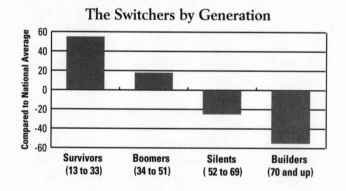

The Switchers by Generation

The Switcher and Religious Faith

Consistent with their generational profile, switchers express great concern for their spiritual development. Finding spiritual teaching and a good church drive this group. However, concern for finding life direction is also very important. Switchers switch because something is missing in their lives. We suspect they have not yet settled. With so many still looking and having changed once, a segment of switchers will switch again.

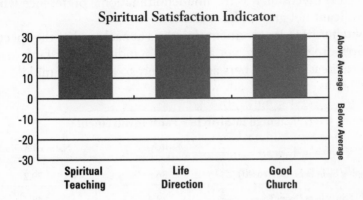

Spiritual Satisfaction Indicator

Where are they going? From where have they come? We know switchers have not rejected a preference. They have simply moved from one to another. Like a game of musical chairs, the switchers leave one tradition and move to another. Presbyterians become Methodists; Methodists, Episcopalians; and Episcopalians, Presbyterians. And like musical chairs, with every round a chair is pulled on the historic traditions.

So who won and who lost? The following graph tells the story.

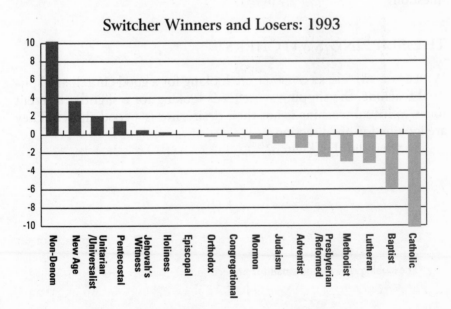

Switcher Winners and Losers: 1993

The greatest blow is to the Catholics, followed by the Baptists. There is not a single historic denominational tradition in the winner's circle. Most of the winning groups are not orthodox Christian at all. Out of six groups having a net gain, there are only two: nondenominational and Pentecostal. It is the nondenominational preference wherein the significant net growth has occurred.

Switcher faith involvement polarizes at each end of the spectrum. Over 36% are decreasing, yet almost 41% indicate their faith involvement is increasing. Switchers are less likely to fall in the middle.

Change in Switcher Faith Involvement		
	Switchers	National Average
The Slipping Switchers (Decreased)	36.8	29.2
The Stable Switchers (Same)	22.4	48.4
The Ascending Switchers (Increased)	40.8	22.4
Source: Percept Group, Inc., Ethos II Survey (1993)		

Switchers are on the move. Where are they going? If we look more carefully at the profiles of those who are increasing (the ascending) and decreasing (the slipping) in faith involvement, we will find clues to this question.[4]

THE SLIPPING SWITCHERS

WHILE THE SWITCHERS OVERALL are looking for a good church and spiritual teaching, the slipping switcher is looking for a slightly different focus. Spiritual teaching is not their desire, nor is a good church. They are looking for life direction.

To what did they switch?

---

[4]The stable profile is too small for projection.

Slipping Switcher New Religious Preference		
	Slipping Switchers	All Switchers
Non-Denominational/Independent	30.5	27.3
Methodist	13.7	12.2
Baptist	11.9	13.7
Lutheran	6.8	6.2
Catholic	6.6	8.1
Presbyterian/Reformed	5.3	6.1
Episcopal	4.7	4.5
Unitarian/Universalist	4.3	2.9
New Age	4.2	4.1
Pentecostal	3.7	5.3
Congregational	3.0	3.3
Total	94.7	93.7

Source: Percept Group, Inc., Ethos II Survey (1993)

The story of William, who switched from Pentecostalism to the Episcopal tradition, provides some insight into the slipping switcher.

Mini-Profile: The Slipping Switcher

William, age 34

What were the reasons or conditions that were the occasion for a switch?

After a lifetime in evangelicalism of one sort or another, my wife and I became exasperated with the overly simplistic "us versus them" mind-set, the deification of the political conservatism, biblical literalism, and the American way, and the capriciousness of "independent" churches. We were captivated and challenged by our experiences in the Episcopal church, which seemed to represent the polar opposite of what we had previously known "church" to be, yet it managed to hold to basic orthodox Christianity. While we are still most at home in the Episcopal church, we are also frus-

> *trated with its tendency to behave more like a club than a church. Unfortunately, we feel there is nowhere else to go, and to leave now will mean abandoning the church altogether. While our faith might survive that transition, we worry about the effect on our children. So we stay . . . for now.*
>
> ### Faith Involvement: Stable to Decreasing
>
> *As measured by traditional church benchmarks (annual giving, attendance, and committee memberships), our involvement has decreased somewhat. My own faith seems more well founded and solid now than it was ten years ago, although again, if you were measuring by classical standards such as personal Bible study and prayer time or being some kind of great spiritual leader for my family, you would probably be disappointed in my current state.*
>
> *It often seems as if the "rules" of belonging to the Christian community were set up by people with a lot more time, disposable income, and energy than I am able to generate and sustain.*

There is a disenchantment in the heart of the slipping switcher. One senses that they want to believe but the barriers are too great.

THE ASCENDING SWITCHERS

THE ASCENDERS ARE THE youngest of the three switcher groups and the most aggressive in their search. The ascending switcher is searching for spiritual teaching *and* life direction *and* a good church.

In their search, where have they gone? Again, most switched to the nondenominational and independent traditions.

Ascending switchers are people on the move. One of the newest church growth strategies in America is the Seeker church movement. Switchers will be attracted to such churches that focus on spiritual development—spiritual teaching and life direction. They are inclined to prefer churches where something is happening.

Ascending Switcher New Religious Preference		
New Religious Preference	Ascending Switchers	All Switchers
Non-Denom/Independent	23.0	27.3
Baptist	15.6	13.7
Methodist	10.5	12.2
Catholic	9.9	8.1
Pentecostal	7.1	5.3
Lutheran	6.8	6.2
Presbyterian/Reformed	6.3	6.1
Episcopal	4.4	4.5
New Age	3.8	4.1
Congregational	3.2	3.3
Total	90.6	90.8

Source: Percept Group, Inc., Ethos II Survey (1993)

Finally, the fact that they have already switched suggests they are likely to keep looking—and switching—until they are satisfied.

Mini-Profile: The Ascending Switcher

Richard, age 48, and Susan, age 45, a married couple

Previous Preference: Presbyterian

New Preference: Methodist

Describe the reasons or conditions that occasioned your switch.

There was a change in the pastor-leader of the church. Even though we stayed almost two years after a new pastor was in place (certainly enough time to give the new person time to prove himself), we were not happy with the quality of the sermons. Since the Sunday message was the most important opportunity to learn and grow in Christ, we were convinced that we needed to go elsewhere to get that message.

Our reason for switching from the Presbyterian denomination to the Methodist denomination did not occur because we had a need to change our religious preference. The reason we left our church we had attended for nine years was because of the pastor. After two years of trying to be objective and give the new pastor time to develop his preaching ability and sermon content to a level we felt should be challenging, interesting, and spirit filled, we grew very discouraged. We became spiritually depressed and no longer had enthusiasm for church or our spiritual walk with God.

Have there been any highlights?

After we searched for a new church for several months, the Methodist church we now attend has provided a friendly, comfortable place to worship. We have again become enthusiastic about attending worship. The sermons are interesting and challenging. The service is spirit filled.

Have there been any disappointments?

We were very disappointed to have to leave lots of friends and neighbors in order to obtain better sermons.

Faith Involvement: Increased

We tended not to be involved in the church and were more or less just attenders. Over the last ten years, we became willing to participate in more church events and joined the choir. Perhaps this was as much related to getting to know people as it was the teaching of the Bible.

Over the past ten years, my faith involvement has varied. For approximately seven of those years, we were involved in various church leadership roles, attended church regularly, and participated in Bible study groups. After becoming discouraged, we began to lose our enthusiasm and spirit for involvement. Since changing churches, once again we have begun to become excited about our faith involvement. We have started attending a Bible study class before worship. We are also looking for areas of service in the church where we might be of help.

THE NEWCOMERS

NEWCOMERS, THE SMALLEST OF the six types, are the *real* new blood within the American church. All other church growth was at the expense of another tradition. Previously the life of faith was outside the newcomers' experience. Something happened in their life to change that. What? This is the key question as we look at this small group.[5]

---

[5]Due to the size of the newcomer sample, no subprofiles may be reliably generated.

Newcomers are twice as likely to be survivors. They are also heavily oriented toward boomers. They are less likely to be either silents or builders.

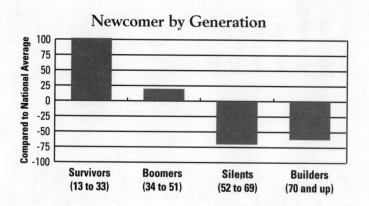

Newcomer by Generation

THE NEWCOMER AND RELIGIOUS FAITH

NEWCOMERS ARE LOOKING FOR life direction and spiritual teaching. Yet a search for a good church is *not* as important. Why isn't finding a good church as important to them? Perhaps because they found one.

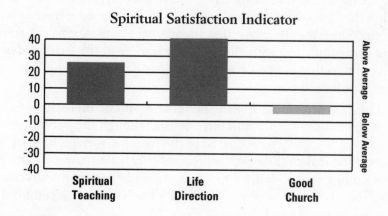

Spiritual Satisfaction Indicator

In the early eighties, newcomers had no preference. Fifty-four percent of the newcomers' hearts and minds were anywhere but on religious matters. The other forty-six percent were at least interested; they just had not landed. Both now are insiders. What are they?

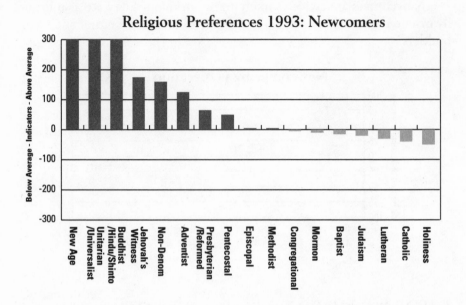

Religious Preferences 1993: Newcomers

In terms of actual percentages, the real winner again is the nonde-nominational preference. One in five newcomers came new to these churches. However, three of the historic mainline Protestant traditions also picked up newcomers beyond their national average. This suggests either that these traditions have been more aggressive in reaching unchurched people or unchurched people are simply returning to the church. While we are aware that many of these traditions are actively doing evangelism, our suspicion is that it is more of the latter. A denom-inational tradition in one's background may determine where one ends up, *at least initially*.

The two preferences with the most dramatic increases were the New Age and the Unitarian-Universalists. Though the actual percent-ages are not high, when compared to the national average, both of these shoot off the scale. While each represents only 0.8% nationally, the New Agers comprise 7.5% of all newcomers, and Unitarian-Universalists 6.4%. Together they represent 14% of all newcomers, second only to the nondenominational preference!

Has the new faith involvement of newcomers resulted in greater participation in a local worshiping community? Not necessarily. Forty-two percent insisted that they did not actively participate in a local con-gregation. How does one account for this? In what does a person participate if the preference is New Age? Faith involvement within the loosely defined New Age movement can mean just about anything except participation in an established religious body.

But consider another question. Suppose the newcomer's point of entry is a very large nondenominational church. Is it possible to simply attend the worship celebrations without becoming an active participant in the life of the congregation?

In summary, there are really two groups within the newcomer profile. One lines up behind the more esoteric New Age movement, and the other around the more conservative nondenominational traditions.

Given their younger age, newcomers may migrate into one of the other types as another decade passes. We already know of one individual who stumbled onto a women's Bible study one evening and started to actively attend and participate. She had no church background and knew little about what it meant to be a Christian. After several months of involvement, she finally decided that she wanted to become a Christian. She subsequently joined a Presbyterian church. A newcomer! Yes, but not for long. Upon observing the way some of the women treated a leader whom she respected, she left in disgust. We will hear from her in the next chapter.

This scenario will be repeated time and again. Persons having had a life-changing encounter with God subsequently encounter the church. This second encounter may be disastrous. Because they have no long-standing loyalty to the church, an encounter with the dark side of the church may estrange them all over again.

Of course, many in the church will be tempted to see in this story the parable of the sower. This young woman was simply seed sown either on "rocky soil" or "among thorns." She simply did not really believe. But let's look at the text.

> *The one who received the seed that fell on rocky places is the man who hears the word and at once receives it with joy. But since he has no root, he lasts only a short time. When trouble or persecution comes because of the word, he quickly falls away. The one who received the seed that fell among the thorns is the man who hears the word, but the worries of this life and the deceitfulness of wealth choke it, making it unfruitful.*
> MATTHEW 13:20–22

First, the seed that fell among the rocky places: Jesus explains that this person falls away because of trouble or persecution and, under the pressure, denies the faith. This was not the issue for this young woman. She had not been distracted, nor has she given up her faith.

Second, the seed among the thorns is the person who falls away because of worries about this world. But again, our young woman did not depart from the church for this reason. There was deceitfulness, but it was the deceitful behavior of supposedly mature Christian women. She was not deceived by the seduction of wealth.

She left the institutional church for two reasons. One, it was not what it proclaimed to be. Two, it was merciless in its dealings. It was not God nor the Gospel that drove her away.

It was us!

CHAPTER 14

Changing Faith II:
The Outsiders

I am looking for a Christian church where the ideology is not a harsh, human interpretation of the Bible.

A Floater

THE LOYALISTS, THE SWITCHERS, and the newcomers share a common commitment to a religious preference. They are on the inside—even if dissatisfied. But there is a growing percentage of people in America for whom faith and religion have no part in their life. They have "no preference." They stand on the outside of our historic religious traditions. Some are floating, some are disillusioned, and some simply indifferent. Though all three have told us they have no religious preference, each comes to this point from a different place and along a different route.

From the point of view of the church in America, these people represent our largest failures and greatest challenge. They have concluded that institutional religion in any form is meaningless to their lives. This is very different from the insider types. Religion is valued and meaningful for insiders, even if they are struggling to find a place of comfort. But the outsiders reject this notion. As we look at each of these three types, we will sense under their responses hurt, pain, anger, and disillusionment . . . or just plain ambivalence.

We might be tempted to conclude that these represent a small group within the culture and there are always those for whom the

Gospel is a message of death, not life. We would not disagree.[1] But the reality we must face is this: it is in the direction of these three outsider types that religious faith in America is moving! Unless we become much clearer about who these people are and what lies behind their animus, we will simply face a larger and larger percentage of the overall population heading in their direction. However, we may not like what we discover when we begin to listen to them.

THE FLOATING

FLOATERS HAVE NO SPECIFIC religious preference but maintain some level of interest. They encompass almost 6% of the American population. While both survivors and boomers are highly represented, in reality floaters are mostly aging baby boomers.

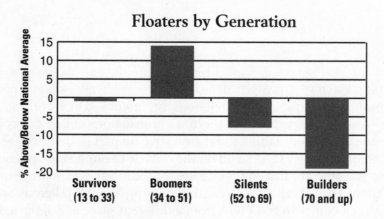

Floaters by Generation

| | Survivors (13 to 33) | Boomers (34 to 51) | Silents (52 to 69) | Builders (70 and up) |

Floaters and Religious Faith

As for spiritual concerns, floaters are quite clear. They are looking for life direction. They are *not* looking for a good church, and they are *not* searching for spiritual teaching.

---

[1]Paul the apostle, in reflecting upon his own ministry, was able to say with some confidence, "But thanks be to God, who in Christ always leads us in triumphal procession, and through us spreads in every place the fragrance that comes from knowing him. For we are the aroma of Christ to God among those who are being saved and among those who are perishing; to the one a fragrance from death to death, to the other a fragrance from life to life. Who is sufficient for these things?" (2 Cor. 2:14–16 NRSV).

Spiritual Satisfaction Indicator: Floater

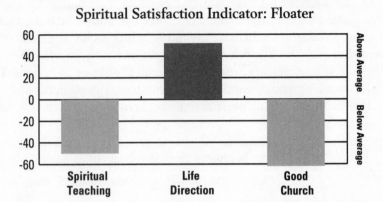

Faith Involvement

Floaters are persons from one of three sources, and these three sources correspond to the direction of their faith involvement. The first source had no preference and was not interested ten years ago. If that was their position today, they would be our sixth type, the indifferent. But they have now moved at least closer, indicating at least some interest. These are the ascending floaters.

The second source is tragic, for they were once insiders. They formerly had a preference but do so no longer, though they maintain some interest. These are the slipping floaters. We suspect that the slipping floaters have simply stopped for a rest on their ultimate journey out of the church and perhaps faith altogether. From where did these floaters come?

Sources of the Floater

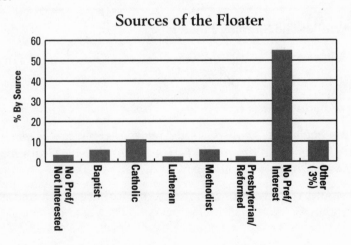

The third source comprises over half of all the floaters. This group forever floats just on the outside. They are the stable floaters, though calling them stable stretches the meaning. It is this characteristic of the floaters that led one church researcher to write them off. They will never become part of the church, because all they ever do is float. They are always seeking and never finding. Though we question his ability to simply write them off, his perspective on them is nonetheless valid.

Change in Floater Faith Involvement			
	The Floaters	National Average	Comparative Index
The Slipping Floaters (Decreased)	33.7	29.2	115
The Stable Floaters (Same)	57.1	48.4	118
The Ascending Floaters (Increased)	9.2	22.4	41
Source: Percept Group, Inc., Ethos II Survey (1993)			

THE SLIPPING FLOATERS

THE SLIPPING FLOATERS ARE significantly younger than their counterparts. Is there any meaning in this? Throughout all of the profiles, we have noted that younger people are the most likely to be in motion. This is a specific example. Only for this group, their movement is outward.

Mini-Profile: The Slipping Floaters

Stephanie, age 36

Former Preference: Methodist

What are you looking for?

I am not looking for an organized religious experience as much as I am looking for a spiritual experience. Most religions leave me frustrated and empty (including New Age).

Why would you say you are interested but have not found a place to land?

> *I have not found a place to land because I haven't looked very hard. I also don't think there is anything out there for me.*

Under what conditions would you find yourself able to commit to a particular preference?

> *I would "commit" if there was a place where I felt comfortable with my spiritual beliefs.*
>
> *P.S. I made a special effort to place my child in a preschool with a Protestant religious preference so that she could receive this information as part of her education. However, this has already resulted in a "mother-daughter" argument in that she insists God is a boy and I try to point out that we don't know that for sure.*

Faith Involvement: Decreased

> *The big change in my faith involvement came about ten years ago. I was happily attending the Methodist church (even sitting on the board). My then current—now former—husband became involved in a super-fundamentalist church. I drifted away from the church, got divorced, disillusioned, et cetera. I have not found anywhere to settle since then.*

THE ASCENDING FLOATERS

BELOW IS A MINI-PROFILE of an ascending floater. This young woman found God. We met her previously as the disgusted newcomer. Having come from no church background at all and having given herself to a church upon her conversion, she was immediately disenchanted and has already left the institutional church. We share her thoughts because we suspect she does in fact represent a population of floaters who want a relationship with God, but she finds the behaviors within the institutional church to be at odds with what she has discovered about this God. As you read her comments, listen for the authentic pain and longing that is there.

Mini-Profile: The Ascending Floaters

Georgianna, age 34

Former Preference: None

What are you looking for?

> *I am looking for a Christian church where the ideology is not a harsh, human interpretation of the Bible. I'm not interested in hearing that people who don't fit squarely and neatly into the "perfect" Christian ideal are damned. I'm not interested in listening to hellfire and brimstone threats. I would want a church that is accepting of people as they are, with all their faults and mistakes, and leaves judgment to God. I want a church that would be more concerned with being active with pastoring people with AIDS, providing food for the hungry, counseling for families, et cetera, than raising money for new buildings. I want a church that doesn't make people feel awkward about wearing casual clothes to worship. I want a church that is focused on providing support and guidance to those seeking grace, not on the ego of the pastor and congregation.*

Why would you say you are interested but have not found a place to land?

> *I am interested in finding such a church because I believe in God and I have so much more to learn. I am scripturally quite ignorant. I haven't attended church for about two years and yet have been feeling a "pull" to start going again. I feel a void that I think could be filled by finding a good church.*
>
> *I also have not been actively looking. My husband is not feeling this particular need at this time, and I have wanted a church that would be "ours," not "mine."*

Under what conditions would you find yourself able to commit to a particular preference?

> *I would be very slow to make a commitment to a church. I have attended only one church during my lifetime, and I made a commitment to that church too quickly.*
>
> *I would be able to commit to a church if (a) I felt it met the characteristics I was looking for, (b) I felt comfortable with other*

congregation members, and (c) if my husband was willing (at least at a minimum level) to belong (or at least did not object to our future children being part of that particular church).

Faith Involvement: Increased

I didn't believe in God ten years ago. I had no faith and no involvement of any kind with any church. Now I do believe in God, and while I'm not active or involved with a particular church, I'm confident that I someday will be.

FLOATING SUMMARY

WE SAID THERE WERE three distinct groups within the floating type. But so what? To answer the question, let's return to the most significant spiritual concern of the floating. They are looking for life direction.

Slipping floaters tell us this: *"We did not find reasonable answers to the story of life in the church."* Consequently, these people are drifting. They are still interested, but they have abandoned any sense of religious preference as an anchor. Like it or not, we have failed these people. We suspect that these floaters are our next type in the making: the disillusioned.

The stable floaters are very likely to be in the same place in ten more years. These folks simply want to graze on the edge of religion. They do not want to take it seriously. There is perhaps a deep level of self-deception at work in their hearts. While they envision themselves as interested—translate open, tolerant, and exploring—for many it is a journey that exists for the purpose of journey.

Where will the ascending floaters go? We do not know. Those we do know continue in the netherworld between authentic faith and aversion to institutional religion. Perhaps it is up to us.

THE DISILLUSIONED

WHAT IS THE NEXT STOP after the slipping floaters? Total rejection of faith and tradition. This is our next type: the disillusioned.

A Story

It didn't seem to matter what the subject was; Carla would take an opposing view. Her constant antagonism, however, was only a thin veil for the obvious pain that lay just under the surface. This was so obvious that even though we were conducting a focus group with eight other people in the room, she was not disruptive. Somehow she communicated an authenticity in her contrariety, and the response of the group was actually supportive of her. Even those of us behind the one-way mirror felt empathy.

This was one group out of ten conducted during a large research project for the Western Territory of the Salvation Army. Leaders within the Army felt they had lost touch with their original vision: the urban poor. They had many social service programs for the truly down and out. But our urban centers are populated with thousands of people living on the economic margin, who may only on occasion need social service support. Still, the Army is also a church, and part of their original mission was to provide a worshiping Christian community as part of an integrated investment in poor communities. We were commissioned to assist them in rediscovering these people so they could reestablish themselves in concert with their original vision but consistent with the modern environment.

The focus groups endeavored to discover what kinds of needs and struggles were common to those who lived in our urban centers. We then invited them to assist us in designing a church that would work for them. Powerful information was shared. And then the moderator asked what they personally did for spiritual nourishment. Some standard answers were given as she went around the table. Then she came to Carla. Something almost sacred occurred at that moment. First of all, her relatively hostile facade dropped as she began to tell us that she went into her room alone to pray. As she said the words, everyone could sense the emotion that was beginning to erupt from deep within. "I don't trust anyone else ... and especially not the church. So I talk to God alone."

Carla had been hurt—deeply—and the church was part of that pain. Her hurt ran so deep that she almost fell apart when the session led too close to its harsh edge. In order to protect herself from further pain, Carla rejected the church. She had not rejected what the church was supposed to do: lead people to God. She had rejected the institutional form of the church. Carla represents almost 3% of all people in the U.S. who were part of the church at some point in their past but who have rejected it. Their profile is always one of pain and deep disappointment.

With a median age of forty, the disillusioned are the second youngest of the six types. They are a very educated group. One in three of the disillusioned is single.

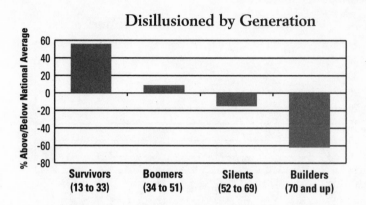

Disillusioned by Generation

THE DISILLUSIONED AND RELIGIOUS FAITH

ONE THING IS VERY clear. The disillusioned do not want spiritual teaching or a good church. No single type reflects greater animosity toward these two concerns than the disillusioned.

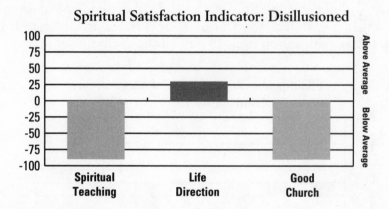

Spiritual Satisfaction Indicator: Disillusioned

Only 1% are looking for a good church, compared to nearly 14% nationally! And less than 1% long for spiritual teaching. They do seek life direction. Like the floating who are slipping away, the disillusioned long to find life's meaning, but for whatever reason have decided the church offers nothing of value on the subject.

This brings us to that most painful question that we have to ask of each type. Who are the losers? (There are no winners. We have lost these people.) In other words, with which of our traditions have they been the most disenchanted?

Sources of the Disillusioned

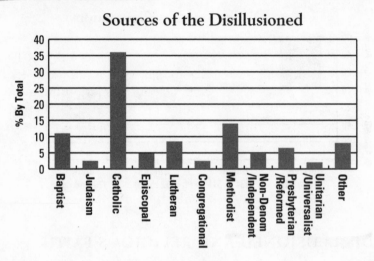

Given the nature of the disillusioned, we may find additional insight if we review actual denominational membership within the larger Christian bodies in the U.S. The biggest loser is the Roman Catholic Church. In 1983, one in three of the disillusioned indicated Roman Catholic membership, but by 1993, that number had dropped to less than one in ten. The United Methodist Church picture is not much better, with a drop from 15% of all the disillusioned to 3%.

Changes in Denominational Membership: Disillusioned 1983 to 1993

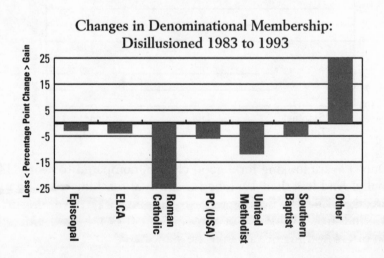

The value of this information—if value can be so described—is in knowing which traditions are being rejected.

DISILLUSIONED SUMMARY

THE CHURCH HAS FAILED the disillusioned. We must remember that these people maintained a religious preference as recently as 1983. Whether they attended or were active in their faith is not the issue. *The issue is simple: We lost them.* Or better, they have rejected the message of the church as they have understood and perceived it. Quite frankly, it does little good to provide ourselves with explanations or justifications. Certainly some of them are valid. But the fact remains, these people have been completely and thoroughly disenchanted with any form of religious faith. *If Carla is an example, and we believe she is, we lost them through hurting them.*

If there is any point of potential future connection with the disillusioned, it will revolve around their desire to find meaning in life. It is possible that a certain number of these people will return to the church as they get older. But we wonder. The disillusioned have an anger at the church that we do not see in any of the other types. They are bitter in their utter rejection.

THE INDIFFERENT

OUR FINAL TYPE REPRESENTS 8% of the population. These are the people the church simply does not reach. They are not in the least bit interested. They are indifferent to the issues the church addresses.

More than any other type, this is a baby boomer group. Age groups on both sides of the boomers are underrepresented. Over a quarter have never been married.

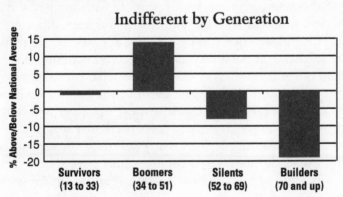

Indifferent by Generation

THE INDIFFERENT AND RELIGIOUS FAITH

NOT SURPRISINGLY, THE INDIFFERENT see little if any value in spiritual teaching or a good church, though their rejection of these is not as strong as the disillusioned. Unlike the disillusioned or the floaters, the indifferent are not overly concerned about finding life direction either. *Spiritual matters, no matter how defined, simply do not interest them.*

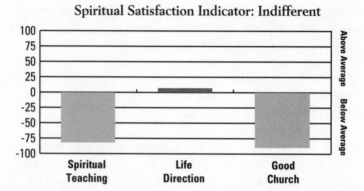

Spiritual Satisfaction Indicator: Indifferent

INDIFFERENT SUMMARY

WHAT CAN WE CONCLUDE about the indifferent? The painfully obvious is that the church does not reach them. They perceive no spiritual need. The indifferent present us with a dilemma. Unless there is some level of felt spiritual need that poses a question to the individual heart, regardless of how the person defines that need, it is difficult to provide an answer of any kind. Supposing we are willing as a church to listen with open hearts; what will we hear?

In each case, we have pointed out how one group within a type may roll into the next with time. Is this possible with some of the indifferent? Perhaps. But how or why? Indifference is very different from disillusionment. Indifference can be emotionally neutral. Rejection is emotionally loaded. Is it possible that under certain circumstances, the indifferent may find themselves confronted with life issues beyond their current situation that challenge them to the core of their being? Would they under such circumstances be more open perhaps to a message that provided a larger context to their particular story?

One wonders, for example, how many jailhouse conversions are of persons who under different circumstances may have fit the indifferent profile. Or what about the busy businessman or businesswoman whose life success is of such magnitude that they are unaware of a gradual but real erosion of the life structures and relationships they have built? Is it possible that under certain circumstances—such as a divorce, a downturn in business, a loss of position—such an indifferent person may be suddenly very aware of larger life issues?

The obvious answers to all of these is yes. We all know of actual examples. Our purpose here, however, is not to convince the reader of what is already known. Our purpose is to tie the indifferent profile to this well-known scenario. Within it we may find an intentional strategy for reaching the indifferent person.

CONCLUSION

THE FLOATING, DISILLUSIONED, AND indifferent represent 17% of the American population. Each profile presents the church with special challenges. If we are correct, this is where faith in America is headed, apart from a significant intervention of the divine. It is not acceptable for the leadership of the church to be unaware of these people. We know of people who are technically still within the church who will very probably join the ranks of this group.

We must consider the factors moving people in this direction. Though we might like to tell ourselves it is the secularizing forces of postmodernism, we suspect that for a large portion of these people, the factors are first internal to the church itself. To what extent is our intransigence on issues that are of little consequence in the large scheme of things driving people away? Such a response, we believe, manifests our failure so far to adapt to the transformations that are reshaping cultural life in America.

This is not to say that the pressures of postmodernity on our culture are of no consequence in the increasing gap between people and the church. But the impact may well be different from what we think. People whose belief systems under premodernity or modernity would not allow them to step outside the bounds of faith may find, even if unaware, that the postmodern world offers them the choice to step outside systems that are too often dysfunctional!

When Paul declares, "For we are the aroma of Christ to God among those who are being saved and among those who are perishing; to the one a fragrance from death to death, to the other a fragrance from life to life" (2 Cor. 2:15–16 NRSV), is he not assuming that it is Jesus that people are either attracted to or rejecting? Dare we assume it is Jesus that is being rejected?

PART THREE:

The Church in a Defining Moment

CHAPTER 15

Joseph Who?

Then Joseph died, and all his brothers, and that whole gener-
ation. But the Israelites were fruitful and prolific; they multi-
plied and grew exceedingly strong, so that the land was filled
with them.
Now a new king arose over Egypt, who did not know Joseph.

Exodus 1:6–8 NRSV

THE AMERICAN INSTITUTIONAL CHURCH finds itself in a position similar to that of the Israelites as a new dynasty arose in Egypt. Not
because we have grown and become a strong force, even a potential
threat. Far from it! We feel under siege and ready to collapse.

So what is the connection? As one pillar of the grand American
story, the church played a significant role in America's past, just as
Joseph had in Egypt's past. White Protestant values helped shape and
form this new world. Even as subsequent waves of immigrants came to
North America, the cultural influence of the predominantly Protestant
tradition continued to prevail.

But the church is no longer a dominant cultural influence. The
tremendous forces reshaping our culture and its grand story have left
the church in a very different position. Why has our place decreased?

"Now a new *king* arose over Egypt, who did not know Joseph."

Out of gratitude for Joseph's role in saving the country from starvation, the Egyptians had allowed the children of Israel to live in peace,
to prosper, to increase, and to practice their faith.

But when a king arose who no longer "knew Joseph," this favored
position collapsed. There was a significant cultural and political shift—
a transformation—that no longer gave favored status to God's people.
Where they had been a protected and supported people, they found
themselves outcasts. Far from being favored, they became objects of
scorn and ridicule.

THE MARGINALIZATION OF THE CHURCH

THE INSTITUTIONAL CHURCH IN America finds itself in a similar place. At the brink of the twenty-first century, the king who knew not Joseph is the collective culture of which we are a part. The combined impact of the Information Age, postmodern thought, globalization, and racial-ethnic pluralism that has seen the demise of the grand American story also has displaced the historic role the church has played in that story. As a result, we are seeing the marginalization of the institutional church. What does this mean?

There are many smaller church denominations in the U.S. that have lived on the cultural margin for their entire history. When we reflect, for example, on many of the Holiness traditions, some Pentecostal groups, and most Free Church traditions, we find the numbers relatively low. Most do not think of them as ever having been in the central cultural flow. They have always lived on the margin of American cultural life—present but not in the cultural mainstream.

The new phenomenon *is the movement of the mainline Protestant denominations to the margins.*[1] Many do not yet realize this has occurred. Living on in dreamland, many among the Protestant denominations still believe their collective voice is influential. True, there is still *some* influence, but less so all the time. The real change is that these denominations are just one among many voices. *There is no favored status.* The larger social trend is suspicious of voices from religious groups—any religious groups.

One really cannot speak of "mainline churches" any longer. If mainline means in the mainstream of the cultural flow, then we must face the facts: In our lives as people of faith, we are no longer there.

Now this shift is neither "good" nor "bad." It just is. We can consume tremendous emotional, spiritual, and financial resources lamenting, but it will not change. The marginalization of the church is a direct by-product of the forces reshaping our world. We could no more go back than the Catholic Church could force Europe to return to the pre-Wittenberg-door era.

Yet there are voices attempting to do just this. They bemoan days past when our culture was based upon strong Judeo-Christian princi-

---

[1]We use the phrase "mainline Protestant denominations" as a general banner under which would fall most large Baptist traditions, the Episcopal Church, the Lutheran denominations, Presbyterians, the United Methodists, and the Congregationalist traditions.

ples. Suppose a leader of the children of Israel asked for a hearing before the new king of Egypt to protest the ill-treatment. Imagine him speaking eloquently of the long relationship they had enjoyed based upon the good works of Joseph—all true. Yet imagine the Israelite leader's chagrin when the king interrupts and says, "Joseph who?"

As we step into the twenty-first century, it does not matter what role the church historically played in American culture. We must come to terms with the fact that the institutional Christian church and especially Protestant mainline churches are no longer in the cultural mainstream. If we have the courage to look, we will see that the church as a social institution is on the outside looking in.

A DEFINING MOMENT COMES

DRAWING ON OUR EARLIER models of change, we contend that the church as an institution—be it conservative or liberal, Protestant or Catholic—is in a transformational moment itself. It is a time of chaos and discontinuity. The turbulence is great, and the formal structures we have known are cracking.

Shifting the metaphor, the institutional church as we have known it is dying. We do not mean that the church will cease to exist. Theologically we are quite certain that God will be faithful to finish what has been started and that the church will be the primary vehicle through which that will occur. But we are equally certain that it will not be through the existing structures and traditions we have known— that is, through our particular American form of the church.

This is an ominous statement. But the changes that are occurring leave us no other option. Institutional cosmetic surgery—a nip here, a tuck there—will not save it. Yet such tactics typify many current responses. The most common strategy is to put a modern face on the same old structures and traditions. Such measures may result in momentary bursts of success, but they will not provide long-term results. If one could step back from it all, he or she would see that these bursts occur within a larger trajectory of demise. Too many of our efforts to attack our disease are pitiable denial, comparable to the alcoholic who, having destroyed his family and career, suggests that perhaps he ought to cut back some on his drinking.

We are even willing to suggest that some of the more popular models of ministry today—such as the "mega-church" concept, the "Seeker" church, and the new "Cell" church—are only tactical attempts to breathe new life into old structures. And they enjoy some success. We are not in opposition to these strategies. They do in fact represent some of the more positive attempts to address the changing cultural environment. We hope that they are effective, even if we believe they are only momentary structural adaptations on the way to the graveyard. Is it possible that they are more a reflection of the generational cycle than attempts at the real, substantial restructuring the church must embrace?

What about the literally thousands of churches across America in which no such progressive strategies are attempted? Let's be frank. In reality, many of them will not see the dawn of the twenty-first century. Many more will pass away by the end of the first decade. We have looked at the demographics. There is no future for most. If, for example, the average age of the members of the average Presbyterian church is sixty-five, how many years can it have left?[2] Now think about that for a moment—the average age of the *average* Presbyterian church. That means that there are hundreds of churches where the average age is higher! And the picture for the United Methodists or Episcopalians or Lutherans is no different.

Let's stop the denial!

Yet everyone wants to talk about starting new churches. It is without a doubt a whole lot easier than dealing with an old and dying congregation, just as having babies is more fun than dealing with an aging and feeble parent. But it is not the primary need. When honest, church leaders will tell us that the real issues for them are the hundreds of little congregations that are already living on borrowed time.

No one wants to close a church. There is something fundamentally wrong about it. We feel as if we have failed. Making matters worse, those remaining in churches that need to close are inevitably dear old saints. The prospect of "taking their church away from them" doesn't make any of us feel particularly heroic! So we look for new churches to start and tell ourselves a little tale that goes like this: "When people get older, they come back to church. We just need to wait for the young people to come and care for all of these little churches."

But the changes transforming our world reflect more than the young who have temporarily wandered away to "sow their oats." They are not coming back, certainly not in numbers large enough to bail out thousands of empty shells. The data simply do not support it, and the

---

[2]We believe that the actual national average age is higher, but our point is made with a more conservative figure.

transformational changes that are occurring support that data. *The place and role of the church in America has changed, and we will not go back!* We just haven't accepted our death yet.

But we are coming to a moment when we will need to address it, when we can no longer simply try to outrun the obvious. That moment is being forged by the confluence of the transformational changes and the generational cycle. We are entering a defining moment in our history, a moment in which we must make a decision.

Before we begin to discuss the meaning of the moment, it would be helpful to provide a framework within which to think about what it means. The change we are facing is so basic that it is at the paradigmatic level.

SHIFTING PARADIGMS

I AM LOATH TO even bring up the subject of paradigms. It is the favored interpretive overlay given to every change encountered in the past few years. Every difference in the way we think or do something has been reduced to the phrase "paradigm shift." We have trivialized the concept, as Thomas Kuhn, who first outlined the concept, complained in frustration some years ago.[3]

For Kuhn, a paradigm shift was more than a new way of thinking about something. A paradigm shift is nothing short of a revolution. In a revolution, everything is turned upside down. All of our assumptions come into question, and many are abandoned. In Part One, we outlined two kinds of change: continuous (incremental) and discontinuous (chaotic). When a paradigm shift occurs, the change is completely discontinuous and generates chaos everywhere.

Joel Barker says, "When a paradigm shifts, everything goes back to zero."[4] When a paradigm shifts, the rules change, the game changes, and what we believe changes. If we have operated under a paradigm that is passing and do not understand the change, we will find ourselves lost and confused about the future and our role in it.

Barker provides us with a good working definition of paradigm and how one functions in our life.

---

[3] Thomas Kuhn, *The Structure of Scientific Revolutions*, 2d ed. (Chicago: University of Chicago Press, 1970). This is a summary of his comments in the postscript.

[4] Joel Arthur Barker, *Future Edge*, (New York: Morrow, 1992), 140. Also published as *Paradigms: The Business of Discovering the Future* (New York: HarperBusiness, 1993).

A paradigm is a set of rules and regulations (written or unwritten) that does two things: (1) it establishes or defines boundaries; and (2) it tells you how to behave inside the boundaries in order to be successful.[5]

Conventional understanding (that is, "the rules") placed the church in the mainstream of American culture—one of the three pillars in the grand American story that developed morally responsible citizens. The "rules" insisted that people of faith and prayer were more likely to be good, ethical people. Such people contributed to the development of the "good society." Though we were supposedly careful not to intermix church and state, the two nonetheless coexisted in most of our social institutions. The boundaries were defined, and the church knew how to behave within them. Under this paradigm, for example, prayer found a meaningful place within the public school setting, because it was assumed that people who pray are more likely to be good, responsible people. This was the role of the church for an industrial age.

But we have already observed how all of this is changing. As we enter the twenty-first century, the church is confused about the boundaries and how it is to behave. It has lost the favored status position. The old set of rules (the old paradigm) has failed. As our postmodern world continues to unfold, the culture looks to the church, especially the so-called mainline denominations, less and less for clues in the realms of moral and spiritual direction.

A new paradigm outlining a new role for the church in our society is emerging, whether we like it or not. Rapid change, personal reality creation, globalization, changing understandings of faith, restructuring, and all of the other reshaping forces have broken the paradigm under which the church in America has existed for so long. We did not ask for this change. We did not ask for a new paradigm. Generally, those whose life and work is governed securely by an existing paradigm do not want it to change. That is why Kuhn insists that paradigm changes come about through revolution instead of incremental evolution.

To better understand this, we can step back and see how the church has moved through two previous paradigms.

Paradigms Lost

Loren Meade, founder of the Alban Institute, has written a small but insightful book titled *The Once and Future Church*. He chronicles

---

[5]Ibid., 32.

the developmental history of the church in mission through two major paradigms. He asserts that we are in the transition period leading to a new paradigm that has not yet fully jelled.

1. The Apostolic Paradigm

First came the Apostolic paradigm, forged in the difficult and challenging period after the first generations after Jesus. Jesus had sent his followers out "to serve and convert the world, to care for the sick, the prisoner and the widow, the fatherless and the poor."[6] In the process, all kinds of structures and ways to organize emerged. Many of the titles used in different traditions today had their functional genesis in this period, such as apostle, teacher, healer, bishop, presbyter, deacon, pastor. Meade points out that the search of the early Christian community for an "identity in mission" caused turbulence.[7] The church as the ekklesia were the "called out" ones who were to share the Good News of Jesus with the communities in which they lived, while demonstrating its values in their daily lives.

Under this paradigm, the community of faith was a series of local congregations of Christians living in a hostile environment. Mission for the early church was next door and across the street. As Meade puts it, the frontier of mission was a church's own community. Congregations provided mutual encouragement and support, sometimes financial, as each engaged in mission where they lived.[8]

2. The Christendom Paradigm

With the Christianization of the Roman Empire under Constantine in A.D. 313, the Apostolic paradigm begins to fade, and a new paradigm begins to emerge. Meade calls this second the Christendom paradigm. Unlike the hostile relationship between the local community and the congregation in the Apostolic paradigm, in the new paradigm your neighbor is a Christian by law. Empire and church have become one. There is no longer any demarcation between a community of believers and the social environment in which they live. Indeed, the notion of local communities of faith increasingly carries no meaning.

---

[6] Loren Meade, *The Once and Future Church: Reinventing the Congregation for a New Mission Frontier* (Washington, D.C.: Alban Institute, 1991), 10.

[7] Ibid.

[8] Paul the apostle collected contributions for the church in Jerusalem from the churches he had planted elsewhere (Rom. 15:26–27).

The Christendom Paradigm

The Dimensions	Empire Period	Recent Period as Relates to the Church in the U.S.
1) The unity of the sacred and secular	No distinction between secular and sacred. Bishops had secular responsibilities. Kings had religious responsibilities..	Though separation of church and state, reality that religious establishment has always been highly influential from the beginning in American culture. Resulted in a cultural religion of God and Country. Has both a liberal and conservative face, but both seek to maintain the key place of religion in the culture.
2) Mission is a far-off enterprise	Mission field outside the Empire. Mission was foreign policy and carried out by princes and armies with the help of missionaries. Regular person not involved in mission.	Mission to far-away pagan lands has been a significant force in American religion in 19th and 20th centuries through emergence of missionary societies. Local and regional groups organized to support mission "over there." Understood that part of mission was to propagate our understanding of democracy wherever mission occurred.
3) Congregation as parish	No longer a close community under local threat. Congregation became geographic region called a parish. Everyone in it was a member of the church. No other institution in a community was outside the church. All fell within the bounds of a parish.	Especially mainline churches have turf. Pastor's role model that of Chaplain to care for the people who belong to their congregations. New members assumed to be converts already. Consequently, little emphasis on evangelism . This has been less the case in the free churches where there is a commitment to convert the unbelievers in the increasingly apostate mainline churches.

The Dimensions	Empire Period	Recent Period as Relates to the Church in the U.S.
4) The drive for unity	Vast Empire/church required tighter administration. To insure unity, standardized structures developed. No place for differences.	Each national religious body created and sustained a culture of oneness in the church and its mission within their own denominational structures. (E.g., A Presbyterian presence means more than a Christian presence.) Some attempts at ecumenical bonding, though generally have failed.
5) The religious role/place of the laity	Ordinary persons did not join the church, were born into it. Entire community effort was to nurture all in the parish in the faith. Educational and legal systems supported the faith and appropriate conduct.	Still strong expectation by clergy to be loyal citizens and supportive of church and state Not become too concerned in theological matters. Loyal to denominations. Little to do with mission other than to financially support, pray, encourage young to go into full-time Christian service and perhaps make short mission trips "over there." Some attempts at ecumenical bonding, though generally have failed.
6) The calling of the lay person	To be good citizens. Pay taxes. Support efforts to expand the Empire into pagan regions (to convert to Christianity). To be obedient and to pray.	To be good, law-abiding, tax-paying, patriotic citizens. Conform to social institutions and obey community leaders. Avoid immorality and disloyalty. Know one's place in life.

189

Meade suggests that two immediate changes occur. First, the individual person is no longer involved in the "frontier of mission." When your neighbor is a Christian by law, what is there to do that is missional? Second, the mission frontier is moved to the outer boundary of the empire.

The missionary frontier on the edge of the empire now becomes the responsibility of the professional—the soldier's job for the political realm, and the specially designated missionary's job for the religious realm. In addition, however, the missionary understands that winning souls to the Lord is the same task as winning nations to the empire.[9]

What is the role of the local Christian? Be a good citizen, which equals being a good Christian, and faithfully support the efforts of the empire and the church in converting, by politically conquering, the pagans.

Within the Christendom paradigm, six key dimensions emerged. These went through some evolution as time passed, but there is still a remarkable similarity between them and the current U.S. situation. The primary changes were (a) the breakup of the empire into nation-states, and (b) the breakup of the church into denominations.

It is actually these latter manifestations that are of interest in this discussion. Consequently, what we offer on pages 188–89 is a comparison table built around these six dimensions.

If we are honest, we all see in this paradigm features and themes we are familiar with and perhaps still support. To therefore suggest, as Meade does, that this paradigm is passing creates great discomfort. Indeed, it is that very feeling of discomfort that is at the heart of much of the current struggle within many congregations and denominational structures. At every level of the institutional church in America, the continued demise of the Christendom paradigm creates unbearable pressure. *It is the discomfort of death.*

For those of us who were not raised in the church but were born during or after the fifties, there has been and will continue to be a certain amount of confusion created in interactions with those who want to hold on to the old paradigm. I do not say this pejoratively. But for most of my adult life, as a Christian and involved since college in Christian ministry, I have found myself perplexed by attitudes held by those who have been in the church all of their life. It was not until I began to

---

[9]Meade, *The Once and Future Church*, 14.

understand that we were in a time of change that the continued dissonance became understandable.

Perhaps an example will serve to illustrate this. I came of age in the midst of the last spiritual awakening in the generational cycle. It was a time marked by social protest and the feeling that questioning authority was not only our right but our ethical obligation when its objectives appeared morally wrong. And so many of them did, from our point of view.

I began my serious Christian pilgrimage in January 1970 as part of the youth revivals of that period. When I entered into the life of the church, this same social protest framework that was part of the youth culture of the time came with me and stayed for many years. In the early eighties I received a call to serve in my first pastoral position as an associate pastor in very conservative Orange County, California. I remember being stunned one Sunday morning. It was the Fourth of July, and morning worship revolved around a God-and-country presentation. It had never occurred to me that these people I worshiped with each Sunday viewed the civil authorities quite differently than I did, until this marriage of the sacred and secular was brought into worship that morning. I felt as if I had more in common with the people of the New Testament in their attitude toward government than I did with my fellow believers in 1980! (Of course, in characteristic young boomer style, I assumed they were less spiritual and had succumbed to cultural religion. And of course, I told them so. But that is another story!)

3. Paradigm in Flux

Upon reading Thomas Kuhn's *The Structure of Scientific Revolutions,* I finally began to make sense out of the confusion I so often felt. The discovery was actually quite simple. Those who were raised in the church and were a part of the institution looked at the world through a different set of filters—what Kuhn would call a paradigm—than I did. The mental framework by which I interpreted the world was different from that of those who had grown up in the church or who had been serving in the church for many years. We were experiencing the tension that occurs when a paradigm collapses.

What causes a paradigm to break down? Let's look at Barker's definition again.

> A paradigm is a set of rules and regulations (written or unwritten)
> that does two things: (1) it establishes or defines boundaries; and (2)

it tells you how to behave inside the boundaries in order to be successful.[10]

Within the Christendom paradigm, the role of Christians and their relationship to the civil authorities is well defined. The boundaries were set, and the rules of behavior were well established. Kuhn points out that when a paradigm prevails unquestioned, it is able to answer a set of questions consistently. The Christendom paradigm functioned to a lesser or greater degree through much of the first half of the twentieth century, though the rumblings of the impending shift have been occurring for a long time.[11] But with the advent of the sixties and its spiritual awakening, the challenges to the paradigm came out into the streets.

Paradigms, according to Kuhn, start to falter when they begin to encounter anomalies. An anomaly occurs when we apply the paradigm's rules and procedures and find that we fail to accomplish the expected result. The Christendom paradigm was not working for many of us, though we did not know what the problem was. We spoke of the "establishment church" that had sold its soul to the culture. We compared what we saw in the church with the authentic community experience we saw in the New Testament. In the New Testament, we saw Christians persecuted by the culture. In the establishment church, we saw it as one with the culture. The modern church seemed obsessed with material wealth and large facilities. We called for the casting off of the "old wineskins." Our elders heard these declarations as rebellion and a failure to appreciate the efforts of those who came before us. It was a strange and wonderful time.

Today I realize these were the marks of the paradigm under stress and cracking because of the weight of the transformational changes that were at work in the world. The transformational seismic waves have simply been assisted during the last twenty-five years of the twentieth century by the spiritual awakening in the current generational cycle. As we stand on the edge of the next century, the entire boomer generation of idealists is fully entering midlife, and the oldest are on the verge of elderhood. What is most likely is that as a generation, we will continue to push the edges, thus further crumbling the Christendom paradigm. If we do well, the result could be good. If we do not do well . . .

---

[10]Barker, *Future Edge*, 32.

[11]One could argue that various movements, such as the Reformation, the Enlightenment, and so forth, have all chipped away at this paradigm.

But it is not just the rambunctious boomers calling for revolution anymore. Today, men and women of all ages are struggling with the changes. Instead of the language of revolution, we now easily discuss the difficulties of the church in the language of mortality—"life" and "death."

We are rapidly moving into our defining moment, in which we must make a decision. How do we want to die?

CHAPTER 16

The Decision

*Sow for yourselves righteousness; reap steadfast love; break up
your fallow ground; for it is time to seek the LORD, that he may
come and rain righteousness upon you.*

Hosea 10:12 NRSV

MORE AND MORE WE have lost our home in the familiar paradigm
of Christendom, but we have no clarity about how to find a
new home in the turbulence of the emerging world."[1] Some of us are
longing for a new paradigm to emerge to take the place of the one we
are losing and provide again a clear identity in mission. Others are pin-
ing away for the "good old days," when the church was one of the three
pillars of the community. And the net effect of these two? Conflict,
confusion, and very little effective ministry.

We would propose one other model for what is happening. During
the Reformation, the church went through a fundamental restructuring
of its life and mission. We have already seen how the transformation of
that period was epistemological, with the foundation of truth shifting
from biblical tradition to autonomous human reason. Such intellectual
changes were bound to play a key role in the life of the church and its
thought, just as in that period the church was bound to play a role in
what transpired in the culture.

We find ourselves in a similar moment. The emergence of postmodernism is pushing us through another epistemological revolution.
But at the same time, the church finds the equilibrium it had established with the culture (as one of the three pillars) being disrupted.
Again, we find ourselves not knowing how to be the church, because
we don't quite know how we are supposed to live in the world.

---

[1]Meade, *The Once and Future Church*, 23.

As of now the new paradigm has not emerged with clarity. It may not occur in our lifetime. But we do know that what has been will be no longer. And we believe that *there is a choice* within the flow of the inevitable. That is, we assume there is the possibility of response to the changes. There is a decision to make.

THE WIDENING GAP

PERHAPS AN ILLUSTRATION WILL present this more clearly. We often speak of a widening gap between what is needed or expected by a particular social environment and how we respond.

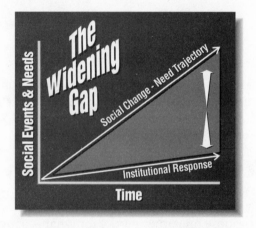

The top line on the graph represents the angle of growing social change and the accompanying needs. The second reflects the rate at which an institution can respond. There *is* a response, but the angle of response will never allow the institution to catch up. Indeed, with time the gap only widens. If we simply continue working on the same assumptions—the same paradigm—as we always have, over time the gap will be so wide as to be virtually unclosable. Church leaders work harder and harder, yet with diminishing returns. They tell us that for all of their efforts, they realize they are losing ground. But on this model, no matter how hard one works, the gap is only going to widen.

The following chart summarizes the changes we have discussed. All of these changes contribute to the widening gap. The only hope is that the angle of the institutional response can be adjusted so that the gap can begin to close.

PASSING REALITIES		EMERGING REALITIES
The Generational Cycle		
Inner-driven (Generational Cycle)		Emerging crisis (Generational Cycle)
Transformations Within American Culture		
Braun based economy		Brain based economy
Unassailable truth		Unsurpassable truth
Means of production = power		Access to information = power
Nuclear family	The Growing	Plurality of options
Anglo-European majority	Gap	No majority
Hierarchical systems of control		Networks of relationships (Virtual Organizations)
Nationalism		Globalism
Church in the mainstream of cultural life		Church on the margins
Transformations Within the Church		
Denominational loyalty		Tradition shopping and declining faith
Supply-driven model of ministry	The Growing Gap	Demand for services - Need driven model of ministry
Lower serves the higher		Higher serves the lower
Clergy dominated		Clergy-Laity in partnership
Faith as dominate		Faith as minority

So what needs to happen? We need to make decisions, strategic decisions, that will allow us to actually change the trajectory of response. To put it simply, we need an adequate response to the reality of these changes.

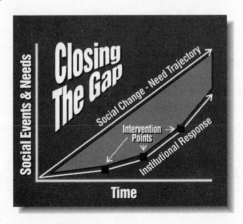

Yet therein lies the rub and the challenge of the defining moment. We often hear an argument upon introducing the concept of the widening gap. It goes like this:

> We are the church. Consequently, we should not even try to move along the same trajectory as the culture. To do so would compromise the Gospel and what the church stands for. If the culture is moving further and further from God, then we most certainly should let it go. We must not try to accommodate ourselves to the social trajectory of the world culture.

If the issue was accommodation to the values and beliefs of the culture at the expense of our biblical and theological beliefs, we would certainly agree. But is it really these essential issues that are at stake? It is our contention that we too often use the theological and biblical compromise as a red herring for confronting the real issue.

What is the real issue? *We don't want to confront the degree to which we have enculturated the Gospel and our traditions.* The cultural ethos of the grand American story has been woven around the essential concerns of the Gospel, and the two have become one. We simply refuse to do the work of separating them back into their constituent parts. As a consequence, the distance between the culture that is emerging and us grows, while our ability to connect with that culture diminishes. The real issue is this: *It is not the core of our message nor our identity that is at stake in the widening gap. It is our cultural comfort zone!*

THE DEFINING MOMENT

IT IS THE GROWING gap that is pushing us into the defining moment. As we enter that moment, we have a choice to make. As we said in the beginning, there are only two options: *We can die as a result of our hidebound resistance to change, or we can die in order to live.* Rooted in the core of the Gospel is this very message.

> *Very truly, I tell you, unless a grain of wheat falls into the earth and dies, it remains just a single grain; but if it dies, it bears much fruit. Those who love their life lose it, and those who hate their life in this world will keep it for eternal life.* JOHN 12:24–25 NRSV

It is a matter of faith. If we are able to embrace the significance of the current defining moment, we will see in it the call of God on the church. But it is a call not unlike the call we each are given when we first encounter the Holy Spirit. We are called to follow Jesus into death. Indeed, without a death there can never be a resurrection—the centerpiece of our hope. This principle is all-pervasive in the Scriptures, perhaps because humans have a penchant for avoiding it. Therefore we must emphasize the point again. There is no other choice but death. If we do not choose to die, we will die anyway.

In the opening chapter, six commitments were outlined. The first two involve gaining an understanding of the dynamics of change in our culture and the faces of change. As we move into the time of decision to die, we turn our attention toward the next two commitments. These two focus on the areas where the death must occur.

- We must accept that the traditional place of the institutional church in American society is dying, and with it the institutional church itself.
- We must be willing to let our traditional forms and structures that are the foundation of the institutional church die.

However, we must understand that the challenge before us provides us with both a call to die and the hope of new life. We must not forget the Frenchlick error.[2] The Gospel is always a promise of life, but it is always life out of death. From the perspective of the Gospel, death is always painful but it is never final. It is this very truth that will allow us to consider the many ways we are dying and must die.

---

[2]See chapter 1, p. 17.

CHAPTER 17

What Must Die?

Fool! What you sow does not come to life unless it dies.

Paul the apostle, 1 Corinthians 15:36 NRSV

W HAT MUST DIE?
When we speak of dying, it is as metaphor for the "letting go" or abandoning aspects of our experience and expectations of what the church is and should be. The dying does not just represent particular "things" that we must abandon. Real death is experienced in the heart. If we are to let go of so much we hold dear, it will cost us in our souls. It will be excruciatingly painful. Death always is painful. That's why we work so hard to avoid it. But then, isn't that what is so compelling about the Gospel? God promises to bring life out of our death!

Some of us may not be able to make the choice. But if we are willing to die in order to live, it will take specific, intentional action in some particular areas of our life. Not all of these areas are equally applicable to all traditions, denominations, or churches. In reality, different traditions within Christ's church have already addressed some of these issues. Some due to forethought, some due to the challenges of the inevitable and the need for survival. In working through the list, perhaps the rule of thumb should be "If the shoe fits, wear it!"

One last point before we jump into the list. We don't assume that the list we have constructed is exhaustive in any sense. Nor do we assume that we have even begun to fully define each issue. We may have accomplished no more than simply creating awareness of deep and complex issues. But if that is all we accomplish, our goal will have been met.

SO WHAT MUST DIE?

1. *The Expectation of a Favored Position in the Mainstream of Culture*

Accept the inevitable that, unlike in the past, in the twenty-first century the church will no longer enjoy the place of significance in the eyes of the culture. The church in Europe, and to some degree Canada, has had to relate in this manner for years. Now it will become the norm in America as well. In response, we must reimage the church in the role of the prophet to the culture, not unlike the role the church played relative to the culture in the pre-Constantinian period.

This will, of course, be more difficult for some traditions than for others. Some already are struggling to play this role. We have watched as bishops in the Catholic Church have stepped into the role of prophet, challenging the assumptions of the culture, yet doing so with the understanding that they do not stand in the mainstream of the cultural flow. And regardless of how one feels about the particular positions they take on some matters, they do model for us what must become normative for all. In contrast to the religious right's political efforts, which have become so militaristic and driven by fear, the bishops have demonstrated courageous compassion for the culture. And in contrast to some of the more liberal Protestant denominations, they have demonstrated a willingness to insist that not all stories are equal, though all should be respected.

In the twenty-first century, the influence of the church will be from the outside looking in. But it is not less important! One could argue that our role has never been more significant and crucial!

2. *The Model of Theological Education That Primarily Emphasizes Theological Method*

In the future, ministerial training must teach sociological method as well as theological method. Both are essential skills for the church leader of the twenty-first century. Given the rapidity of change and the growing cultural and racial-ethnic diversity that are increasingly normative for life in America—if not the world—it is incumbent on our institutions of theological training to restructure their curriculum along the twin trajectories of theology and sociology. It is not enough to be good biblical exegetes and well versed in the history and traditions of the church. To serve congregations today and provide the leadership necessary for tomorrow, pastors of the future will need to also become skilled in what the late Ian Pitt-Watson called "the exegesis of life."[1] *The unspoken assumption has been that pastors know the people and their needs. This is true no longer.* The diversity is simply too great.

There are places where this is occurring, but generally not at the core curriculum of a theological education. Fuller Seminary has cross-cultural and church growth studies, but neither are part of the School of Theology, home of the traditional master of divinity program. St. Paul Theological Seminary in Kansas City comes the closest with Dr. Tex Sample, who is both a theologian and sociologist teaching within the core curricular areas. Dr. Arlin Rothauge, former director of congregational development for the Episcopal Church, is working with Seabury West to develop a specific program around congregational development issues.

The restructuring efforts must be more intentional than mere integration-of-faith-and-life courses. The very methods of sociological and demographic research must be considered tools as essential in ministry as theological method.

No sooner do we say this than we immediately confront one of the issues of the Information Age: too much information. To accomplish this transition, seminaries must make the same shift American education is making. Educators are abandoning the "fill the empty vessel" model of education. The challenge of education in the Age of Information is not filling the vessel. It is simply not possible. There is too much information. Rather, educators within the seminary will have to adopt a model that trains future pastors in mastering the use of information technologies and the vast wealth of information that is available to solve the many unique problems they will face.

3. The Denominational Expectation That the Local Serves the Regional, Which Serves the National, Which Serves the International

To put it another way, the model must be stood on its head. It is a perfect example of the Christendom paradigm. Under the Christendom paradigm, the local resources of a Christian society are captured to further the expansion of the kingdom of God. There is no Christian society any longer. In the emerging postmodern era of religious pluralism, mission is next door and across the street. The only future for denominational structures is in adjusting their priorities to serve the

---

[1] Ian Pitt-Watson, *Preaching: A Find of Folly* (Philadelphia: Westminster Press, 1976), 68 ff.

local congregation. This does not mean that we cease to support mission in other places. Rather, the flow must move in both directions. But priority must be given to the local congregation. Without vital congregations, there is no support base for any kind of world mission.

We have noticed the pressures on higher governing bodies around the country as a result of budget cuts. A question that is often asked is, Why is the structure needed? Or in more blatantly self-serving though understandable terms, the local congregation that is expected to support regional and national budgets wants to know, What will this governing body do for us?

We have, on the other hand, also noticed that in those bodies where the shift of priorities is toward the congregation, such questions are not so prevalent. One example is the Synod of Lincoln Trails within the Presbyterian Church (U.S.A.). The program staff of the synod determined that they must exist to meet the needs of their "client." They then proceeded to define the "client" as the local churches and presbyteries that fall within the synod's jurisdiction.[2]

4. The Obsession with Bombproof Certainty of Truth

The side of the church that has tied its future to absolutism will continue to paint itself, and those who follow it, into a corner. We need to be released from this form of foundationalism. In a world in which the field of knowledge doubles every eighteen months, the potential for a new info-bomb to reorder our basic assumptions—our paradigm of reality—is great and to be expected. A rigid commitment to an unassailable worldview, such as is typically the case in more conservative circles, increasingly runs the risk of shattering all faith—needlessly. We believe that the future lies in abandoning modernist foundationalism and adopting an epistemological position based on the principle of unsurpassability—and in learning to live with relative confidence and a certain level of faithful agnosticism.

As we explained in Chapter 7, "A Reality for Every Occasion," such a view is not the same as wishy-washy relativism—what we have called radical relativism. Rather, it is the best form of certainty we can expect in a universe that we increasingly recognize is infinitely more complex than would have been thought in earlier times. If we expect people of intellectual integrity to find a place in the community of faith, we must

---

[2]We refer the reader to the Rev. Jay Hudson, associate executive of the Synod of Lincoln Trails.

pursue this course. Without this position, the schism between science and faith will grow ever wider, and many people of faith will fall into the widening gap.

5. The Radical Relativism That Has Allowed the Essence of the Gospel to Be Reduced to a Mere Religion Indistinguishable from All Other Religious Ideas

This means reestablishing the role and authority of the Bible over matters of faith. Some of the more radical forms of feminist thought have highlighted for us the dangers of completely leveling the playing field of ideas—making all equally valid and valuable. This is simply not true, and out of faithfulness to the Gospel and people who need to hear the Word of God through the confusion, we must be willing to say, "It is this, not that."

Though we realize it is probably impolitic to say so, we suspect the reimaging conference of the mid-1990s is an example of where we have lost our way in this regard. While we share the concern with our sisters who are struggling to develop language that does not create barriers to their faith experience, we do believe that to simply adopt images and ideas of what would have been considered pagan practices before radical relativism leveled all traditions and made them equal threatens to lose the distinctiveness of the Gospel in a world of stories.

In response to this, we believe that the future here—as in the case of the rigid absolutist—lies in a commitment to a rigorous theological method based upon the principle of unsurpassability. While experience is important, our faith must still be supported by the teachings of the Scriptures and the teachings of the church as it has struggled to interpret them in their particular historical contexts. If we do not maintain a tight connection with our theological traditions and scriptural authority, we will have no basis for appropriately judging one story over another. We must exercise the courage to boldly assert that not all stories will fill the spiritual vacuum felt so deeply in the human soul. Recognizing that there are many things we can learn from other traditions is not the same as insisting that all stories are equally valid. No one has ever been as open and compassionate and engaging of persons of divergent worlds as Jesus. Yet though he met people where they were, he still led them to the well where living water was to be found.

6. *Authority Based upon Position Alone*

In a postmodern world, authority is granted to those whose exemplary life, message, and work carry a high level of moral authority. Borrowing a concept from organizational management, authority in the future will be granted to people, not to positions. It will not be enough, and indeed will most likely be counterproductive, to claim authority based upon position—even if the position is biblically supportable. We may take umbrage with this, insisting that if the Bible establishes a position, that's the end of the discussion. But in a postmodern world where people "choose" what to believe, such a position may find itself making bold declarations to empty seats.

This concept will be especially difficult for many of our clerical colleagues. As a group, we tend to wrap the expectation of authority in the mantle of "call." However, such concepts increasingly bear little weight for people—even in the church. Our advice to our fellow clergy is simple: get used to it. If we have any authority in the twenty-first century, it will be authority granted to us. Biblical support for spiritual authority is certainly important. But in all matters, including biblical authority, we are going to have to get used to a world that will expect to choose. Unilateral demands, no matter how well supported biblically, will be ineffective.

This leads to one other issue that we clerics are not going to like: performance. Leadership of the church will increasingly be subject to the same evaluations as any other enterprise. This is already quite well entrenched in many of the independent and Baptist traditions. But the pressures are growing for those in the other mainline Protestant traditions as well. Pastors of local congregations will be scrutinized for their performance. Those who fail to line up with expectations—some formal and many informal—will find themselves out of "work." The same is true for executive program staff in regional and national offices. The pressure to deliver the goods will increase.

7. *The Attitude That Says the Church Is for Us*

This is the Christendom paradigm. If we insist that the church be for us, then it will *only* be for us. Local congregations must see themselves as being there for the community. From the standpoint of local congregations, community development is a subset of congregational development, especially in our urban centers.

This point may seem easy and obvious, but it is the first one to directly touch people in the local congregation. And our experience over the years would suggest this may be the toughest challenge of all. Those currently in the positions of power, both formal and informal, have been raised on the chaplaincy model. Just listen sometime to a group that is looking for a pastor, especially in mainline churches. The top issue is inevitably a pastor who will "take care of us."

Our firm was asked to do a study of the community served by the Presbyterian church I attend. Part of the goal was to build a new sanctuary. There had been two prior attempts that included conceptual designs for the building, but both had been postponed. On the third attempt, the church decided to get input from the community on a range of issues, including preferred architecture. After holding a couple of focus groups and analyzing the demographic and ethos information on the community, we made some recommendations.

As a result of our work on the study, I was asked to serve on the newly formed building committee. When we began to discuss concepts, I heard ideas that troubled me. We had committed to be a church for the community, not for ourselves. Yet as we discussed design, I kept hearing what "we" wanted—and I knew from having conducted the research that part of what we wanted was the very thing the community disliked. When I pointed that out, some felt frustration, insisting that "we only get to do this once, and we should get to build the church we want." *But if we build a church for us, it will only serve us. If we build the church for others, we will not be disappointed.* To their credit, they decided to build a church for others.

8. The Entrenched Gatekeepers

Every church has gatekeepers; indeed, every church must have them. Functionally, gatekeepers protect the vision and mission of a local congregation. However, there are two kinds. The first are the formal gatekeepers, who function in most churches as an administrative board guiding the direction and setting policy. The second kind of gatekeeper is more insidious and ultimately more powerful. They are the informal gatekeepers who decide what will really happen. In too many congregations across America, these people are allowed to hold the church captive to their own particular will and values. Some are aggressive and mean-spirited, and some are passively aggressive. Either way, the impact is the same. Those who emerge with new ideas, with new enthusiasm, or with new programs find they are blocked. Even when the official board supports an effort, if the informal power structure opposes it, it will fail. These people must be confronted and graciously moved out of their dysfunctional position of control. This, of course, will take courage. These are powerful people, and they have their ways. But their ways are killing congregations everywhere!

Likewise, we have had enough of the denominational gatekeepers who strategically place themselves in positions of power to further their own agendas regardless of what would be best for their denomination. Too many agencies are staffed with well-meaning managers or mean-spirited ideologues. The former struggle to provide any sense of direction; the latter impose upon their churches social and political agendas close to their hearts but often far from the central message of the Gospel. Denominational leaders must demonstrate the courage and clarity of vision to neutralize these negative efforts.

9. The Perception That the Culture Is the Enemy

While sinful accommodation to the culture is always a danger for the Christian, it is equally sinful to view the culture as the enemy. In reality, *such a viewpoint inevitably sees real people as the enemy.* We will be hard-pressed to love those whom God loves if we are castigating them for being of the Devil. Of even greater concern is how the recipient of such behavior is supposed to respond when one moment he or she is called evil and the next we are telling them Jesus loves them. In the mean-spiritedness of the current culture, we have lost our ability to separate people from the systemic evil in which they may or may not knowingly participate. We would do well to study the painful but beautiful story of Hosea as a model for how to view the culture.

> The LORD said to me again, "Go, love a woman who has a lover and is an adulteress, just as the LORD loves the people of Israel, though they turn to other gods and love raisin cakes." HOSEA 3:1 NRSV

Nowhere in my life has this principle been more painfully illustrated than in my role as a school board member. I serve because I believe it is my responsibility as a Christian to give myself to my community. I believe that in serving faithfully, the Gospel will be modeled. Over the years, this strategy has allowed me to have very open discussions about my faith with many individuals within education without raising the church-state controversy. But into this mix comes the religious right, mostly boomers on their moralistic bandwagon. Using a technique they openly endorse—the stealth campaign—they are working to overthrow school board candidates across the country. My experience with this movement has been painful and embarrassing. It is not the desire of the religious right to participate in the political process that troubles me; I welcome this as an expression of responsible service. It is what I believe to be unethical and mean-spirited tactics that creates the pain and ultimately embarrasses me. I simply do not believe that this is how Jesus would behave.

A school board member in Los Angeles County told me how the religious right came before her board over a curriculum issue, a right that all members of the community have. In their presentation, they announced that the materials used were offensive to the Christians who live in the district. Pain crossed her face as she said, "I thought I was a Christian. My faith is important to me, and I am active in my church. But I was made to feel that only those who agreed with their point of view were Christians." This is a common complaint.

We live in a postmodern world. The culture is pluralistic, and this will not change. If, in our discomfort with the growing diversity, we make the culture the enemy, we misrepresent the Gospel and we frustrate efforts to proclaim it. We do not represent Jesus. We represent our own fear and rigidity. Nothing more.

10. The Gospel As Religion

This issue is really an extension of the prior principle. But it is of such supreme importance that it requires further focused attention. It is, perhaps more than any other issue, close to our hearts. An entire book could and should be written on this principle. No matter what we say, it will not be enough, and we run the risk of trivializing it.

If honest, we would all have to confess that we shape the Gospel around our own culture. This is not necessarily wrong. The church in every age and every culture must recast the essential story of the Gospel in terms that make sense to real people in real cultures.

Yet this effort becomes dangerous when two things occur. First, we forget that we have done it. And second, we believe that our rendition of the story, with all of the traditional and cultural trappings we have added, is the Gospel. *When this happens, we have turned the Gospel into our own religion.* The church in America is deeply guilty of this. We will call people to follow Jesus, but we will also communicate either directly or indirectly that this means a whole host of other things as well. What is on the additional list is determined by the tradition. In some denominations, there is the assumption that the entire received tradition is sacred and not to be corrupted.

How many times have I heard the phrase, "But that is simply not Presbyterian." So? Are we Presbyterians willing to let the entire Presbyterian Church die because the segment of the population that is

209

likely to be impressed with our Presbyterianism is dying? Are we called to make sure that there will always be a Presbyterian church, or are we called to be faithful to the Gospel? Some may feel that we are making the issue too black and white. We recognize this, but the question remains. When our Stated Clerks cut off a Hispanic pastor because he is not as schooled in the finer points of the Book of Order, has the Gospel been served? Or are we simply protecting ourselves against change? Have we not built a religion around the Gospel and assigned gatekeepers to protect it? I love the Presbyterian Church and its theological tradition. But sometimes we lose our way. Sometimes our tradition becomes more important than the simplicity of the Gospel. Is it possible that we suffer from the same problem the Pharisees of Jesus' day suffered from? Is it possible that we love our traditional trappings more than the Gospel itself?

We have focused on the Presbyterians, but the story is no different for the Episcopalians, the Baptists, the Lutherans, or the Methodists, and increasingly the Vineyards and the Willow Creek look-alikes.

If one is part of the more conservative side of the church, the list generally includes an assumption of political conservatism, patriotism, and a demonstration of one's love of God by the faithful practice of religious disciplines. While words of God's grace are spoken, the practical message most often outlines all of the things that a good Christian is expected to do. And in some traditions, this is couched in rhetoric of potential damnation for failure.

Where is the Good News?

Are we willing to do the work of disencumbering the simple but overwhelmingly beautiful story of the Gospel from all of our cultural trappings? This is the real focal point of our choice to die. If we are unwilling to address this issue, particular traditions will simply die.

Summary

In the table at the top of the next page, we have provided the areas that we believe must be addressed—areas to let go of—if we embrace the commitment to die in order to live. Each area has been classified along three trajectories.

Areas of Change	The Type of Change			The Level Where the Change Must Occur			The Target	
	Theological-Philosophical	Cultural-Traditional	Structural	Local	Regional	National	Liberal	Conservative
1 The Marginalization of the Church in Society	X	X		X	X	X	X	
2 Theological Education as Exclusively Bible and Theology	X	X	X	X	X	X	X	X
3 Denominational Principle that the Lower Serves Higher		X				X		
4 Bombproof Certainty of Knowledge	X	X		X	X	X		X
5 Relativizing of and Acceptance of All Stories	X			X	X	X	X	
6 Authority Based Upon Position	X	X	X	X	X	X	X	X
7 The Church Is for Us	X	X	X	X			X	X
8 Dethrone the Informal Gatekeepers		X	X	X	X	X	X	X
9 The Culture as Enemy		X		X				X
10 The Gospel as Religion	X	X	X	X	X	X	X	X

MAKING THE CHOICE

THE SECOND QUESTION PROVOKED by the willingness to consider making the choice was, How do we choose to die if we don't want to die by default? The simplistic answer would be, Embrace what has been said above, to the extent that there is any wisdom in it. But that is a simplistic answer. We have already said that the real difficulty in the death metaphor is in the heart, not in identifying areas where we need to let go of some things. In reality, the choice to die is a spiritual choice requiring the kind of willing resignation that our evangelical and pietistic brothers and sisters model so well for us.

But how does that look on an institutional level, be it a local church, a regional governing body, or a national institution? We received a copy of the strategic plan developed by one of our clients, the South Georgia United Methodist Conference. They provide a powerful model.

The opening section is titled "A Call to Confession." In the introduction, they pose the following question for themselves:

Will we South Georgia United Methodists allow God's dynamic Spirit to capture our imaginations? There is no question that God will be heard; if not by us, then by others. God's will cannot ultimately be thwarted. These are the questions: Will we South Georgia United Methodists rise up and share the good news in this transformational age, or will we become irrelevant? Will we place ourselves, our churches, our resources at God's disposal or will we simply protect the status quo?[3]

The report proceeds to outline three danger signals: swirling social change, declining membership, and a model of ministry that is still tied to an agrarian culture, all issues we have addressed previously. Following each danger signal, they repeat the *Kyria* ("Lord have mercy. Christ have mercy.") The section then concludes with these words:

> The predicament is that in our Annual Conference and in our local churches we are doing business and ministry essentially the same way we did fifty years ago, in spite of swirling changes. We see the changes. We have even acknowledged the changes. However, we have remained unchanged. We have sinned.

> The Bible teaches that in confession there is hope (Psalm 32:5). The Bible also teaches that acknowledgment of our sin can bring us to a point of turning and salvation (1 John 2:1–2). Are we willing as South Georgia United Methodists to confess our sin? Having confessed our sin, are we ready to march into the future fulfilling God's vision for the churches of our conference?[4]

Quite frankly, we cannot improve upon this. If we will confess our sin, our hearts will be open to what must come next. Confession clears the heart and prepares us for a faithful response.

If we say that we have no sin, we deceive ourselves, and the truth is not in us. If we confess our sins, he who is faithful and just will forgive us our sins and cleanse us from all unrighteousness. 1 JOHN 1:8–9 NRSV

The first act in our decision to die involves confession. We must acknowledge that we have sinned.

- We have loved death more than life.

---

[3]Report of the Futuring Committee to the South Georgia Annual Conference, June 13–16, 1994, 2.

[4]Ibid., 4.

- We have loved our traditions more than God.
- We have loved our institutions more than people.

We must ask forgiveness.

We must repent, turning our backs on those things that keep us from moving ahead faithfully.

CHAPTER 18

The Road to Life

While it is fashionable in our "postmodern world" to deride those who hope to ferret some meaning from the mystery of being human, no one can deny that mystery. We arrive here, after all, with few clues as to where we came from, and with even fewer clues as to where we are headed.

Phillip L. Berman[1]

W E HAVE SEEN THE face of death. Before proceeding, we must reiterate again the principle. There must be a death before life. But if we follow the road through the valley of the shadow of death, what will life on the other side look like? Whatever shape our new life will take, it will be consistent with the fifth commitment: *We must wrestle to forge new ways to proclaim the Gospel in this changing world.*

The road to life will be marked by three principles.

1. THE UNSURPASSABLE STORY

"I'VE DONE THE MATERIALISTIC thing and found it to be empty. As I enter midlife, I am wrestling to know what life is about."

These are the words of a midlife boomer, spoken during a focus group. It is a consistent theme among unchurched people. During many different focus groups around the country, we consistently heard people wondering what life is, where meaning is to be found, and whether authenticity is possible. Like the quote that opens this chapter states, people are struggling to "ferret some meaning from the mystery of being human." For those within the church, the answers seem so

---

[1]Phillip L. Berman, *The Search for Meaning: Americans Talk About What They Believe* (New York: Ballentine, 1990), 5.

215

clear—but not to a culture that has rejected the central role of the church. While the questions remain to haunt them, the traditional structures designed to address these queries have lost their place. Yet within these questions are two critical clues about the task of the church as we wrestle to find our place and role in the twenty-first century. Together these two clues provide us with our first principle down the road to life.

First, *to make sense to modern, unchurched people, we need to hear what they are asking.* They are not asking how one is justified. They are not asking how to have their sins forgiven. They are asking about life. What it is and if it can be found. They are looking for ultimate meaning for their lives. Of course, the church believes it has answers to guide searchers in this quest. Indeed, justification and the forgiveness of sins are supremely significant, but that is not the point. In the post-Christendom, postmodern world, we cannot speak in classic doctrinal categories. People are not versed in these issues and are not interested. It is a consumer world that is increasingly noisy and complex. In this world, people feel confused and overwhelmed. Yet they long for a story that provides a point of integration for them in a world awash in complexity.

One of the primary responses to the rising complexity of our modern culture is reductionism. In the face of complexity, many will look for simplicity. But too often what they will adopt is merely simplistic. Yet it is the coping mechanism of a postmodern, technically sophisticated world. Remember, in a postmodern world, there is a reality for every occasion. There are stories galore that promise to provide a point of integration for the inner soul. Is it not curious that as we step into the twenty-first century, where technological and scientific advances are moving at unchartable speed, we also see a renaissance of the mythological? Any modern bookstore will highlight the books of Joseph Campbell, the premier intellectual authority on mythology and the role it plays in the human soul.

Remember also that a trademark of postmodernism is the abandonment of a grand narrative, a big story that gives meaning to all of the particulars of life. Nevertheless, the desire for a story to give meaning to life is fundamentally human. We may have abandoned the modernist notion that on our own we can construct *the* grand story, but we cannot remove the need each of us has for a story.

It is this very fact that drives the efforts of so many. The failure of the grand story has not removed the void. In a manner consistent with a postmodern world, people will scan the world of ideas in search of a story that connects with their hearts. And they will be quite creative in their combinations. *Newsweek* reported that even the Internet has been conscripted for religious pursuits.

> On the Internet, devotees can find Bible-study groups, meditation instruction and screens of New Age philosophy. A self-described futurist in Amherst, Mass., who calls herself Doctress Neutopia, has created her own on-line religion.[2]

Our culture needs a story that is unsurpassable in its ability to speak to the longing of the human heart. Here is the opportunity for the church if it will embrace it. Accept the fact that our story will be seen as simply one story in the marketplace of stories. And embrace the challenge of telling again the story of the Gospel as the grand story. It will not be a barrier to our culture if we present it as *the* great story. In a postmodern world, there is a story for every occasion. It is only a barrier when we are miffed that we have to take our place in the marketplace of stories, enjoying no favored position. For example, when we continually make a big issue out of school prayer, we are perceived as trying to coerce people. We must let these issues go. If we can't let them go, we will fail in our mission. If we can, the opportunity to proclaim again the story of Jesus, and the hope of life that is in him alone, will open before us. It is the unsurpassable story. No other story answers the question, What is life? or the question, Where is meaning to be found?

The second clue is: *We must speak the Gospel—the unsurpassable story—in language that answers their questions, not ours.* We cannot quote verses at people and suppose they have heard. To say that Jesus is the life is both true and at the same time meaningless. It is we who must translate. We cannot expect them to understand us. We must demand of ourselves that we make sense to them about the things that concern them. This points to the necessity of authenticity. To the extent we will not do the work of translation, we speak inauthentically, and that is how we are heard. We proclaim that we love them, but we speak nonsense. What do they understand from what we say? Money. What comes through our babble is an image of the church that always has its hand out.

Of course, we assume that those within the church understand the Gospel in the depths of their souls. But do they? To listen to much of

---

[2]Barbara Kantrowitz, "In Search of the Sacred: America's Quest for Spritual Meaning," *Newsweek* (November 28, 1994).

the religio-babble that is spewed forth today, one wonders. Over the years, I have asked various groups to whom I was speaking a simple question: "Why is it important that Jesus forgives our sins?"

The response was predictable: "So we can go to heaven."

But I would ask, "Why is that so great?"

Which, of course, was immediately followed with: "So we can be with God."

To which I responded with the same question: "Why is that so great?"

Of course, my question verged on blasphemy to many, but "Why?" or "So what?" is nonetheless a valid and deeply significant question. (We challenge the reader to try this little question exercise on a group sometime and see where it leads.) If we cannot answer the whys and so whats, then we do not in fact know the Gospel, nor do we appreciate why it is the unsurpassable story. Furthermore, we will not be able to speak authentically to our culture. What people long for is the meaning and source of real life. While they may not be able to articulate their concerns, it is the futility of death that gnaws at them. Something deep within our humanity longs for life, yet we seem inescapably destined for death. This is why Jesus died and why forgiveness is so important. It is so that we can live, truly and authentically! (We will address this topic in greater detail in the next chapter.)

The central issue is authentic storytelling. If we will tell the story of the Gospel in terms that make sense, and if we will free that message of our cultural and traditional trappings, we will find a world ready to listen. But this again places before us our current challenge.

> For those who want to save their life will lose it, and those who lose their life for my sake, and for the sake of the gospel, will save it. MARK 8:35 NRSV

2. LOCAL CONGREGATIONS — THE NEW HORIZON OF MISSION

THE SECOND PRINCIPLE ON the road to new life requires a reordering of institutional priorities. While mission has historically been something done "over there" or somewhere else, that is changing. The horizon of mission has moved very close. This brings us to a very significant place for some—though not all—within the Christian tradition. Many of the Free Church, Baptist, and evangelical traditions have understood for some time that being a Christian was more than being baptized as an infant within a particular religious tradition. Their evangelistic emphasis on making a personal commitment of faith is more consistent with the kinds of communities in which congregations find themselves today. For this reason, they are somewhat ahead of the more traditional denominations wherein one's faith was an apriority and a private matter. However, even for those from an evangelical tradition, the horizon has shifted.

The changing environment is part of the reason the horizon of mission has come close. It is also one of the anomalies contributing to the breakdown of the Christendom paradigm and the endeavor to form a new paradigm. Evidence of a new paradigm struggling to emerge can be seen. We are in fact able to discern a few of the new "rules."

The Primary Unit of Mission

The most important "rule" has been alluded to already. *The primary unit of mission as we move into the twenty-first century must be, indeed will be, the local congregation.* No longer will the primary flow move from the local church up the denominational ladder and out to mission elsewhere. Just the opposite must occur, at least initially. Increasingly, denominational leaders are being forced to ask, "What must we do to serve the local congregation?" instead of asking, "What can we do to help the local congregation serve the denomination?" Mission is on our doorstep.[3]

The transition to the local congregation as the primary unit of mission can also be very difficult for the people in the congregation. The Christendom paradigm that so clearly defined the local congregant's role as supporting missions elsewhere can cause one to feel it is self-indulgent to turn attention to the home front. I was amused recently in a congregational meeting in which the mission of the local congregation was the topic. The pastor was making the argument that our commitment to the Great Commission had implications for how we spent our resources, both near and far. On a more practical level, then, money spent on a pastor's salary was every bit as much a part of fulfilling the Great Commission as sending money to our missionaries.

Someone objected, "No, this is not right. One is operational spending and one is missions." A curious bifurcation. Why is it operational

---

[3]Mission on Our Doorstep is a special capital funds campaign of the Presbytery of Los Ranchos. It is a program designed to raise capital to fund the development of new congregations.

spending if we spend some of our resources on a youth pastor who works hard on behalf of the kids inside our church as well as in the community but missions if we send it to a missionary who works with kids in Young Life, in the same community? Surely the distinction must be more than a mere accounting structure! But is it?

Some are concerned that it feels as if we are just spending the money on ourselves, and that seems somehow self-indulgent and unchristian. I suppose that might have been true under the Christendom paradigm.[4] But that paradigm is in shambles. We must be the church for others. If we embrace the notion that the local congregation is the front line of mission in the twenty-first century, then we must see mission as *all* that we do. We must begin to frame our understanding of mission as both near and far, as both time and money, and as both prayer and personal involvement.

The Primary Agents of Mission

A second rule is also clearly emerging. If the local congregation is the primary unit of mission in the twenty-first century, *then the individual members of the local congregation are the primary agents of mission.* We have the opportunity to again image the lay person as playing not just a supporting actor role but a lead role in the mission of Christ's church in the world. The Pauline notion of being ambassadors for Christ takes on renewed meaning, not just for those who enter into "full-time Christian work" but for those who work, period. Each one of us must be captured by the vision of playing this role in every activity we undertake.

Having been raised on the concept of the "priesthood of all believers," under which model the congregation does the ministry, I was somewhat disoriented when, upon entering the Presbyterian ministry, I found the assumptions of the congregation—as well as of those who guided my preparation for ordination—very different. The priesthood of all believers was not a common assumption. The model of pastor was (and is!) still that of the chaplain, the caregiver. The prevailing model of the Christendom paradigm hangs on. The pastor does the ministry, and the lay people receive the ministry. He or she is there to meet our

---

[4]We don't really believe this, because we do not believe that the assumptions of the Christendom paradigm were very consistent with reality. Mission has always been both near and far. Christianity as a predominate cultural force is not the same as people having genuine faith. But this is another discussion for another time.

needs. The medical metaphor of pastor as caregiver contributes to this image. After all, most of us only go to the doctor when we have a medical problem. Likewise, many only really engage the pastor and the ministry of the church when they sense a "spiritual" problem.

Within this cluster of images of the pastor is the assumption that he or she is there to serve the congregation. But we believe this is not only unbiblical in its inadequacy but dysfunctional for the twenty-first-century church. The pastor as servant is great if he or she is modeling servanthood. But in too many congregations, the pastor is servant and the congregants those served, period. God help the pastor who fails in this. The whining and criticism is unending.

There is nothing wrong with any of the caregiver functions. Indeed, they are consistent with the Gospel. They become a problem, however, when they are the essential functions. As the new paradigm struggles to take shape, we are sure these functions will remain, but they must move to a secondary position. The primary role of the pastor will look more like the one under the Apostolic paradigm. Pastors will be teachers and disciplers, preparing the congregation for the work of ministry. The pastor will be the servant of servants. The congregants will be the ministers. The pastor of the twenty-first century must reflect many of the attributes of an entrepreneur struggling to open a niche in the marketplace of religious ideas.

It is not just within mainline churches that the principle of the priesthood of all believers has failed to take hold. It is just as true in many of the evangelical and nondenominational church traditions, even though it has been discussed more frequently within the latter. Some years ago I was actively involved in ministry in an independent church with an evangelical foundation. A group of us were very committed to the church and to ministry. We read Howard Synder's three books. The first, *The Problem of Wineskins,* gave us a powerful model for ministry as lay people. It also revisioned the role of the clergy. Being young and naïve, a friend bought a copy for the church's library and handed it to one of the associate pastors. Sitting in this pastor's office sometime later, I noticed the book sitting on his bookshelf. I asked why it wasn't in the library, since it had been given for that purpose. His response, I believe, tells why fifteen years later the priesthood of believers has a long way to go, even within evangelical traditions. He said, "I just don't think such books are appropriate for our people." Howard Synder fell under the ax of the censor!

Why does the priesthood of all believers fail to excite many church leaders? Whether in the mainline churches or the independent and evangelical churches, the reason is the same: It's about power and position. It's about pride and fear. Under the Christendom paradigm, the clergy enjoy a certain authority and position. Such notions challenge those of us who are clergy in our authority role. For some of us, that is simply too threatening. Indeed, we would rather strangle something that is emerging than give up our favored position.

But we are grasping after fading glory. The Christendom model of pastor as "person of distinction" in the community is gone. Our attempts to hold on to the end of what is fading away are pitiable. We have lost our favored position already. As the Christendom paradigm passes, so does the Christendom paradigm's role for the clergy. We must rediscover our role as clergy, and it will probably be more similar to the role of coach than that of chaplain or strong, authoritarian leader. As clergy, this means change. It means wrestling with a new self-image of the pastoral role. It also means challenging our congregations in their image of the pastoral role.

There is surely a form of dysfunctional equilibrium in the pastor as servant and the congregant as served. But it will not do in the twenty-first century. The members of each local congregation must be prepared to be the primary agents of mission.

3. BECOME COMMUNITY ORIENTED INSTEAD OF INSTITUTION ORIENTED

THE THIRD PRINCIPLE ON the road to life flows out of the first two. *The church of the twenty-first century must shift its focus from an institutional orientation to a community orientation.*

You may be thinking, "Wait a minute. We are community oriented. We are a community church!" Perhaps, but there is an important yet subtle distinction between being a church in a community—the institutional model dressed up—and being a community-oriented church. (We have been amused by the number of denominational churches that take the denomination's name out of their name and in its place use "Community.")

Recently our firm conducted a one-day training event for our clients in the use of our information and strategic planning tools. We were making the point that in the future, several congregations within a particular community should learn to collaborate, to work together in mission within their community and for the community. The critical factor is the ability to think not about "my church" but about "our community."

To make the point, we conducted a mock focus group with several of the denominational executives in attendance. A very distinct difference in the language used emerged early. Without our saying anything other than they needed to work together to develop a mission strategy, most of them immediately began to talk about "our community" and its needs and how different churches with different strengths might be deployed. However, one executive simply could not speak in those terms. Without fail, he always referred to "my church." And curiously, while the others were able to imagine collaboration, his comments were consistently qualifications. For example: "I don't know if doing [whatever] would be in the best interest of our church" or "I don't know if I could support such an effort in my church."

We must be willing to take our place as members of a community, being present to serve that community, not to build a big institution. This may be hard on some egos, but we believe the Bible sides with us. If mission is next door and across the street, then we need to give ourselves away to the people who live next door and across the street. Our institutional survival must be second—or better yet, irrelevant—to our thinking.

In urban centers, this means that community development becomes a primary strategy of congregational development. The context in which we develop the spiritual maturity of our congregations must be the transformation of our communities. While we realize that there are many who have been doing this for some time, it is not the norm. *But it must become the norm!*

These three principles are all large ideas. They are in fact an expression of idealism. But we are in a time in the history of the church when we need a serious dose of big-view idealism. We are currently caught in the quagmire of a dying system. In such moments, we need people who can fly high and call us to gaze again into the wonderful and sublime.

Entering Our Defining Moment

As the defining moment unfolds, we are quickly approaching a significant confluence of both the transformational moment in which we find ourselves and a key point in the generational cycle. Over the next twenty years, the church as we have known it will either be reborn through our historic structures or it will die and emerge in some other form completely. The particular trajectory will be in large part due to how the current adult generations play out their roles.

At the turn of the century, most silents will have entered their elder years of sensitivity, most boomer-idealists will have entered their midlife moralist phase, most survivors will have entered rising adulthood. The millennials will still be in their protected youth. The current inner-directed era will be closing, and the next crisis era will be just around the corner.

So what will happen? We don't know what *will* happen, but we have some fairly good ideas about what *could* happen—and much of it depends upon how the boomers in the church behave. An idealist generation (the boomers) in its elder years emerges as visionary leaders to guide us through the next secular crisis. Concurrently, a reactive generation (the survivors) emerges out of a period of burned-out alienation to provide the necessary pragmatism to translate the vision into a workable reality—something idealists do not do well. And just when the all-for-one-and-one-for-all civics (the millenials) enter young adulthood, society calls on their sense of collective destiny to go forth into battle. This is the best scenario in the generational cycle.

How does that relate to the future of the church? As the defining moment draws us closer to the need to make decisions, increasingly the need of the hour will emerge as the need to forge a new vision for what the church could and should be in relation to the postmodern world. Another way of saying this is that the church will need to revision itself. We hear the calls to "return to our Judeo-Christian heritage." This phrase encapsulates a particular vision of life and the church. But we have seen that the kind of world in which this vision prevailed no longer exists. We will not return to it.

But without an overarching vision, the church (or any institution, for that matter) loses its way and becomes lost in confusion. (We will explore the meaning and role of vision in the next chapter.) It cannot go on for long without a new vision. The new paradigm that Loren Meade speaks about fits in the discussion at this point, for a new vision and the new paradigm are related. The vision provides the overarching meaning, and the paradigm the rules of engagement.

The most likely generation to provide leadership in this revisioning period is the idealists—that is, the boomers. And the most likely generation to put it together and make it work on a practical level is the survivors. And the most likely generation to carry this forward into the world is the up-and-coming millennials. And finally, the most likely generation to first enjoy the transformed church will be the yet-to-be-born adaptives. This is the ideal scenario.

Now the problems. The first cohort of the boomers will not reach elderhood until 2004. In the meantime, more and more of us will move into our midlife moralism. Quite frankly, we are not convinced that we boomers can behave ourselves long enough to let life season our moralistic zeal. Our greatest liability is our tendency to shoot at anything we find within our moral universe. The survivors will too often be the target. Yet we must depend on them to make the transition. If we so brutalize this younger generation that they simply want nothing to do with us, it may prove to be a problem later when we really need them. On another front, if we turn our full attack too much on the existing structures of the church, there may be nothing left to revision.

Coming at this from the perspective of the culture outside of the church, both the boomers and the survivors may find the unreformed church simply too unacceptable to even join it in time to participate in its revisioning. If the existing builders and silents will not face the fact that the world has changed and their churches will never return to a former era, it may be simply too late.

We enter our defining moment.

Are there any recommendations we could offer the various generations on this rather precarious road to life? Some.

Memo to the Builders

We are grateful for your faithfulness, but the structures you built and maintained so faithfully are choking us to death. We would ask that you let go. It is time to accept their death. But death, whatever form it takes, does not have to be a repudiation of your efforts. Death accepted as the forerunner to resurrection is worthy of humble celebration. Just as when a saintly loved one departs there is grief with joy, so also you must consider the end of much of what you have built as a cause for grief with joy. Such a response will be your final act of faith. However, if you cannot do this, if you cannot let what you have built die where necessary, you have simply condemned it to death anyway without the joy that comes from the hope of resurrection. This is the face of the defining moment for you as a generation.

Memo to the Silents

We would plead that you not allow us boomers to push you out of the way in our moralistic zeal. The best hope we have that boomers will provide the kind of gift to the church that is most needed is if we are kept in check. We must mature a few more years. But this is a tall task for the silents, for we outnumber you significantly. The challenge you face is exacerbated by your own fears. As indicated earlier, you have enjoyed a long ride on the coattails of the postwar economic boom engineered by the builders. As that world passes away, you will find yourselves watching the activity from the sidelines, as if the world simply forgot you were there. If your pain and anger continue to manifest themselves in blocking behaviors, you will only intensify the pressure to push you aside. The challenge will be to move through your anger and accept that it has been a good ride but the ride is over—let emerge what must. If you silents can do this, then you will be in a position to mitigate some of the boomer zeal and perhaps even mentor us in the ways of graciousness that we will need in our elder years.

In reality, while the defining moment for the builders is in letting it go, for you it will be in making sure the letting go happens in the most gracious and humane way. In some ways, the pain of this death will be greater than the pain the builders will experience. For you will have to participate in the killing.

Memo to the Boomers

To the boomers, we say, "Let's keep our heads, folks." As a generation, we have always felt that we had a key role to play in the great scheme of things. Frankly, most of that may be an overly inflated sense of self-import. But we do have an important role at a very important point in the history of the church. It is not just the normal role all idealists play in the generational cycle. It is the role of revisioning the church for a new age. But we are not ready yet. We must be about the business of learning, of listening, and of building relationships. We must fight against our natural inclination toward self-righteousness and look for ways to positively contribute to the communities where we are. And especially, we must love the survivors and stop the criticism. The defining moment for boomers will require coolheadedness and careful compassion. It will require us to step out of our fragmented and hostile polarizations and find in the Gospel a common vision. The difficulty of this for us is the face of our death.

Memo to the Survivors

Avoid burning yourselves out while learning to make it work. Be warned against the tendency to build your young lives around anti-boomerism. In the end, it will be you that gets hurt, not the boomers. Most of all, recognize that you too have an appointed role to play in the very near future of the church. This will be the defining moment for you. Initially it will include making sure we boomers don't do something exceedingly crazy. Later you will be called upon to build the new superstructures of the revisioning effort that must occur. While it is likely that your future selfless service will go relatively unrecognized, please know that it is essential and that the church needs you to provide it.

Chapter 19

Prelude

*Where there is no prophecy, the people cast off restraint, but
happy are those who keep the law.*

Proverbs 29:18 NRSV

THE MOST IMPORTANT PROBLEM in the church today is a fundamental lack of clear, heart-grabbing vision. The church in America has
no vision. It has programs and institutions and property and ministers
and politically correct hymnals, but no vision.

This brings us to the last of the six commitments we believe the
church must make: We must do the work of revisioning the church for
the twenty-first century—from the local congregation to the national
denominational office. Indeed, building upon the commitments and
principles that have preceded, the institutional church's first concrete
step will require a revisioning of its role and place. The task is revisioning because the once-prevailing vision is simply no longer valid. We
must envision again in light of all that has been addressed. In a very real
sense, we must return and reflect upon the most essential components
of God's grand story and find again our place and role in it.

A VISION FOR LIFE

FIRST, WHAT IS THE core of God's grand story?

When we conduct focus groups with various segments of the
American population, we ask participants why they think people get
involved with a church.

The following represent some of the responses we have heard.

- Raised in the church; it's part of my identity
- Belief in God and Jesus

- The Gospel
- Place where I find personal meaning for my life
- Heaven
- Healing of personal pain
- The promise of the kingdom of God

There is a common theme among all of them: The church and what it stands for represents something qualitatively better than what this world on its own has to offer. They sense that in it there is a promise of something. What is that "something"?

The Great Exchange

Isaiah tells us, in the passage that Jesus read in the synagogue in Nazareth at the beginning of his ministry,

The Spirit of the Sovereign LORD is on me, because the LORD has anointed me to preach good news to the poor. He has sent me to bind up the brokenhearted, to proclaim freedom for the captives and release from darkness for the prisoners, to proclaim the year of the LORD's favor and the day of vengeance of our God, to comfort all who mourn, and provide for those who grieve in Zion—to bestow on them a crown of beauty instead of ashes, the oil of gladness instead of mourning, and a garment of praise instead of a spirit of despair. They will be called oaks of right-eousness, a planting of the LORD for the display of his splendor. ISAIAH 61:1–3*

Isaiah envisions a series of exchanges in which God promises to substitute one thing for another. In every case, the exchange is a negative condition for a positive condition.

Negative	Positive
oppressed	good news
brokenhearted	bind up (make whole)
captives/prisoners	declare year of the Lord's favor
mourn	comfort
ashes	garland
mourning	gladness
spirit of despair	mantle of praise

This text points to Israel's growing hope of the coming kingdom of God, wherein all that is wrong because of sin and evil is made right. The Lord intends to make right what is wrong. He will heal where brokenness in any form exists. The negative list reflects the current condition, what we call the "what is." The positive list reflects the condition of hope, a condition yet in the future. We call this the "what ought to be."

The Goal of Salvation

We can see this same pattern in the theology of Paul the apostle. There is a "nowness" about the negative, and a "thenness" about that which will be true when God completes the work of salvation.

I consider that our present sufferings are not worth comparing with the glory that will be revealed in us. The creation waits in eager expectation for the sons of God to be revealed. For the creation was subjected to frustration, not by its own choice, but by the will of the one who subjected it, in hope that the creation itself will be liberated from its bondage to decay and brought into the glorious freedom of the children of God.

We know that the whole creation has been groaning as in the pains of childbirth right up to the present time. Not only so, but we ourselves, who have the firstfruits of the Spirit, groan inwardly as we wait eagerly for our adoption as sons, the redemption of our bodies. For in this hope we were saved. But hope that is seen is no hope at all. Who hopes for what he already has? But if we hope for what we do not yet have, we wait for it patiently. ROMANS 8:18–25

If we follow the same procedure as was used with the Isaiah passage, we again acquire two interesting lists. Only this time we add the elements of "now" and "then."

Negative (Current - Now)	Positive (Future - Then)
present sufferings	the glory to be revealed
creation waits	revelation of children of God
creation subjected to futility	creation set free
bondage and decay	freedom
creation groans in labor pains now and we too groan in similar pain	our adoption, the redemption of our bodies
hope	fulfilled hope

In Paul's theology, all of creation (including the children of God) are finally set free from all of the pain and agony that goes before us and follows after us. The great enemy of humanity and all of God's creation is death. Paul looks forward to a qualitatively different world where life has swallowed up death. This is the "hope of the Gospel." This is the goal of salvation.

> *When this perishable body puts on imperishability, and this mortal body puts on immortality, then the saying that is written will be fulfilled: "Death has been swallowed up in victory."* 1 CORINTHIANS 15:54 NRSV

The hope of the Gospel is that through faith in Jesus Christ, one day we will be whole and fully alive. Today we are broken and suffering the reality of death on every front of our lives, but one day we will be set free of death. We will finally be whole persons, filled with the life of God. Death will be no more. This grand story promises that God will exchange our sin and brokenness for life and vitality.

Is this not the longing of every human heart? This is what the modern person seeks: life. They want to know where life is to be found. The very thing the Gospel promises is the very thing every person pursues. So why isn't the church the obvious answer? Perhaps because we do not understand the core of the grand story ourselves? Is it possible that what we really envision is nothing more than the survival of our little churches? Are we really even aware of the central promise of the Gospel? Are we even preaching this message from our pulpits?

Not often!

Yet without this central story as the focus of our vision, we have no reason to exist. We recently were meeting with a congregation and asked them if they had a vision for their church. Their response was very telling and typical. Their vision: a sanctuary full of people who could help carry the financial burden of the church! If it wasn't so pathetic, one could feel holy rage over such a notion. We suspect that if a survey was done of one hundred typical churches across America, the response would not differ much. There is very little vision in the land, and it shows in the hearts of God's people.

The Mission Context

The biblical hope of the Gospel (the "what ought to be") provides only half of the vision. Earlier we saw that in the Bible, there is the juxtaposition of the "what ought to be" with the "what is." The "what is" is the particular mission context where we live and work. Both of these are necessary for real vision to emerge. With only the anticipated side of vision, we are left with a disconnected, sweet by-and-by. We must understand the context of mission beyond general ideas of death, brokenness, injustice, and the like.

This is one of those points where the church of the twenty-first century must stretch. Under the Christendom paradigm, knowing anything about the community was meaningless. Episcopal churches were in a community to serve the needs of the Episcopalians. The Presbyterian, Baptist, and Lutheran churches were there to serve their respective members. Again, mission under the old paradigm was out there, not close in. This has all changed. Now the community in which a church is located is important.

Years of experience tell us that this is the most difficult transition in thought for mainline Protestants as well as Roman Catholics. Too often, even when these bodies seek demographic information, it is to discern the demographic profile that is distinctively theirs. They hope that in finding where their "niche" is located, they can increase their membership. For many it is difficult to grasp one simple demographic reality: their individual demographic profiles are a diminishing species.

The future requires a more general engagement of local community, modeled on a "foreign missions–cross-cultural" model. In other words, local congregations must do the work of discovering who lives in their communities. This is the new mission context: what we do as a congregation in our own communities.[1] Included in this are the ministries we maintain to reach our community with the Gospel (if we in fact are involved in such efforts). It also includes the ministries and programs we maintain for the spiritual development of our own congregation.

What do we need to know about our near mission context? Quite simply, *we need to know about people*. The people in the community around the church, and the people who are part of the life of the church. What do we need to know about people? Think relative to the gap between "what is" and "what ought to be." It is not enough to know general things. Of course, we all know that all people need God and one another. But beyond that, *we must know how sin and death are peculiarly manifested in our particular mission context*.

The answer to the question of what we need to know cannot be stressed enough. There is far too often a perceptual gap between who

---

[1]There is a near and a far to mission context. There is always a faraway mission context that we support through mostly financial efforts. But we can no longer afford to ignore the near context and its critical importance.

a local congregation believes to be in their community and who is actually there.

How does one close this gap? By systematic listening. We were conducting a pair of focus groups in Seattle, Washington, a few years ago. The target group was boomers. They loved the open-discussion format and expressed a desire to have that experience in the church. When probed on that issue, they relayed their frustration that the church is a "telling place." It does not listen. It's true, we *are* far better at telling than listening. After all, we have the truth; what is there to learn? We have it; they don't. They come to us. We give it to them. To what do we need to listen? If the church is going to revision itself for the twenty-first century, it is going to have to learn to shut up and listen.

In review then, there are two elements that comprise a clear vision: the hope of the Gospel (what ought to be) and a significant understanding of a particular mission context (what is). We have looked at both of these. Any efforts at revisioning the church must evidence deep understanding of both of these elements. This challenge is germane to the full spectrum of the institutional church, from local congregation to national denominations. All must revision themselves, and that vision must emerge out of a clear understanding of the grand story and our particular environment. Without such vision, we wander—aimlessly and heartlessly. With such a new vision, our hearts will be reborn, for we will see again that God intends to close the gap between "what is" and "what ought to be" in our own lives and in the lives of all whom he sends us to serve.

CLOSING THE GAP

SUCH A GRAND VISION calls us to mission. It gives us ultimate purpose. And what is that purpose? To close the gap between what is and what ought to be. In other words, everything we do in ministry together has validity only to the extent it helps us close the gap. It is this singularity of direction in response to our vision that is our mission.

It is also at this point that many churches in America are completely lost. So many do not have a clue as to why they exist. We once asked a local congregation's strategic planning group why they existed. Their answer? "Because the presbytery started a church here forty years ago." Now there is a clear sense of mission!

Vision calls us to mission. Instead of doing church activities because "someone has to do it" or because somebody started a church here forty years ago, we do those activities that have the greatest likelihood of assisting people in becoming whole and fully alive in the current environment. Our actions as individuals and as members of Christ's church in the world ought to be aimed at closing the gap between what is and what ought to be in some real and substantial way.

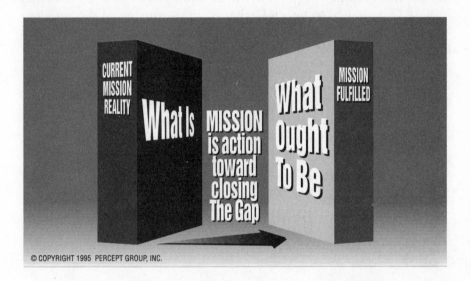

© COPYRIGHT 1995 PERCEPT GROUP, INC.

How does this look in our daily experience?

- When a person hears and embraces the Gospel due to your efforts, an action has been taken to close the gap. In what sense is the gap closed? In the ultimate sense, a person has moved from death to the hope of real and full life.
- When a kind word is spoken, life has broken through death.
- When a Black person can forgive the White population for years of abuse and prejudice, life has broken through death.
- When a White person can see the impact of systemic evil on Black communities and repent, life emerges out of the White person's death and begins to flow into Black communities.
- When a hungry person receives food because in faith we have sought to alleviate someone's suffering, life and health have broken through.
- When in response to an attack on our person we respond with grace, life has cut off death midstream.

Until Jesus returns, this is what we as the church of Jesus Christ are to be about. Our mission is to work where we must, in faith, believing that through our efforts, God is bringing life out of death.

If the institutional church in America is to be reborn in any sense, the first manifestation of new life will be a collective vision that is driven by both "what ought to be" and "what is." In the process of this revisioning, a new sense of mission will unfold. Ultimately, mission is translated into the particular ministries and programs that we actually do.

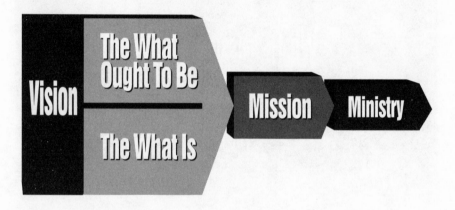

Where this occurs, evidence of life will arise out of the ashes of death—first within the institutions themselves and subsequently in the lives of women, men, and children in the communities where we live.

It must happen in this order, however. Revisioning must occur before anything else. If it does not, we have not yet fully embraced our own death. It is the prelude to all else.

CHAPTER 20

Stop!

"Hear this, O Job; stop and consider the wondrous works of God."

Job 37:14 NRSV

S TOP!
Do nothing yet.
Do not begin to strategize.
Remember the Frenchlick error!
In the opening chapter, we set forth three questions:

- What is the place and role of the institutional church in such a changing social and cultural environment?
- How are we to respond to the magnitude of changes and stresses we face, while remaining faithful to the Gospel?
- How will our churches look?

We could summarize the first two answers like this:

- The place of the church will be on the margins. The role will be that of prophetic moral influence as we rediscover the central grand story of the Gospel.
- Our response must be one of embracing the inevitable death of what we have known, repenting of the recalcitrance that has tried to avoid it, and in faith accepting a redefinition of what it means to be the church in America.

The answer to the third question is yet to unfold, but it depends upon the first two. They will either be empty shells or revitalized centers of life.

A TIME FOR GRIEF

THE TYPICAL HUMAN RESPONSE to ideas such as those presented here is activism. But activism is not what must come first. If it does, we have adopted the error of Frenchlick. Putting activism first means that we have failed to see clearly the nature of the defining moment. In characteristic denial, we will seek to minimize its seriousness by circumventing our death. Acknowledging the stages of grief, we must wrestle to face the reality of our situation and allow ourselves time to grieve.

We must let the anger pass as well. There is so much anger in the church today. The older generations are angry at the younger for rejecting their life's work. The younger are angry because of the barriers the older have erected to ward off change. Anger is part of the process. But we must call it for what it is: an expression of our fears. It reflects the faces of uncertainty about our world and the mission of the church.

We must reach in faith toward acceptance. Like a patient who faces a terminal disease, we must embrace the inevitable. The historic institutional church in America is passing into history. It will not return except as a part of the larger history of Christ's church in the world. It is essential that we allow ourselves the freedom to arrive at this level. It cannot be forced.

Acceptance is a matter of faith. It believes that though there is a death, God promises resurrection. It hears in the cries of sorrow the hope of the Gospel.

Death and Life

The apostle Paul understood his entire ministry in just these terms. He tells us in 2 Corinthians 4 that every day his life was put in danger. At times, he seemed to be at the point of breaking. He summarizes, "So death is at work in us, but life in you" (2 Cor. 4:12 NRSV). In other words, because he was willing to put his life on the line daily, the Word of Life had come to the Corinthians.

Paul teaches us that as the church, we too will participate in Christ's suffering, in his death. In calling us to mission, Jesus also calls us to die. It is a great paradox of the Gospel that if we obediently carry forth the word that leads to life, to wholeness and full life, we will die. But he also tells us that in giving up ourselves to die, we have the promise that we too will live.

It is written: "I believed; therefore I have spoken." With that same spirit of faith we also believe and therefore speak, because we know that the one who raised the Lord Jesus from the dead will also raise us with Jesus and present us with you in his presence. 2 CORINTHIANS 4:13–14

But even more, in the very process of our death, we are becoming our true, whole selves.

For our light and momentary troubles are achieving for us an eternal glory that far outweighs them all. So we fix our eyes not on what is seen, but on what is unseen. For what is seen is temporary, but what is unseen is eternal. 2 CORINTHIANS 4:17–18

While these passages capture Paul's personal reflections on his life, they apply equally well to both our individual lives as well as our corporate life as the body of Christ. God has nothing less than our perfection in view. All else is secondary. Each of us will become that which we are intended to become: beings of magnificent glory and filled with life.

However, the same is the end of God's work with the true church as well.

Husbands, love your wives, just as Christ loved the church and gave himself up for her, in order to make her holy by cleansing her with the washing of water by the word, so as to present the church to himself in splendor, without a spot or wrinkle or anything of the kind—yes, so that she may be holy and without blemish. EPHESIANS 5:25–27 NRSV

It is faith that allows us to believe that even the death of the historic institutional church in America is part of the preparation of the church. As Christ's body, we will be holy. Nothing, not even our historic institutions, will get in the way.

While we are not optimistic about the future of today's institutions, we are optimistic about the future of the church. As Ray Stedman said many years ago, "Resurrection power works best in graveyards." As we scan the American countryside, we see a whole lot of graveyards! What an incredible opportunity.

Let us remember that the death the institutional church is facing is like the death each of us must face each day in our pilgrimage. Christ calls us to put to death those things in our lives that inhibit us from becoming all God intends for us to be. Dying to self in the Scriptures means recognizing the many ways we avoid accepting our need of God and inadequacy of self. The beauty of the Gospel is that God gives us "beauty for ashes." Out of the ash heap of our lives springs forth new life and wonder.

In the same manner, the institutional church must face its "self." It must die to its "self." But if in faith we let our institutions go, out of the ash heap God will raise new institutions to serve a new day. So let us pray as Henri Nouwen instructs us:

> Help me, O Lord, to let my old self die, to let die the thousand big and small ways in which I am still building up my false self and trying to cling to my false desires. Let me be reborn in you and see through you the world in the right way, so that all my actions, words, and thought can become a hymn of praise to you.
>
> I need your loving grace to travel on this hard road that leads to the death of my old self and to a new life in and for you.[1]

So STOP!
Confront the denial.
Name the anger.
Feel the grief.
And in faith accept the inevitable with hope.
May God grant us each the grace to be moved again in our hearts by the wonder of the Gospel's simple beauty and profound power to bring life out of death.

---

[1] Henri J. M. Nouwen, "A Cry for Mercy," reading found in Rueben P. Job and Norman Shawchuck, *A Guide to Prayer for Ministers and Other Servants* (Nashville: The Upper Room, 1983), 149.

APPENDIX A

Generations

What is a generation?
We begin with the most fundamental unit of the generational cycle: the generation. Generational discussions have become quite popular, mostly because of the near-obsessive concern with the large baby boom generation. A working definition of generation can be loose or specific. When discussing the boomer generation, demographers have generally referred to the period between the end of World War II, 1946, and the last year the birth rate exceeded four million—that is, 1964. Curiously, there has been less definition of other generations by demographers. This specific generational demarcation is driven exclusively by fertility rates.

A looser definition suggests merely a group of people who were born and live approximately in the same period of time. More specifically, a generation is often marked as the period of time from the birth of parents to the birth of their offspring. In other words, all of those persons born as one's contemporaries. The problem with this definition, though more specific, is that it floats too much to be of much use for general reflection purposes. It works well within individual families; it does not work when considering a whole population.

Strauss and Howe have developed a much more helpful definition as the foundation of their generational theory. It is not unlike the last definition provided above, but they add more definition to the boundaries on each end. They define a generation as "a cohort group whose length approximates the span of a phase of life and whose boundaries are fixed by peer personality."[1] (A cohort represents all births within a single year. A cohort group comprises all of the birth years within a generational group together.) For our purposes, the span of a phase of life averages around twenty-one to twenty-two years. So a generational cohort group would encompass all persons born in about a twenty-two-year period.

---

[1] Strauss and Howe, *Generations*, 429.

But there is more to their definition than this. How do we determine when to start or stop the twenty-two-year count? Strauss and Howe contend that each generation is marked by a peer personality, a personality that is forged in a critical moment such as a war or revolution or spiritual awakening or some other significant moment in history. Where a generational cohort group falls in their phase of life when such a decisive event occurs will fix or further confirm the general personality of a generation.

For example, how would the beginning of World War II have impacted young men and women of fighting age? Would the experience of that war impact their collective personality? Could that impact continue throughout their lives?

But what if we ask the same question of the children still at home under the custodial care of a mother and father during the war? How would the experience of the war shape them? Would it be different from that of the young adults who built the machines of war or who fought on the battlefields?

Or what about the impact of the student revolution of the late sixties? Did this event impact the generation we know as the boomers? Is it not true that this generation is forever marked as the Woodstock generation? Or what about the elder generation that was in power at the time? Having fought and won World War II, this generation went on to build major institutions in America, the very institutions the boomers were rejecting. As the elder generation steeled themselves against the onslaught of the boomer attack, were they not defending their life's work as a generation? Were they not indeed defending the values that translated into their accomplishments?

Strauss and Howe and others contend that such historical events do impact the collective psyche of cohort groups, depending upon their phase of life, and that it is this impact that forges them into a separate and identifiable generation with their own peer personalities.

> The peer personality of a generation is essentially a caricature of its prototypical member. . . . A generation has collective attitudes about family life, sex roles, institutions, politics, religion, lifestyle, and the future.[2]

Continuing, they provide this concise definition:

---

[2]Ibid., 63.

A peer personality is a generational persona recognized and determined by (1) common age location; (2) common beliefs and behavior; and (3) perceived membership in a common generation.[3]

PHASE OF LIFE

A common demographic way of viewing populations is by where they fall at any given moment in the progressive "phases of life." There are different schemes available that break this down into different groupings, some with more groups and some with less. The level of detail is a function of the need for noting distinctions. For example, if the focus of an inquiry is to determine how children are distributed along the age continuum, a more detailed phase of life scheme will be necessary.

One scheme used by Percept in its reports is designed to roll up age groups into key characteristics during certain moments.

Before Formal Schooling (0-4)	Required Formal Schooling (5-19)
College Years, Career Starts (20-24)	Singles and Young Families (25-34)
Families, Empty Nesters (35-54)	Enrichment Years Singles/Couples (55-64)
Retirement	Opportunities (65+)

For intergenerational comparison, such a scheme is too detailed. Strauss and Howe provide a four-phase model that is much more helpful for such a purpose. The primary organizing principle of their model revolves around the central role played by people within each phase.

Phase of Life	Age Span	Central Role	Primary Activities of Role
Elderhood	66+	Stewardship	supervising, mentoring, channeling endowments, passing on values
Midlife	44 to 65	Leadership	parenting, teaching, directing institutions, using values
Rising Adult	22 to 43	Activity	working, starting families and livelihoods, serving institutions, testing values
Youth	0 to 21	Dependence	growing, learning, accepting protection and nurture, avoiding harm and acquiring values

Source: *Generations*, Strauss and Howe

[3]Ibid.

However, it is not this tidy, for each generation exercises this central role differently. A generation's peer personality will greatly influence the particular expression of their central role. To understand this, we turn to the generational types.

GENERATIONAL TYPES

Strauss and Howe insist that there are four generational types through which society cycles in fixed order every eighty to ninety years. The following table was constructed from descriptions and definitions found in their book.[4]

---

[4]Ibid., 74, 430.

Generational Type	Key Peer Personality Formation Moments	Resulting Personality Characteristics at Key Phase of Life Points
The Idealist	encounters a spiritual awakening entering rising adulthood and a secular crisis entering elderhood	A dominant, inner-fixated generation • childhood of increasing parental indulgence after a secular crisis • comes of age inspiring a spiritual awakening • fragments into narcissistic rising adults • cultivates principle as moralistic midlifers • emerges as visionary elders guiding the next secular crisis
The Reactive	encounters a spiritual awakening entering youth and a secular crisis entering midlife	A recessive generation • grows up as neglected and criticized youths who generally get in the way during a spiritual awakening • matures into risk-taking, alienated rising adults • mellows into pragmatic midlife leaders during a secular crisis • emerges as respected reclusive elders
The Civic	encounters a secular crisis entering rising adulthood and a spiritual awakening entering elderhood	A dominant, outer-fixated generation • childhood in an era of growing awareness of need to protect children from harm in the period following a spiritual awakening • comes of age overcoming a secular crisis • unites into a heroic and achieving cadre of rising adults; • sustains that image while building great social institutions as powerful midlifers • emerge as busy elders who are the target of attack by the next idealist generation during the next spiritual awakening for all of their materialistic values
The Adaptive	encounters a secular crisis entering youth and a spiritual awakening entering midlife	A recessive generation • smothered by over protective parents during a secular crisis • matures into risk-adverse, conformist rising adults • becomes indecisive midlife arbitrator-leaders during a spiritual awakening • maintains influence as sensitive elders, though suffering from increasing disrespect by the idealist generation following them

APPENDIX B

Whatever Happened to the Family?

Whatever happened to the American family? As we prepare to step into the twenty-first century, this is a question on everyone's mind. Curious, if one thinks about it. It was not many years ago that it would have been illiberal to even raise the question. Coming out of the spiritual awakening of the seventies and through the "Greed is good" eighties, the self-centered orientation of the adult population maintained that our own personal, spiritual, and emotional health was of greatest importance. If we felt unhappy in relationships, we were cajoled to make a change. If children were involved, they would adapt.

For years it was politically incorrect to suggest that the breakdown of the mother-father structure was unhealthy for kids. A report by a noted psychologist in the early eighties suggested that children were just as happy and likely to succeed coming from divorced households as from married couple households. Ergo, divorce was not such a bad thing. If truly honest, we were really saying, "My personal happiness must take priority." If we were happy, that of course was better for our kids. But alas, we were wrong. We have "discovered" that divorce does put inordinate stresses on children. If we really bothered to ask the kids, they always told us that mom and dad staying together was what they wanted most. More recent findings now insist that children from divorced families are more likely to struggle than those raised in two-parent households.

THE GRAND STORY AND THE FAMILY

Time and research confirmed what has been known in most human societies forever: no institution is more basic to the formation of a person than the family. Yet we are very aware that like all other institutions, it is in turmoil. What is its future? Perhaps more to the point, what will it look like? Its future form is somewhat uncertain, but we can understand in general terms why it is in trouble.

Like any institution, the formation of a family purposes to fulfill a vision of what could be. In this respect, it must connect to a grand story. From a theological point of view, families are God's idea, rooted in creation. Both creation stories emphasize the essential and central role of the man-woman relationship as a formative structure for all of human life.

> *Then the man said, "This at last is bone of my bones and flesh of my flesh; this one shall be called Woman, for out of Man this one was taken." Therefore a man leaves his father and his mother and clings to his wife, and they become one flesh.* GENESIS 2:23–24 NRSV

In the joining of a man and a woman, the family institution is formed, creating the most fundamental formative structure for the care and nurture of children. This is made clear in the first creation story, in which God creates humankind as male and female and commands them to multiply themselves while they govern the creation.

> *So God created humankind in his image, in the image of God he created them; male and female he created them. God blessed them, and God said to them, "Be fruitful and multiply, and fill the earth and subdue it; and have dominion over the fish of the sea and over the birds of the air and over every living thing that moves upon the earth."* GENESIS 1:27–28 NRSV

By connecting with this creative plan, woman and man and the families that extend from them connect with a story that gives them meaning.

Inherent within the grand American story was this central theological assumption. Families were God's idea. America was a nation of faith and trust, and families would be the foundation of all human relationships. Family meant mother, father, and children. All social life revolved around these central relationships. An individual was either being raised to forge his or her own family, was in a family, or was the grandparent of a family. Always at the center was the "nuclear family."

However, the American form reflects a transition from the biblical understanding of family. The biblical stories occurred within an agrarian environment. Therefore the normative structure for the family revolved around the patriarch. Though it was true from the beginning that a man and woman would "leave and cleave," leaving did not mean what it meant for industrial society. "Leaving" might mean moving next door. Within the social fabric of community, grandparents would still play the primary role. The grandfather was the head of the family. Family meant an interconnection of many "husbands and wives." The model of the family in biblical times was not the nuclear family that has been a central institution of the historic grand American story. With the advent of the Industrial Age and the city, "leave and cleave" took on an added geographic dimension. Couples literally "left" and went where there was work. With this transition, the role of grandparents shifted. In fact, one could argue that they lost their central role in the family structure. To this day, grandparents and parents struggle to know how to relate to each other.

Of course, in earlier times people's lifespans were shorter. But throughout the twentieth century, average lifetimes have increased dramatically. So whereas in the past, few years would have been available upon completion of child rearing, now many seniors enjoy full second lifetimes. For much of my three boys' childhood, they enjoyed knowing not only all four of their grandparents (and still do) but also, for years, not less than four of their great-grandparents!

NEW ARRANGEMENTS FOR LIVING

America was founded within the midst of the industrial revolution of the modern era. Consequently, as its institutions were shaped and formed, the nuclear family model became normative. This model, which *we* think of as the "traditional family," prevailed for most of our nation's history. However, during the second half of the twentieth century, it began to lose ground. As we disconnected from the grand American story, we also disconnected from our traditional idea of family. Contributing to its demise has been the radical relativism of the last thirty years. While we rode our wave of self-indulgence, we let the family slip into disarray. We followed the subliminal mantra that it was only the rigidity of our Puritan foundations that insisted that maintaining families was so important. Like everything else that was relativised (including our central moral and spiritual institutions), so was the historic notion and role of the traditional nuclear family.

Consequently, as we enter the twenty-first century, we are in the midst of restructuring the way we live our lives and form our intimate and nurturing relationships. The traditional American model of the nuclear family is going through a transformation. The same forces pushing us out of the Industrial Age are reshaping it. Moreover, the inner orientation of the generational cycle prevailing in the final decades of the twentieth century amplified the effects of the transformation. As a result, in a mere thirty years' time, we have seen the way we structure our living arrangements radically altered.

So what will it all look like? One cannot be certain. We are still in the midst of the transformation. Furthermore, to what extent the many alternative structures are permanent or simply reflect the generational cycle is equally uncertain. However, we can at least observe the options that are current and that have been emerging. Within these structures, we will see incipient forms of our future.

We approach this discussion along two tracks. The first is a survey of the various optional living arrangements adopted by adults. We have added some new ones in the past few decades. The second track focuses on the new frameworks within which we bear and raise children.

ADULT LIVING ARRANGEMENTS

Adult living arrangements have evolved into a full array of options along a continuum. On one end is singleness, and on the other is marriage. But in between fall several alternatives, all of which are increasing. Indeed, the only option not increasing as we step into the twenty-first century is marriage itself.

Single in America

Single–Never Married: The number of single adults has increased 75% over the past twenty years. While singleness for most is a temporary state, adults are nonetheless far more likely to be single in the nineties than in 1970. Part of this increase reflects normal behavior within the generational cycle. During inner-oriented eras (awakening and inner-directed), the percentage of singles rises, and it declines during outer-oriented eras (crisis and outer-directed). By the beginning of the second decade of the new century, the percentage of singles may flatten. There is a difference, however. We have come to accept that singleness is a real option that many women and men choose intentionally.

Single–Divorced: Divorce has increased throughout the entire twentieth century. However, being divorced for most is a temporary condition. I served some years ago as an intern in a large singles ministry under Pastor Ron Ritchie. Obviously, divorce is a big issue in a singles ministry. In discussing the issue of divorce and remarriage, he made this comment: "People get a divorce because they want a marriage." He was right. In reality, 70% of those who have been divorced will remarry.

The divorce issue is somewhat confusing. For example, while only 7% of the population was divorced in 1985, a full 25% of all persons who had ever married had also been divorced. It is sometimes difficult to ascertain what is being said when people quote divorce numbers. Therefore for simplicity, we provide a chart reflecting the percentage of people divorced and not yet remarried in a given year.

Percentage of Population Divorced: 100-Year History

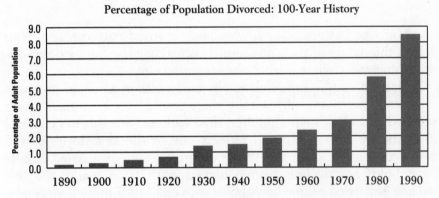

While the single–never married percentage appears to ebb and flow with the generational cycle, the rising divorce rate suggests the impact of the postmodern world and the end of the grand American story. It has become more socially acceptable to depart from unhappy marriages. We suspect this trend will continue into the twenty-first century, though the increases may flatten during outer-oriented eras.

MARRIAGE IN AMERICA

While marriage is still the preferred form of intimate adult relationship, since 1960 fewer and fewer persons fifteen years of age and older marry. This may seem distressing, but as the following one-hundred-year-history graph shows, we have simply returned to earlier levels. The twenty years immediately following World War II saw a significant increase in the percentage of adults who were married. By 1990 the level had returned to that of 1920.

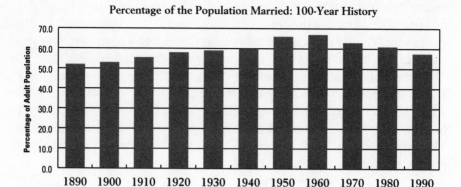

Percentage of the Population Married: 100-Year History

Marriage patterns, like single–never married patterns, appear to reflect the swings of the generational cycle. They rise during outer-oriented eras and decline during inner-oriented eras.

Married couple households, obviously, either do or do not have children in the home. Historically, there would have been many more married households with children than without. But this has changed dramatically since 1970 and reflects one of the key stories of the restructuring of the family. While the percentage of married couple households has declined somewhat since 1970, in reality the real decline is married couple households with children. Empty nesters now comprise the largest of the two. These are married couples whose children have grown and left the "nest."

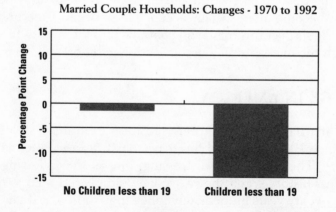

Married Couple Households: Changes - 1970 to 1992

COHABITATION: THE NEWEST ARRANGEMENTS FOR LIVING

Topping off the transformation of the traditional family is the emergence of cohabiting as an acceptable lifestyle choice, what is increasingly called becoming "domestic partners." There are two forms.

Opposite-Sex Cohabiting Couples: These are men and women choosing to live together within an intimate relationship without the covenant of marriage. Since 1970 there has been significant growth of this kind of relationship.

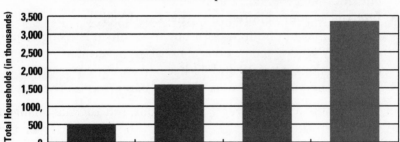

Number of Unmarried Couple Households: 1979 – 1992

Same-sex Cohabiting Couples: Like the unmarried couple households, this is a growing lifestyle choice among homosexual adults. Though the Census Bureau has only recently begun to track this alternative, already we can see its expansion. However, this may not be "real" growth. The statistics may only reflect the "coming out of the closet" phenomenon. That is, the number of homosexual relationships may have been around for a long time, but the growing social tolerance of this alternative lifestyle is reflected in more open disclosure.

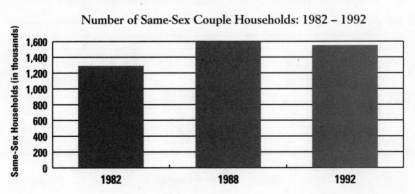

Number of Same-Sex Couple Households: 1982 – 1992

PARENTING FRAMEWORKS

With changes in the ways adults live together (or don't), it was inevitable that the framework within which parenting occurs would also change. The past few decades have seen a phenomenal restructuring of the parenting environment. Consider these key facts.

- In 1991, 50% of all children did not live in the traditional mother-father family—where mother and father are also the birth parents.
- The number of children in poverty has grown to 20% of all children, and children in poverty are more likely to be in single parent (mother, generally) households.
- One out of four children today lives with only one parent.
- The number of children born out of wedlock is rising rapidly, especially among teens. Over 24% of all never-married women between the ages of 18 and 44 have given birth at least once.
- More fathers are becoming primary caregivers as the roles of mothers and fathers evolve.

MARRIED COUPLES WITH KIDS

We have already seen that the traditional nuclear family of mom, dad, and kids declined significantly since the 1970s. But even where this primary structure still exists, significant change is occurring. A father who works and a mother who stays at home with the kids is the most traditional notion of the family. However, this model is being eclipsed by the continual increase in women participating in the labor force.

Changes in Married Couple Employment Structures: 1976 – 1992

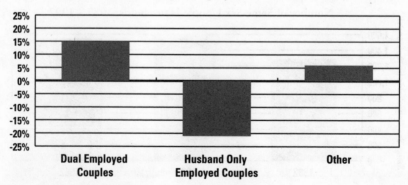

According to the Census Bureau, the greatest structural change to the family since the 1970s is the number of dual-employed couples *with* kids—referred to as DEWKs.[1] The most pertinent question is, Why the shift? Generally, there are two reasons: (a) as it becomes more acceptable for women to work in the professional world, they have done so; and (b) the economic strains of the times have made it necessary for both husband and wife to work. We find it ironic that some within the church who have criticized so many women for going to work are from the generation in which it was economically feasible to stay at home. For a majority of American families, this is no longer possible.

As of the 1990 census:

- Seventy-three percent of all children lived in two-parent families. (This does not mean both parents are the birth parents of the children.) This reflects a decrease. For example, in 1970, 89% of all White children lived with two parents, but by 1993 this had dropped to 77%.
- In the African-American community, in 1970, 59% of all Black children lived in two-parent households; by 1993 this had dropped to 36%. *In other words, two out of three Black children do not live in a two-parent household!*[2]

SINGLE PARENTS WITH KIDS

Single parent households are growing (the majority, single mothers). Since 1970 the number of single parents with children under 18 has more than doubled, from 12% in 1970 to over 27% by 1993.[3] This is a trend to watch as we step into the twenty-first century. There are several reasons for this. First, single parents, especially women, are more likely to suffer from poverty than any other group other than single senior women. And second, because they have children, children are directly impacted.

---

[1] Amara Bachu, "Fertility of American Women: June 1992," Census Bureau, xv.

[2] "African-American Children Comprise A Slightly Larger Share of the Nation's Children, and About One-Third of Them Live in Married Couple Families," Census Bureau press release, September 15, 1994. Information was received via Cendata (CB94-144).

[3] "Marital Status and Living Arrangements: March 1993," Census Bureau press release, July 20, 1994. Information was received via Cendata (CB94-108).

How does one become a single parent? Single parenthood is usually the result of one of four events: (1) divorce, (2) out-of-wedlock birth, (3) separation, or (4) widowhood. Of these four, 72% are from items one and two. And even these two are experiencing dynamic change. As recently as the early 1980s, a child was twice as likely to live with a single parent because of divorce than from being the offspring of a never-married mother. By 1993 the two had virtually come together, with 37% living with a divorced parent, and 35% with a never-married parent.[4]

This points to another emerging trend of special significance for the future. The percentage of never-married women having children is growing. There are two kinds.

The Murphy Brown Phenomenon—Never Married, with Kids: This is named after the popular sitcom character that Candace Bergen plays, a sophisticated, single career woman who decides to have a baby. However, while she wants a baby, she does not want a man. Babies yes, men no! This growing choice among professional women in the age group 30 to 39 increased from 23% in 1982 to 37% by 1992.

Children Having Children: Perhaps the most distressful trend is children having children, unmarried teenage girls becoming mothers. Pregnancy and childbirth is generally not the preferred, intentional choice—at least not in the sense of the Murphy Brown types. Experts suggest the problem is that these teens have no goals—they don't have their eyes on the future at all.[5]

While distressing, this particular phenomenon may reflect the generational cycle. In watching many interviews with young, unmarried teen mothers, one is impressed with the love and concern they show their children. Though it is too early to tell, we suspect that they are expressing toward their children what most of them did not receive as children: security and bonding with one's parent, and the attention a child needs for healthy development. However, within the generational cycle, this reflects predictable behaviors. The neglected generation tends to become the most doting of parents.

Whether they will be successful in this is, of course, questionable. The economic realities are not stacked in their favor. Single parent households are far more likely to either be poor or are at risk of slipping

---

[4]Ibid.

[5]"Babies Who Have Babies: A Day in the Life of Teen Pregnancy in America," *People* special issue (October 24, 1994).

into poverty—and doubly so if the parent is female. Consider the following graph of average family income.

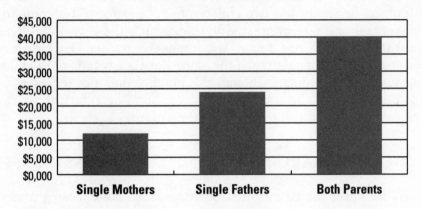

Average Family Income: 1994

COHABITING COUPLES RAISING CHILDREN

Both new household types of cohabiting adults are choosing to "raise a family." This is a relatively new trend, but it is growing in popularity.

Cohabiting Opposite-Sex Couples: While the majority of unmarried couples do not have children, the number of unmarried households with children has grown steadily since 1970.

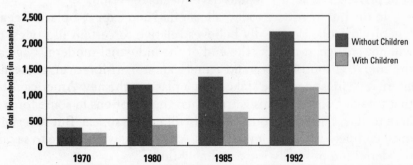

Unmarried Couple Households

Same-Sex Couples with Children: As same-sex couple lifestyles become more mainstreamed, many are choosing to "raise a family." Lesbian women are using various methods to become impregnated—either by a male donor or a test-tube implantation. During one focus group with poor single mothers, a young women revealed that she had "used both of the fathers of her two children to get pregnant." Listening to this woman, one was impressed by how much those two children meant to her. But "loving a man" was impossible for her. Gay men are pursuing adoption of children, if they have not already fathered a child previously with a woman. Though this practice does not represent a large percentage of the total adult population of parents, it is a new family structure that will most likely stay with us.

OUT OF THE MARGINS AND INTO THE MAINSTREAM

As we enter the twenty-first century, adults are choosing many alternative ways to live together. Consequently, our definition of "the family" is evolving. Though there have always been a certain number of alternative lifestyle arrangements, never in American history have they been socially acceptable alternatives. How could they be, under the grand American story? God (Christianity), country, and family: these three were the foundational values. A departure from any one of them meant social rejection and even ostracism. No more! What were once marginalized lifestyles increasingly have a place in the mainstream of American culture. For example, as we close the twentieth century, we know of several openly homosexual persons holding public office. This is new. Undoubtedly, there have been other gay and lesbian persons in public office in other times. But their lifestyle would have been kept private. Disclosure would have meant rejection.

In the public square today, all can find and expect a place. Regardless of what one personally believes relative to certain lifestyles, this will not change. It reflects the end of the industrial-modernist age and the moral vision of the grand American story. Moreover, these new alternative lifestyles have staked out a place in the new American story that is taking shape. If this is true, then these options in some form are here to stay. The "traditional" model will not disappear. But it certainly must compete with the new options. At best, we would have to say that the definition of family is exceedingly fluid.

APPENDIX C

Population Projections—
Births, Deaths, and
Immigration

POPULATION PROJECTIONS: 1970 TO 2050

As a total population, we are projected to increase from 249 million in 1990 to over 392 million by 2050, a 57% overall increase or an annualized average increase of less than 1% per year (.95%). But is that a big increase or a little increase? That depends. To what are the projections compared? If we compare our growth projections with some other countries, the percentage change is negligible. Many Third World countries will see significantly greater percentage growth. However, among the industrialized nations, our percentage growth tends to be at the top, so much so that population "under-growth" is becoming an issue in many European countries.[1] In the large scheme of things, our growth is negligible.

CENSUS BUREAU NET MIGRATION PROJECTIONS

The Census Bureau calculates, based on existing national policy, an annual net migration figure for the total U.S. and by each of the various racial-ethnic groups. We provide the Middle Series assumptions in the table below. Please keep in mind that these numbers are based upon the best available information and current practice. The projections may change, depending upon changes in U.S. policy. Furthermore, these

---

[1]R. Scott Fosler, William Alonso, Jack A. Meyer, Rosemary Kern, *Demographic Change and the American Future* (Pittsburgh: Univ. of Pittsburgh Press, 1990), 26–27.

numbers only include legal immigration. Illegal immigration numbers are only projected and are not included here.

Net ANNUAL Migration Assumptions:	
White (non-Hispanic)	193,000
African-American (non-Hispanic)	61,000
Asian/Pacific Islander (non-Hispanic)	304,000
Hispanic	322,000
Total	880,000

Source: Census Bureau Middle Series as of 1994

The following table compares the difference in country of origin between immigrants who came to America in the 1960s and those coming in the 1990s.

Top 10 Countries of Birth for Legal Immigrants: 1960 and 1990

1960				1990			
Country	Immigrants	% of Total	Ancestry	Country	Immigrants	% of Total	Ancestry
Mexico	32,684	12.3%	Hispanic	Mexico	56,549	8.6%	Hispanic
Germany	31,768	12.0%	Euro-Non Hispanic	Philippines	54,907	8.4%	Asian/PI
Canada	30,990	11.7%	Euro-Non Hispanic	Vietnam	48,662	7.4%	Asian/PI
United Kingdom	24,643	9.3%	Euro-Non . Hispanic	Dominican Republic	32,064	4.9%	
Italy	14,933	5.6%	Euro-Non Hispanic	Korea	29,548	4.5%	Asian/PI
Cuba	8,283	3.1%	Hispanic (Mainland)	China	28,746	4.4%	Asian/PI
Poland	7,949	3.0%	Euro-Non Hispanic	India	28,679	4.4%	
Ireland	7,687	2.9%	Euro-Non Hispanic	Soviet Union	25,350	3.9%	Euro-Non Hispanic
Hungary	7,257	2.7%	Euro-Non Hispanic	Jamaica	18,828	2.9%	Hispanic
Portugal	6,968	2.6%	Euro- Hispanic	Iran	18,031	2.7%	Near East
All others	92,236	34.8%		All others	314,747	48.0%	

Source: INS Annual Report (1960) and Statistical Yearbook (1990) and Percept Group, Inc.

NO MAJORITY HERE

We must not think that the time in which our national population reflects no singular racial-ethnic majority will simply "pop up" at some vague moment in the future. There are already many places in America where no clear majority exists. Indeed, if one were to assess where many of our dying churches across the country are located, our suspicion would be that a majority of them would fall in these areas of no majority!

Using Percept's proprietary unit of geography, the ImagineArea,[2] the table below lists those with at least one hundred thousand people where there is no singular racial-ethnic majority as of 1994. It indicates that already, close to one in ten persons in America lives where there is no racial-ethnic majority. Our purpose in providing these ImagineAreas is simple. It is important to understand that the changing of the American face is not in the distance.

---

[2]Sometimes, for special purposes, it is helpful to create your own geographic unit, such as your parish boundaries. After all, the primary reason for drawing zip codes or census tracts is for planning and management of some particular function. For example, the post office formulates zip codes based upon people and distance from a central post office. While this is a great geographic unit for their purposes, namely mail delivery, it is not as useful for other purposes. Census tracts are designed to assist Congress in congressional districting. Again, great if politics is your purpose. But our concern is with ministry, with proclaiming and demonstrating the Gospel in and amongst people. Geographic units designed for other purposes do not easily serve such a task. As our firm has worked with churches and regional governing bodies in planning for congregational development, we began to ask ourselves the question, Is there a unit of geography specifically designed to assist in mission planning? There wasn't. So we have developed our own custom unit of geography. We call it an ImagineArea. Each ImagineArea, shaped like a circle, is specifically designed to identify where population centers are located and at the same time cover as much of the population in as few ImagineAreas as possible. The primary purpose of the ImagineArea is to stimulate the imagination. Specifically, we hope that such geographic areas provoke missional reflection. We develop ImagineAreas for both national analysis as well as regional analysis. The national ImagineAreas are circles with a fifteen-mile radius.

	Place	ST	1994 Population	1994 % Non-Anglo	1994 Population Non-Anglo	1994 % White	1994 % African American	1994 % Hispanic	1994 % Asian/ Other
	ImagineAreas With No Single Racial/Ethnic Majority: 1994								
1	New York	NY	9,469,086	55.4	5,244,927	44.6	24.0	23.8	7.6
2	Los Angeles	CA	6,350,204	69.3	4,401,326	30.7	12.2	43.5	13.6
3	Oakland	CA	2,358,069	50.9	1,200,965	49.1	13.2	15.0	22.7
4	Houston	TX	2,296,568	55.8	1,280,796	44.2	24.1	26.3	5.4
5	Hialeah	FL	2,095,577	65.1	1,364,221	34.9	22.0	41.5	1.6
6	San Antonio	TX	1,220,359	57.1	696,581	42.9	7.1	47.9	2.0
7	Fresno	CA	621,963	51.2	318,632	48.8	5.3	33.5	12.4
8	SW Hialeah	FL	611,415	65.2	398,398	34.8	13.9	48.7	2.6

Total U.S. Population : 1994   259,842,688
Total Population in Non-majority ImagineAreas   25,023,241
Percentage of Total U.S. Population   9.6%

Sources: Percept National ImagineAreas, Census Bureau, National Decision Systems

GRAYING AMERICA

Perhaps the greatest issue on the aging horizon is the structural imbalance of working-age people to retirement-age people. This is a serious problem waiting to happen. Most of us remember the discussions in the early eighties over the pending failure of Social Security. The resulting Social Security reform legislation accelerated the tax rate increases, began taxing certain benefits for the first time, and started the process of lifting the legal retirement age in regular increments into the twenty-first century. Immediate disaster was averted, but there is a second one in the making. The entire Social Security and Medicare social safety net is dependent upon a ratio of working to nonworking people. If the number of nonworking seniors becomes too large, it places an unbearable burden on those of working age. As the large age cohorts born between 1946 and 1964 move into retirement years, the imbalance may become too great. It may in fact break the system. The only way to fund the social safety net is to raise taxes or cut benefits. Since both are strategies currently being employed, where is the flex room in the future?

The growth of the senior population is illustrated in the following graph.

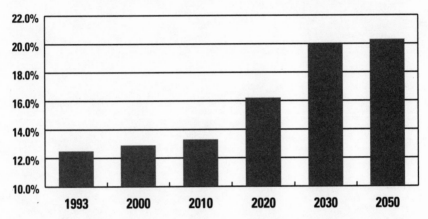

Projected Percentage of the Population: 65+

The total sixty-five-and-older population is projected to increase from 12.6% of the total population in 1993 to one in five by 2050. The resulting increase in seniors, most of whom will not be income-generating individuals, results in a changing ratio of working-age adults to retirement-age adults. Whereas in 1990 there were five working-age adults for every senior, by 2050 this will have dropped to 2.6, or in half! It is not that there will be a reduction in the raw numbers of working adults, it's just that there will be so many more seniors to support.

Ratio Working-Age Adults to Retirement-Age Adults						
	1990	2000	2010	2020	2030	2050
Ratio (N to 1)	.5.0	4.6	4.4	3.5	2.7	2.6
Percent Change		-7.9%	-3.0%	-21.2%	-23.5%	-1.9%

Source: Percept, Inc., 1990 Census and the Census Bureau 1993 - 2050
Middle Population Projections by Age, Sex, and Race

While there are more persons over age sixty-five projected, a second dynamic is perhaps of greater import: increasing longevity. The percentage of the population over eighty years of age is also growing significantly. In 1993 there were 7.5 million persons eighty years of age or older. By 2050 there are expected to be 31 million! Instead of representing 3% of the total population, they will represent 8%.

Religious
Preference Profiles

THE LOYALISTS

The Loyalists				
	All Loyalists **72%**	**The Slipping** **29.3%**	**The Stable** **51.1%**	**The Ascending** **19.7%**
Demos	Largest type Primarily Anglo Older couples Older parents	Above average representation from Survivor and Boomer generations	Above average representation from Silent and Builder Genera- tions	Above average representation from Survivor and Boomer generations
Median Age	49	47	54	46
Education	Average	Average	Average	High
Average Household Income	40,930	41,001	40,692	42,297
Spiritual Concerns	Good church Spiritual teaching	Life meaning	Good church Spiritual teaching	Spiritual teaching
Top Three High Index Preferences	Judaism Mormon Catholic	Episcopal Adventist Unitarian/Univer.	Jeh. Witness Mormon Holiness	Unitarian/Univer. New Age Catholic

Source: Percept Group, Inc., Ethos II Survey (1993)

Please note that the sub-profile indices are against the total Loyalist profile. The total Loyalist profile is indexed against the national average.

The Loyalists

	Loyalists - All	Slipping	Stable	Ascending
Total Respondents	11,224	3,245	5,664	2,182
Margin of Error for Profile	0.83%	1.54%	1.16%	1.88%

RELIGIOUS PREFERENCES

Religious Preference: Now

	Loyalists - All	Slipping	Stable	Ascending
No Preference/Not In	0.0	0.0	0.0	0.0
Adventist	0.6	0.7	0.6	0.5
Baptist	17.7	18.9	17.3	16.7
Buddhist/Hindu/Shinto	0.3	0.2	0.4	0.2
Catholic	30.6	29.5	29.6	34.8
Congregational	2.7	2.9	2.7	2.2
Episcopal	3.4	4.0	3.2	2.8
Holiness	0.9	0.6	1.1	1.0
Islamic	0.1	0.1	0.1	0.1
Jehovah's Witness	1.0	0.5	1.4	1.0
Judaism	5.2	3.8	6.2	4.6
Lutheran	8.9	10.0	8.6	8.3
Methodist	12.0	13.5	11.4	11.0
Mormon	2.2	1.5	2.9	1.2
New Age	0.4	0.4	0.3	0.6
Non-Denom/Independent	6.1	4.9	6.8	6.2
Orthodox	0.5	0.5	0.5	0.4
Pentecostal	2.1	2.0	2.1	2.2
Presbyterian/Reformed	4.9	5.2	4.5	5.3
Unitarian/Universalist	0.6	0.7	0.5	0.9
No Preference/Interest	0.0	0.0	0.0	0.0

Denominational Membership: Now

	Loyalists - All	Slipping	Stable	Ascending
Episcopal	3.1	3.5	2.9	2.9
ELCA	5.9	6.9	5.4	6.1
Roman Catholic	30.5	29.8	29.2	35.1
PC(USA)	4.2	4.7	3.5	4.8
United Methodist	10.3	11.7	9.5	10.2
Southern Baptist	9.0	9.2	8.5	9.3
None of the Above	37.1	34.1	41.1	31.6

THE SWITCHERS

The Switchers				
	All Switchers 9.4%	The Slipping 36.8%	The Stable 22.4%	The Ascending 40.8%
Demos	Most racially diverse Kids key	Above average representation of Boomers and Builders	NA*	Above average representation from Survivor and Boomer Generations
Median Age	41.0	41.0	44.0	38.0
Education	High	High	Very High	High
Average Household Income	39,718	39,256	42,430	38,964
Spiritual Concerns	Spiritual teaching Good Church Life Direction	Life Direction	NA	Spiritual teaching Good Church
Top Three High Index Former Preferences	Adventist Pentecostal Presb/Reform	Pentecostal Lutheran Catholic	NA	New Age Mormon Judaism
Top Three High Index New Preferences	New Age Non-Denom Unitarian/Univ	Unitarian/Univ Methodist Non-Denom	NA	Adventist Jeh. Witness Judaism

Source: Percept Group, Inc., Ethos II Survey (1993)

*The Stable Profile is too small for reliable projection, therefore, apart from basic age, income and education information, no data is supplied.

Switcher Religious Preferences				
	Switchers - All	Slipping	Stable	Ascending
Total Respondents	1,467	536.0	325.0	592.0
Margin of Error for Profile	2.29%	3.79%	4.86%	3.60%
RELIGIOUS PREFERENCES				
Religious Preference: Now				
No Preference/Not In	0.0	0.0	0.0	0.0
Adventist	0.7	0.5	0.3	1.2
Baptist	13.7	11.9	13.8	15.6
Buddhist/Hindu/Shinto	1.3	1.2	1.4	1.5
Catholic	8.1	6.6	7.5	9.9
Congregational	3.3	3.0	3.3	3.2
Episcopal	4.5	4.7	3.6	4.4
Holiness	1.2	0.9	1.7	1.1
Islamic	0.4	0.7	0.3	0.3
Jehovah's Witness	1.1	0.5	0.9	1.8

continued . . .

	Switchers - All	Slipping	Stable	Ascending
Judaism	0.6	0.6	0.3	0.9
Lutheran	6.2	6.8	4.3	6.8
Methodist	12.2	13.7	13.2	10.5
Mormon	1.0	0.8	0.8	1.3
New Age	4.1	4.2	4.0	3.8
Non-Denom/Independent	27.3	30.5	29.4	23.0
Orthodox	0.1	0.0	0.4	0.0
Pentecostal	5.3	3.7	5.0	7.1
Presbyterian/Reformed	6.1	5.3	6.6	6.3
Unitarian/Universalist	2.9	4.3	3.3	1.3
No Preference/Interest	0.0	0.0	0.0	0.0
Religious Preference: 10 Years Ago				
No Preference/Not Interested	0.0	0.0	0.0	0.0
Adventist	2.1	2.1	1.9	2.3
Baptist	19.6	19.4	20.4	18.7
Buddhist/Hindu/Shinto	0.7	0.5	0.3	1.1
Catholic	18.3	20.2	12.5	19.5
Congregational	3.5	3.0	3.4	4.2
Episcopal	4.5	4.7	5.8	3.8
Holiness	1.1	0.9	1.7	1.1
Islamic	0.2	0.2	0.4	0.0
Jehovah's Witness	0.7	0.7	0.6	0.8
Judaism	1.7	1.1	1.7	2.2
Lutheran	9.3	10.9	9.1	7.9
Methodist	15.1	14.5	15.6	15.4
Mormon	1.5	1.2	0.7	2.2
New Age	0.4	0.4	0.2	0.6
Non-Denom/Independent	7.2	4.8	8.8	8.7
Orthodox	0.3	0.4	0.8	0.0
Pentecostal	4.2	5.0	4.6	3.2
Presbyterian/Reformed	8.5	9.3	9.3	7.5
Unitarian/Universalist	1.0	0.6	2.1	0.9
No Preference/Interest	0.0	0.0	0.0	0.0
DENOMINATIONAL MEMBERSHIP				
Denominational Membership: Now				
Episcopal	5.2	5.3	4.3	5.4
ELCA	5.1	5.2	3.5	5.9
Roman Catholic	10.3	11.6	6.9	11.3
PC(USA)	6.3	4.8	7.5	6.8
United Methodist	12.3	14.0	12.0	11.3
Southern Baptist	8.3	5.7	8.3	10.6
None of the Above	52.6	53.3	57.4	48.7
Denominational Membership: 10 Years Ago				
Episcopal	4.5	4.8	4.6	4.4
ELCA	6.8	9.0	6.8	5.0
Roman Catholic	20.4	22.4	14.0	22.0
PC(USA)	7.9	8.3	8.8	6.8
United Methodist	15.2	15.5	14.8	15.2
Southern Baptist	12.2	11.6	11.9	12.8
None of the Above	32.9	28.5	39.1	33.8

THE NEWCOMERS

The Newcomers			
	All Newcomers **1.8%**	**Increasing Active** **Participation**	**Decreasing Active** **Participation**
Demos	Anglos & Asians Single (25%) Survivors and Boomers	Young couples with children	Single, never married
Median Age	36	Profiles too small for further analysis	
Education	Above Average		
Average Household Income	38,411		
Spiritual Concerns	Life direction Spiritual teaching		
Top Three High Index Preferences	New Age Unitarian/Universalist Non-Denom.		
Other Comments	Increased faith involvement does not necessarily translate into increased participation		
Source: Percept Group, Inc., Ethos II Survey (1993)			

Newcomer Religious Preferences

Total Respondents	275.0
Margin of Error for Profile	5.29%

RELIGIOUS PREFERENCES

Religious Preference: Now

No Preference/Not In	0.0
Adventist	1.3
Baptist	11.8
Buddhist/Hindu/Shinto	2.2
Catholic	11.6
Congregational	2.1
Episcopal	3.5
Holiness	0.3
Islamic	0.9
Jehovah's Witness	2.5
Judaism	2.8
Lutheran	3.9
Methodist	11.5
Mormon	1.4
New Age	7.5
Non-Denom/Independent	19.8
Orthodox	0.0
Pentecostal	3.3
Presbyterian/Reformed	7.2
Unitarian/Universalist	6.4
No Preference/Interest	0.0

Religious Preference: 10 Years Ago

No Preference/Not In	53.9
No Preference/Interest	46.1

DENOMINATIONAL MEMBERSHIP

Denominational Membership: Now

Episcopal	3.2
ELCA	4.2
Roman Catholic	8.4
PC(USA)	5.9
United Methodist	9.0
Southern Baptist	3.9
None of the Above	65.5

Denominational Membership: 10 Years Ago

Episcopal	1.7
ELCA	3.8
Roman Catholic	6.8
PC(USA)	2.2
United Methodist	0.8
Southern Baptist	1.0
None of the Above	83.7

THE FLOATING

<table>
<tr><th colspan="4">The Floating</th></tr>
<tr><th></th><th>All Floaters 5.9%</th><th>The Slipping 33.7%</th><th>The Stable/
Ascending 66.3%</th></tr>
<tr><td>Demos</td><td>Anglo and Asian
Singles, no kids
Aging Boomers</td><td>Anglo, Asian and Other
Singles, no kids and
young families
Boomers and Survivors</td><td>Anglos
Singles, no kids
Boomers</td></tr>
<tr><td>Median Age</td><td>42</td><td>39</td><td>44</td></tr>
<tr><td>Education</td><td>Average</td><td>Above Average</td><td>Average</td></tr>
<tr><td>Average Household Income</td><td>39,628</td><td>40,361</td><td>39,282</td></tr>
<tr><td>Spiritual Concerns</td><td>Life direction, yes
Spiritual teaching and
a good church - NO!</td><td>Life direction, yes
Spiritual teaching and a
good church - NO!</td><td>Life direction, yes
Spiritual teaching and
a good church - NO!</td></tr>
<tr><td>Top Three High Index Original Preferences</td><td>No Pref/Interest
New Age
Unitarian/Universalist</td><td>Episcopal
Catholic
Baptist</td><td>No Pref/Interest
New Age
Unitarian/Universalist</td></tr>
<tr><td>Other Comments</td><td>Floaters are always
seeking, never finding</td><td>The Slipping are the
group within the Floaters
who were more likely to
have a preference in the
prior 10 yrs.</td><td></td></tr>
<tr><td colspan="4">Source: Percept Group, Inc., Ethos II Survey (1993)</td></tr>
</table>

271

Floating Religious Preferences

	Seekers - All	Slipping	Stable
Total Respondents	854.0	285.0	558.0
Margin of Error for Profile	3.00%	5.19%	3.71%

RELIGIOUS PREFERENCES

Religious Preference: Now

No Preference/Interest	100.0	100.0	100.0

Religious Preference: 10 Years Ago

No Preference/Not In	3.8	0.5	5.6
Adventist	0.2	0.4	0.1
Baptist	6.4	12.4	3.3
Buddhist/Hindu/Shinto	0.2	0.5	0.0
Catholic	11.1	24.2	4.5
Congregational	0.9	2.0	0.2
Episcopal	1.5	3.4	0.6
Holiness	0.1	0.3	0.0
Islamic	0.1	0.4	0.0
Jehovah's Witness	0.5	1.6	0.0
Judaism	0.3	0.0	0.5
Lutheran	3.1	5.9	1.8
Methodist	6.1	11.5	3.4
Mormon	0.9	1.8	0.4
New Age	0.5	0.8	0.4
Non-Denom/Independent	2.3	2.6	2.2
Orthodox	0.3	1.0	0.0
Pentecostal	0.9	2.6	0.1
Presbyterian/Reformed	4.3	6.9	3.0
Unitarian/Universalist	1.0	1.6	0.7
No Preference/Interest	55.6	19.6	73.3

DENOMINATIONAL MEMBERSHIP

Denominational Membership: Now

Episcopal	0.8	0.6	0.9
ELCA	1.1	0.9	1.2
Roman Catholic	5.3	6.0	5.2
PC(USA)	2.4	2.7	2.4
United Methodist	2.4	4.3	1.6
Southern Baptist	1.1	2.5	0.5
None of the Above	86.8	83.0	88.1

Denominational Membership: 10 Years Ago

Episcopal	2.4	3.9	1.8
ELCA	2.4	5.3	0.9
Roman Catholic	14.0	25.4	8.4
PC(USA)	5.4	7.3	4.6
United Methodist	6.5	11.9	3.8
Southern Baptist	3.8	7.9	1.8
None of the Above	65.4	38.3	78.7

THE DISILLUSIONED

The Disillusioned	
All Disillusioned 2.8%	
Demos	Anglo Some Hispanic/Latino Aging Boomers
Median Age	40
Education	Very High
Average Household Income	42,385
Spiritual Concerns	Life direction, yes Spiritual teaching and a good church, NO!
Top Four High Index Former Preferences	Unitarian/Universalist Episcopal Catholic Methodist

Source: Percept Group, Inc., Ethos II Survey (1993)

The Disillusioned Religious Preferences

Total Respondents   412.0
Margin of Error for Profile   4.32%

RELIGIOUS PREFERENCES

Religious Preference: Now

No Preference/Not In	100.0

Religious Preference: 10 Years Ago

No Preference/Not In	0.0
Adventist	1.0
Baptist	10.5
Buddhist/Hindu/Shinto	1.2
Catholic	35.9
Congregational	2.7
Episcopal	4.7
Holiness	0.2
Islamic	0.2
Jehovah's Witness	1.9
Judaism	2.5
Lutheran	8.6
Methodist	14.2
Mormon	0.8
New Age	0.4
Non-Denom/Independent	4.8
Orthodox	0.3
Pentecostal	1.8
Presbyterian/Reforme	5.9
Unitarian/Universali	2.3
No Preference/Intere	0.0

DENOMINATIONAL MEMBERSHIP

Denominational Membership: Now

Episcopal	1.5
ELCA	1.4
Roman Catholic	8.7
PC(USA)	1.3
United Methodist	2.9
Southern Baptist	0.6
None of the Above	83.5

Denominational Membership: 10 Years Ago

Episcopal	4.4
ELCA	5.2
Roman Catholic	34.0
PC(USA)	7.1
United Methodist	15.4
Southern Baptist	5.6
None of the Above	28.3

THE INDIFFERENT

The Indifferent	
All Indifferent 7.9%	
Demos	Anglo Asian Native American
Median Age	45
Education	Above Average
Average Household Income	42,780
Spiritual Concerns	Life direction, some Spiritual teaching and a good church, NO!
Top Four High Index Preferences	None

Source: Percept Group, Inc., Ethos II Survey (1993)

The Indifferent Religious Preferences

Total Respondents	1,152
Margin of Error for Profile	2.58%

RELIGIOUS PREFERENCES

Religious Preference: Now

No Preference/Not In	100.0

Religious Preference: 10 Years Ago

No Preference/Not In	100.0

DENOMINATIONAL MEMBERSHIP

Denominational Membership: Now

Episcopal	0.2
ELCA	0.6
Roman Catholic	2.7
PC(USA)	1.6
United Methodist	0.7
Southern Baptist	0.3
None of the Above	94.1

Denominational Membership: 10 Years Ago

Episcopal	0.6
ELCA	0.7
Roman Catholic	3.6
PC(USA)	2.2
United Methodist	1.6
Southern Baptist	0.5
None of the Above	90.9

APPENDIX E

Characteristics of the Emerging New World

W hat is this new world going to look like? By way of contrast, we provide a brief description of the characteristics of the worlds that have passed and are passing and the world that is emerging. Of special interest for our purposes is how the role of religion and of the church was understood in each period.

FROM WANDERER TO FARMER — CIRCA 8000 B.C.– 1650 A.D.

The first transformation was the agricultural revolution that moved humans from being wandering hunters and gatherers to farmers. As this transformation unfolded, people began to gather in permanent villages. Agricultural life emerged as they learned to till the land and domesticate animals. Extended families, or clans, lived together. Such innovations were revolutionary for these earlier societies. The changes completely eliminated the earlier human way of life. Education, to the extent it was provided, was carried out within the family or later, within the religious structures.

In Western society, the role of religion was that of mediator between the Deity and society—generally through the established political structures, whether cultus or king. As Christianity took hold of Western culture after Constantine, it assumed this mediatorial role. It always insisted on the primary position, while human governments were relegated to a secondary position. The truth of the church held higher value and authority than worldly government.

Owning land was the capital or source of wealth as the dust of this transformation settled. Those who had it were the wealthy and the political rulers. Those who did not were forever dependent, and were usually ruled (or oppressed) by those who did.

FROM FARM TO FACTORY — CIRCA 1650–1955

The second transformation resulted in the industrial revolution. In the course of a short three hundred years, the social and economic fabric of life was completely changed. People began to move from their villages to the newly forming industrial centers, the cities. Whereas before the extended families lived in close proximity on the farm and labored together on the land, in this new era, husband and wife with children in tow went where the work was. Husbands left the home to work in factories. Women became the primary caregivers for the children.[1]

The responsibility of education shifted away from the family and was given to the school. The character value of punctuality, the ability to follow directions, and mastery of basic skills, such as computation, were essential for the factory worker of this new age. The role of the school was to instill these and so prepare the children for work in the factories.

The role of the church went through a shift. It no longer maintained the preeminent position in society. It still had an important role, namely to prepare the soul for heaven and insure that good moral character was developed in every citizen. And in this role, it became one of the three pillars upon which the society was founded: the family, the school, and the church. But it had lost its preeminent position of authority through which it could "impose" by simple reference to *tradition*. Indeed, it is a hallmark of the church's challenge in this period that it struggled to find an adequate foundation upon which to anchor its authority over life. At best it had to be satisfied with finding a place in the mainstream of culture. The mainline Protestant denominations in America perhaps were the most successful of all in this regard. In reality, much of what is so often referred to as the Judeo-Christian tradition was really just the structural manifestation of this industrial-age relationship between the church and society. When people bemoan the loss of our Judeo-Christian heritage, what they really bemoan is the fact that society is evolving away from the industrial-age role of the church in society.

---

[1]We find it curious that the family structure we as Christians so often hold up as the biblical standard—dad, mom, and kids—is really a social structure shaped by the emergence of the industrial age.

Industrialization introduced the world to mass production and manufacturing methodologies. Work was parceled out in manageable and trackable units. Output was standardized. The goal of manufacturing endeavors, which gave us the assembly line, was "One fits all." While there were white-collar workers and managers, there were far more blue-collar workers who needed to be "managed." This need resulted in centralized hierarchical management structures to control the flow of information and the work of people. The theme was mass: mass planning, mass machinery, mass media, mass production, and ultimately, massive organizations. Equipment, inventory, and raw materials were the capital of the industrial era.

FROM BRAUN TO BRAINS—CIRCA 1955

This new era supposedly began with a symbolic event that occurred in 1955. It was the first year that white-collar workers outnumbered blue-collar workers.[2] It was the beginning of the "information age," a new revolution in which information and mental ability replaced physical labor as the primary drivers of our social and economic structures. The characteristics of the industrial age are giving way to a new age of information. Customization to fit segments and niches has given birth to a new concept called "Mass Customization."[3] Control mechanisms are being decentralized as decision-making authority moves out to the local environment where the actual "work" occurs.

Why is this possible? The computer, the master information processor and manager. The computer is the centerpiece of the emerging information technologies. In the past it took dozens of middle managers to maintain the flow of information guiding production from beginning to end. Increasingly the computer manages this function, doing its work at the speed of light. Mass(ter) planning has been superseded by strategic planning, which is being superseded by "real time" planning.

On the social level, the centrality of the nuclear family is branching into multiple alternative structures. Schools are being forced to rebuild

---

[2] Alvin Toffler, *The Third Wave* (New York: Bantam, 1981), 14.

[3] B. Joseph Pine II, *Mass Customization: The New Frontier in Business Competition* (Boston: Harvard Business School Press, 1993). This is a must read for church leaders. Though the title suggests the focus is business, this is misleading, for the author spends a great deal of time addressing similar issues for service-based organizations, which is, of course, where the church and its related organizations would fall.

themselves in order to accommodate. The product of education must be a "knowledge" worker who knows how to identify problems and, using information technology, create solutions—custom solutions.

The massive accomplishments of the industrial age are fragmenting. And the velocity of all of this change is overwhelming. The possession of information is power in this new world.

Because we are currently in a transformational period, how things will finally look is still unknown. We cannot stand outside of the period and reflect on what happened or how life ended up being structured. We are in the time of flux in which all of these things are up for grabs.

However, we do know some things. We know that the "three pillars" concept has lost its place in most urban communities. Churches are allowed in communities and most feel they are good for communities, but does this new emerging world really see the role of the church as part of the cultural mainstream? We don't think so! Just as education is struggling to understand its role and the family is being reshaped, so also is the church in a time of fundamental change.

What will be the role of the church in this new emerging world? How will it relate to the culture? This has not yet been determined. This is the challenge of the approaching defining moment. How the institutional church answers the question we have posed will have much to do with this.

Summary Table: Transformational Periods in Human History

Toffler's Periods of Social History	Economic Organizing Principle	Source of Capital	Political Structure	Family Social Structure	Role of Religion and/or the Church	Distinctive Character
First Transformational Change: From Wanderer to Farmer						
First Wave: From 8000 BC to 1650 AD	Agriculture	Land	Village	Extended	Mediator between Deity and Society	Tribal, small communities, family a complete economic unit
Second Transformational Change: From Farm to Factory						
Second Wave: From 1650 to 1955	Industry and Manufacturing	Equipment Inventory and Raw Materials	Nation-State	Nuclear	One of three Pillars. Preparing for heaven and good citizenship	The factory, the assembly-line worker, the city, centralization and massification, the "marketplace"
Third Transformational Change: From Braun to Brains						
Third Wave: From 1955 to ???	Knowledge and Information	Information	Global Village	A Potpourri of Options	To be determined	Decentralization, Demassification, Mass customization, Information technologies and the mind worker

Index